Testing
Code
Security

Testing Code Security

Maura A. van der Linden

CRC Press
Taylor & Francis Group
Boca Raton London New York

CRC Press is an imprint of the
Taylor & Francis Group, an **informa** business

CRC Press
Taylor & Francis Group
6000 Broken Sound Parkway NW, Suite 300
Boca Raton, FL 33487-2742

First issued in paperback 2019

ISBN-13: 978-0-8493-9251-1 (hbk)
ISBN-13: 978-0-367-38901-7 (pbk)

This book contains information obtained from authentic and highly regarded sources. Reasonable efforts have been made to publish reliable data and information, but the author and publisher cannot assume responsibility for the validity of all materials or the consequences of their use. The authors and publishers have attempted to trace the copyright holders of all material reproduced in this publication and apologize to copyright holders if permission to publish in this form has not been obtained. If any copyright material has not been acknowledged please write and let us know so we may rectify in any future reprint.

Library of Congress Cataloging-in-Publication Data

Van der Linden, Maura A.
    Testing code security / Maura A. van der Linden.
        p. cm.
    Includes bibliographical references and index.
    ISBN 978-0-8493-9251-1 (alk. paper)
    1. Computer security. 2. Computer software--Testing. I. Title.

QA76.9.A25.V359 2007
005.8--dc22   2007060350

Visit the Taylor & Francis Web site at
http://www.taylorandfrancis.com

and the CRC Press Web site at
http://www.crcpress.com

Contents

Acknowledgements..xxi

About the Author..xxiii

1 Introduction..1
    Why Is This Book Being Written?...1
    Why Am I Writing This Book...2
    Goals of This Book 3
    Intended Audience...4
    How This Book Is Organized...4

2 Security Vocabulary...7
    Virus or Attack Naming...7
    Security Terminology 8

**3 Software Testing and Changes in the Security
    Landscape 11**
    Software Testing as a Discipline 11
    Security Has Become More of a Priority...................................13
        The Number of Computers Has Increased............................14
        The Use of the Internet Has Increased 14
        More Activities Are Performed Online.................................15
    Security Efforts Have Become More Visible..............................17
        Introduction of the Trustworthy Computing Security
        Development Lifecycle 17
        The Enormous Costs of Security Exploits Recognized..........18
        In-House Software Is No Longer Immune.............................19
    Perimeter Security Just Isn't Enough...19
    Bibliography 21

4 All Trust Is Misplaced...23

5 Security Testing Considerations...27
Security Testing Versus Functional Testing..27
  Change Your Focus...28
    All Consumers Are Not Customers..28
    The Intent of Security Testing Versus Functional Testing 29
    "Positive" Versus "Negative" Testing...30
    Test Overlap and Streamlining..30
  Changing Your Prioritizations 31
    Code Maturity 31
    Code Complexity...32
    Code Coverage 32
  Discovery of Software Vulnerabilities 33
    Accidental Discovery...33
    Insider Information 34
    Deliberate Search Efforts 34
  Assume Attackers Know Everything You Do..35
    Source Code Compromise Is Common..35
    Tools Are Readily Available 35
    Secrecy Is *Not* Security 36
    Vulnerabilities Are Quickly Exploited 37
    Social Engineering Works All Over 37
  Know Your Attackers..38
    What?..38
    Why?...39
    Who?...39
    Create a Matrix...40
  Exploiting Software Vulnerabilities..41
    Trojan 41
      Trojan Horse Virus 42
    Virus 42
      Boot Sector Viruses...42
      Master Boot Record (MBR) Viruses..42
      File Infector Viruses 43
      Macro Viruses...43
      Multi-Partite Virus..43
    Worm...43
    Logic Bomb 43
    The Role of Social Engineering...44
      Active Attacks 45
      Passive Attacks 46
      Phishing...46
      Urban Legends 47
      Nigerian (419) Scams..48
    Lost in the Cracks 48
  Common Security Hindering Phrases...49
    "That's not a user scenario." 49
    "It's hidden. The user can't even see it." 50

"No one is interested in trying to hack this product." 50
"Our developers have a security focus." 50
"The UI prevents that." 51
"It can't get to the back end." 51
"I got an error when I tested it. That means it's secure." 52
Software Development Life Cycle Versus Security-Testing Life Cycle 52
The Generally Accepted Software Development Life Cycle 52
Requirements Phase 53
Design Phase 53
Implementation Phase 54
Verification Phase 55
Release Phase 56
Support Phase 56
The Trustworthy Computing Security Development Lifecycle (SDL) 56
Secure by Design 57
Secure by Default 57
Secure in Deployment 57
Communications 57
Requirements Phase 58
Design Phase 58
Implementation Phase 59
Verification Phase 59
Release Phase 60
Support and Servicing 60
Extreme Programming and Security Testing 60
Black-Box Versus White-Box Security Testing 61
Many Attacks Require Little Coding 61
Security Testing Is a Part of All Testing Efforts 62
The Differences Between Black Box and White Box
Security Testing 62
Guard Your Own Gates 62
Reliance Solely on Outside Protection Is False Security 63
Your Application Must Defend Itself 63
Don't Let Your Application Be the Achilles' Heel 63
Mitigation of Damages Must Be Considered 64
There Is No Perfect Security 65
The Role of Security Testing 65
What Developers Want 65
What Program Managers Want 66
What Management Wants 66
What Testers Want 67
Effectively Presenting Security Issues 67
Carefully Evaluate All Factors 68
Risk 68
Cost to Fix 68
Cost if Exploited 68
Trickle-Down Effect to Dependents 68

Trickle-Up Effect to Dependencies..68
Think Outside the Box...68
    Possible Solutions...69
    Possible Mitigations..69
Pick Your Battles but Continue the War..69
    Make Bug Reports Accurate..69
    Include Appropriate Information..70
    If You Don't Agree with the Decision 70
    Don't Fight Every Decision 71
Foster a Security-Conscious Environment...71
    Be Persistent 71
    Share Knowledge 71
    Advertise Success and Failure..71
Bibliography 72

6 Threat Modeling and Risk Assessment Processes.....................73
Threat Modeling Terms 75
    Assets..75
    Attack Path..75
    Condition 75
    Entry Points 75
    External Dependency...76
    Exit Points...76
    Risk..76
    System 76
    Threat..76
    Threat Model 76
    Threat Profile..77
    Trust Levels...77
    Use Scenario...77
    Vulnerability..77
Initial Modeling of Threats...77
    Document Entry and Exit Points 78
    Document Assets...79
    Document Trust Levels...81
    Document Use Cases and Use Scenarios 81
    Document External Dependencies 82
    Document External Security Notes..83
    Document Internal Security Notes...83
    Model the Application 83
    Create Threat Profile..84
        Create Attack Hypotheses...84
        Classify Threats...85
        Analyze Threats to Determine Vulnerabilities 85
        Prioritize Vulnerabilities..86
        Mitigate Vulnerabilities..86
        Update Threat Model..86

Pitfalls of Threat Modeling...86
    Blindness to Interactions with Downstream Dependents 87
    Threat Model Tunnel Vision 87
    Failing to Track Dependency Changes...88
    All Copies of Data Aren't Addressed as Assets...................................88
        Temporary Files...89
        Database Backups 89
        Log Files...89
        Copies of Production Data Outside Production..............................90
        Failover Data 90
        Who Has Access or Control..91
        Physical Disks or Devices 91
    Security Becomes Single Layered — No Defense in Depth.................92
    Vulnerabilities with Lower Priorities Are Ignored.............................93
    Modeling Becomes a Time Sink...93
    Forgetting Physical Access 93
    Forgetting the Registry...94
Threat Trees...94
    Attack Path...96
DREAD...96
    Damage Potential..97
    Reproducibility..97
    Exploitability...97
    Affected Users 97
    Discoverability 98
STRIDE...98
    Spoofing Identity..98
    Tampering with Data...98
    Repudiation..99
    Information Disclosure 99
    Denial of Service..99
    Elevation of Privilege...99
MERIT..99
    Insider Threat Study Items of Note...100
    Analysis...100
        Attacker Behavioral Aspects..100
        Access Path Control Aspects 101
        Attacker Technical Aspects...102
        Defense Aspects 103
OCTAVE and OCTAVE-S 103
    Phase 1 — Build Asset-Based Threat Profiles...................................104
    Phase 2 — Identify Infrastructure Vulnerabilities 104
    Phase 3 — Develop Security Strategy and Plans................................105
Bibliography 105

7   Personas and Testing...107
    Creating Personas..107

Using Personas...110
Pitfalls of Personas...111
   Persona Tunnel Vision..111
   Personas Are Customers, Not Consumers or Attackers.......................111
   Persona Flaws...111
Security Personas 112
Bibliography 114

8 Security Test Planning 115
Overview of the Process..115
Start Drafting Your Test Documents 116
   Test Plan 116
   Test Case Outline/Test Case Documentation 116
Dissect the System 117
   Separate the System into Security Areas...117
      Incoming Information 117
      Outgoing Information 118
      Dependencies 118
      Interactions/Interoperability..119
Gather Information 119
   Look at Existing Product Bugs and Known Security Issues 120
      Your Own System 120
      Competitive Systems 121
      Systems You Interface or Interact With 121
   Review System Specifications..122
      Begin as Early as Possible..122
      Always Question Security Concerns..122
   Review Existing Test Plans and Cases 122
   Review Existing Test Automation 123
Develop Security Cases..123
   Known Vulnerabilities...124
      Your System..124
      Other Known Vulnerabilities...124
   Unknown Vulnerabilities 124
Prioritize Tests...125
   Use Threat Modeling/Risk Assessment Charts..................................125
   Use Personal Experience Data...126
   Talk to the Developers for Special Concerns 126
Develop a Test Plan of Attack...126
   Using "Normal" or "By Design" Test Methods...............................127
   Using Commercial Tools 127
   Using Custom Tools..127
   Don't Forget Validation Tools 127
   Remember the Downsides 127
   Untestable Code Is Unshippable Code 128
Draft a Schedule 128
   Time to Develop or Learn Tools..129

Time to Perform Tests 129
Time to Investigate Issues 129
Time to Rerun All Security Tests on Release Candidate 130
Review the Plan and Test Cases 130
Review with Other Disciplines 130
Review with Other Testers 130
Share the Plan with Others 130
Run Test Passes 131
Postmortem the Results 131

9   Sample Security Considerations 133
Universal 133
Default Installation 133
Too Many Features Enabled on Install 134
More Risky Abilities Enabled by Default 134
High Permissions Required to Install but Not to Run 134
Hard-Coded Install Locations 134
Authentication 134
User Authenticated Only at Certain Points 135
Access Control Rules Not Enforced Consistently 135
Input 135
Input Contents Assumed Trustworthy 135
Input Formats Assumed Trustworthy 135
Input Sources Assumed Trustworthy 135
Security Validations 135
Validations Are Faulty 136
Validations Are Processed in Wrong Order 136
Cryptographic Considerations 136
Cryptography Not Being Used 136
Home-Grown Cryptography 136
Operational Environment 136
Registry Entries 136
System Pathing 136
Hidden Files and Locations 137
Information Disclosure 137
Verbose Errors Displayed 137
Access to Temporary Files 137
Access to Crash Dump Files or Reports 137
Extraneous Code 137
Debug Code Still Present 137
Test Hooks Still Present 137
Security Bypass Settings 138
Stand-Alone Applications 138
Application Process 138
Processes Run at High Privilege 138
Output 138
Setup Information Saved to Hard-Coded Location 138

State Information Saved to Hard-Coded Location............................ 138
Repair/Restore Information Saved to Hard-Coded Location 139
Output Interceptable before Final Destination................................. 139
Backward Compatibility... 139
Defaults to Less-Secure Versions.. 139
Operational Environment 139
Cached Information Not Safeguarded 139
Information Revealed Unnecessarily 139
Registry Keys Easily Accessible.. 140
APIs 140
Application Process.. 140
Processes Run at High Privilege 140
Default Accounts Used to Run Processes 140
Input.. 140
Data Submission Formats Are Trusted 140
No Validation of Data/Request Source.. 140
Language.. 141
Specific Language Details Relied On 141
Operational Environment 141
Session Cookies Are Weak or Easily Reused 141
Session Persistence.. 141
Specialized Considerations 141
Safeguards on Perimeters Solely Relied On (Proxies, Etc.) 141
Insufficient Safeguards on API Abilities 141
Web Applications/Web Services/Distributed Applications...................... 142
Application Process.. 142
Local Processes Run at High Privilege.. 142
Server Processes Run at High Privilege 142
Default Accounts Used to Execute (Admin, Dbo, Sa).................... 142
Input.. 142
Custom Packet Format Relied On 142
Data Not Encoded Before Action 143
Hidden Form Fields Not Validated... 143
Data Transfer 143
Named Pipes.. 143
Traffic Not Encrypted.. 143
Client 143
Rogue Clients Not Detected... 143
Server Verifies Only Client, Not Data (Client Hijacking)................ 144
No Antirepudiation Validation.. 144
Server 144
Rogue Servers Not Detected 144
Client Verifies Only Server Identity, Not Data (Server Hijacking).. 144
No Antirepudiation Validation.. 144
Remote Administration Available 144
Specialized Considerations 144
Safeguards on Perimeter Only 145

Encryption Keys Stored in Source Code 145
HTML Comments Remain in Shipped Forms 145

10 Vulnerability Case Study: Brute Force Browsing 147
Pseudonyms 147
Description 147
   URL Guessing 148
   Session Replay Attack 148
   Non-URL Forceful Browsing 149
Anatomy of an Exploit 149
   URL Guessing 149
   Session Replay 149
Real-World Examples 150
Test Techniques 150
   URL Guessing 150
   Session Replay 151

11 Vulnerability Case Study: Buffer Overruns 153
Pseudonyms 153
Description 153
   Stack Buffer Overruns 154
   Heap Buffer Overruns 155
Anatomy of an Exploit 157
Real-World Examples 158
   Buffer Overrun 158
   Stack Buffer Overrun/Stack Smashing 158
   Heap Buffer Overrun/Heap Smashing 159
Test Techniques 160
   Find and Document All Entry Points into the Product You
   Are Testing 160
   Create an Attack That Targets Each Variable at Each Entry Point 160
   Pass the Attack Data to Each Entry Point 161
   Look for Any Crashes or Unexpected Behavior 161
   Black Box 161
   White Box 162
Bibliography 162

12 Vulnerability Case Study: Cookie Tampering 165
Pseudonyms 165
Description 165
   Background 165
   Cookie Risks 166
      Cookie Theft 166
      Cookie Poisoning 167
      Cookie Inaccuracies 167
      Cross-Site Cooking 167
Anatomy of an Exploit 168
   Cookie Theft 168

Cookie Poisoning 169
Cross-Site Cooking 169
Real-World Examples 169
Cookie Theft 169
Cross-Site Cooking 170
Test Techniques 170
Black-Box Testing 170
Analyze the Gathered Cookies 170
Compare to Documentation 171
Modify Cookies 171
Cookie Misuse 172
White-Box Testing.. 172

13 Vulnerability Case Study: Cross-Site Scripting (XSS)..................... 173
Pseudonyms.. 173
Description 173
Nonpersistent or Reflected 174
Persistent or Stored.. 175
DOM-Based or "Local" 175
Anatomy of an Exploit.. 176
Nonpersistent or Reflected Exploit.. 176
Persistent or Stored Exploit.. 176
DOM-Based or Local 177
Real-World Examples... 177
Bugzilla DOM-Based XSS 177
PayPal XSS 177
Microsoft Passport 178
MySpace XSS Worm... 179
Test Techniques 179
Question All Filtering and Encoding.. 180
Black-Box Testing 180
Basic Script Test 180
Encoding Test... 181
Returned Code Examination.. 181
White-Box Testing.. 181
Hidden Fields 182
GET Versus POST... 182
Bibliography 182

**14 Vulnerability Case Study: Denial of Service/Distributed
Denial of Service 183**
Pseudonyms.. 183
Description 183
Ping of Death 184
Teardrop.. 184
Ping Flooding 184
Smurf Attacks.. 185

Amplification Attacks 185
SYN Flooding 185
Distributed Denial of Service (DDoS).. 186
Anatomy of an Exploit 186
Ping of Death 186
Teardrop.. 186
Ping Flooding 187
Smurf... 187
SYN Flooding 187
Real-World Examples.. 187
WorldPay DDoS Attack.. 187
Gibson Research Corporation DDoS Attack 188
Chat DoS Attack 189
Test Techniques 189
Network DoS 189
Protocol Vulnerability.. 189
Lack of Limits 190
Think Outside the Typical DoS Box... 190
Circular References... 190
Bibliography 190

15 Vulnerability Case Study: Format String
     Vulnerabilities 193
Pseudonyms.. 193
Description 193
Anatomy of an Exploit 196
Real-World Examples.. 196
Ramen Worm Toolkit.. 196
wu-ftpd (port 21/tcp)... 197
rpc.statd (port 111/udp) 197
lprng (port 515/tcp)... 197
Test Techniques 198
Black Box 198
White Box.. 198
Tools... 199
Flawfinder 199
ITS4 Security Scanner 199
Pscan 199
Rough Auditing Tool for Security (RATS)................................... 199
Smatch.. 199
Splint 200
Bibliography 200

16 Vulnerability Case Study: Integer Overflows and
     Underflows... 201
Pseudonyms.. 201
Description 201

Anatomy of an Exploit 203
Real-World Examples 204
Test Techniques 205
  Black Box 205
  White Box.. 206
Bibliography 206

17 Vulnerability Case Study: Man-in-the-Middle Attacks.................. 207
Pseudonyms... 207
Description 207
Anatomy of an Exploit 209
Real-World Examples 209
Test Techniques 210
Bibliography 210

18 Vulnerability Case Study: Password Cracking............................... 211
Pseudonyms... 211
Description 211
  Default Passwords 212
  Weak Passwords/Password Guessing.................................... 212
  Insecure Password Storage.. 212
  Insecure Password Transmission 213
  Dictionary-Based Attacks.. 213
  Brute Force Attacks... 213
Anatomy of an Exploit 214
  Default Passwords 214
  Password Guessing 214
  Insecure Password Storage.. 214
  Insecure Password Transmission 214
  Dictionary-Based Password Attacks...................................... 214
  Brute Force Attacks... 215
Real-World Examples 215
  Default Passwords 215
  Insecure Password Storage.. 215
  Insecure Password Transmission 215
Test Techniques 215
  Insecure Password Storage.. 215
  Insecure Password Transmission 216
  Password Cracking.. 216
Bibliography 216

19 Vulnerability Case Study: Session Hijacking................................. 217
Pseudonyms... 217
Description 217
Anatomy of an Exploit 219
Real-World Examples 219
Test Techniques 219
Bibliography 220

20 Vulnerability Case Study: Spoofing Attacks 221
Pseudonyms 221
Description 221
  Nonblind Spoofing 222
  Blind Spoofing 222
  Denial of Service Attack 222
Anatomy of an Exploit 223
  Nonblind Attack 223
Real-World Examples 223
Test Techniques 223

21 Vulnerability Case Study: SQL Injection 225
Pseudonyms 225
Description 225
Anatomy of an Exploit 227
  Look for a Possible Vulnerability 227
  Test the Vulnerability 227
  All Errors Are Not Created Equal 227
  The Hunt Continues 228
Real-World Examples 229
Test Techniques 229
  Black-Box Testing 229
  White-Box Testing 229
Bibliography 231

22 Fuzz Testing 233
Assumptions 233
Process Steps 234
  Prioritize and Choose Targets 234
  Set the Bug Fix Bar 235
  Choose Tactics 235
    "Smart" Fuzz Testing 235
    "Dumb" Fuzz Testing 236
    Mutation 236
    Generation 236
    Mixed Fuzz Testing 236
  Build Tools and Test Harnesses 236
  Run Tests 237
  Analyze Results 237
  Fix Vulnerabilities 237
  Repeat 238
Case Studies 238
  1990: UNIX 238
  1995: UNIX 238
  2000: Windows NT and Windows 2000 238
Bibliography 239

23 Background: Cryptography **241**

Encryption... 241
   Authentication... 242
   Integrity... 242
   Confidentiality... 242
   Nonrepudiation.. 242
How Encryption Works 243
   Methodology.. 243
   Key-Based Ciphers 243
   Key-Based Algorithms.. 244
      Symmetric (Single-Key) Cipher 244
      Asymmetric Encryption 244
   Hash Cipher... 245
Encryption Tools 245
   PGP 245
   GPG 246
   S/KEY 246
   SSH and SCP 246
   SSL... 246
Crypto Is Not Always Secure.. 246
   Key Length... 246
   Programmer Error.. 247
   User Error 247
   Obscurity.. 247
   Cryptanalysis... 247
The Future of Crypto... 248

24 Background: Firewalls **249**

TCP/IP.. 249
   Packets 250
   Ports 250
Port Scanners... 250
Types of Firewalls.. 251
   Packet Filtering.. 251
   Stateful Packet Inspection 251
   Application-Level Proxy.. 252
   Network Address Translation (NAT)................................. 252
Drawbacks to Using Firewalls 253

25 Background: OSI Network Model **255**

Application Layer (Layer 7)... 256
Presentation Layer (Layer 6) 256
Session Layer (Layer 5) 256
Transport Layer (Layer 4).. 257
Network Layer (Layer 3) 257
Data Link Layer (Layer 2) 258
Physical Layer (Layer 1) 258

26 Background: Proxy Servers **261**
Types of Proxy Servers 261
  Web Proxy 261
    Specialized Web Proxies.. 262
  SSL Proxy 262
  Intercepting Proxy... 262
  Open Proxy 263
  Reverse Proxy.. 263
  Split Proxy 264
Circumventor 264
Anonymous.. 265

**27 Background: TCP/IP and Other Networking
Protocols** **267**
TCP.. 267
  TCP Packet Fields 268
  TCP Flags.. 268
  Common TCP Application Port Numbers 269
IP 269
  IPv4 270
    Packet Fields... 270
    Addresses 271
    Fragmentation Variables.. 272
  IPv6 272
    Packet Fields... 272
    Addresses 272
  UDP... 273
  ICMP... 273
  ARP.. 273
  RARP 274
  BOOTP... 274
  DHCP 274

28 Background: Test Case Outlining (TCO) **275**
Goals 275
What Is (and Is Not) a TCO 276
Benefits of a TCO 276
Steps in Test Case Outlining.. 277
  Research the Item to Be Tested 277
  Determine Starting TCO Format.. 278
  Draft an Initial Outline 278
  Refine and Drill Down 279
  Write Atomic/Predictive Statements of Behavior.................. 280
  Use Equivalency Classes if Possible..................................... 281
  Review, Review, Review... 283
TCO Formats 284

  TCO Maintenance 284
  TCO to Scenario... 285

Additional Sources of Information 287
  Recommended Reading... 287
  Recommended Web Sites and Mailing Lists 287

Index.. 289

Acknowledgments

A great many people have played a part in my software testing career and thus the birth of this book. I'm certain that I will manage to leave out people because, well, my memory isn't so great that I can remember everyone over 10 years. So forgive me if I omitted you; it certainly wasn't deliberate!

First thanks go to my husband, Chuck, who encouraged me to enter software testing to begin with and has consistently encouraged and supported me in whatever I decided to try, even when it meant he had to take on more household duties, becoming the primary parent to our 5-year-old son, Morgan, and listening to 15 iterations of a single chapter. Thank you for everything and I love you.

James Bach's class on exploratory testing was the inspiration that made me really love testing, gave me the confidence that this discipline was the one for me, and caused me to totally revamp my career. Thank you for getting me started.

The next thanks go to my ex-boss Rich Lowry. There are many times when managers have to give that kick in the rear that their employees need, and it's a pretty thankless job. As the recipient of one of those "reality checks," I want you to know again that you have a played a large part in where I have gone and this book's existence. You told me that I needed to stop taking the easy road and find something to work on that excites and motivates me. I still carry those words with me and try to live by them. Thank you for what I needed most. You were 100 percent correct.

To my friend and ex-manager Stu Klingman. You're the person who taught me to "keep my eyes on the prize" and then gave me chances to achieve those prizes. Thank you for the encouragement and opportunities and just for believing in me. I'd still work for you in a minute!

Thanks to my friend and ex-boss Tamme Bowen, who lent me great amounts of encouragement, friendship, mentoring, and support. You taught me a lot and shared my passion for security. Thank you for your encouragement and support. I did do it!

Thanks to my agent, Neil Salkind at Studio B, for his patient work in selling my idea and encouraging me

A huge note of appreciation is due to my editor John Wyzalek who waited patiently as this new author discovered a few of the truths of writing something this size. Thank you for understanding my desire to make this book the very best it can be and not killing me when it took far longer than I thought it would.

Lastly, thanks to the rest of my family, friends, and co-workers, past and present. You served as guinea pigs, moral support, test readers, and generally kept me from insanity while understanding that this book consumed my life for a while. Thank you for your patience, forbearance, cheese to go with my whine, and just for being there!

About the Author

Maura van der Linden is a software development engineer in testing at Microsoft Corporation, working in their Security Technology Unit on the Malware Response Team. She has a B.A. degree in business administration from California State University–Northridge and over ten years in the software test discipline.

With a wide variety of experiences in testing, she began to write white papers and informational papers on test subjects for other testers and this, combined with her technical reviewing for *MSDN Magazine* resulted in her first foray into publishing, an article in this publication on testing for SQL injection vulnerabilities. The response to that article from other testers cemented the need for a book that is focused on how to get started in testing software security.

Happily married with two sons, a plenitude of cats, and a parrot, Maura lives near Seattle, Washington.

Chapter 1

Introduction

Why Is This Book Being Written?

In recent years, the security of the software we use has become a huge issue, and yet security testing remains almost a black art in the software industry. This is even more true in those companies that produce in-house software but for whom software isn't their primary focus.

For testers, the sudden announcement of "you're in charge of security testing" is all the warning they may have that their professional focus has changed. Or, a tester may decide to learn about security testing to help prevent his or her company or product from being mentioned in an ugly industry headline. Now, these testers need to immediately add a whole new set of skills and techniques to their test arsenal.

Faced with these new challenges, testers generally begin a hunt for more information and possibly some guidelines. As they delve into this virtual treasure hunt, it becomes quickly apparent that this won't be an easy task. The vast majority of resources that are geared specifically toward software security are focused on either development or hacking. The few that are geared toward testers and testing are written for an audience of senior testers and very technical white-box testers. What is there for the testers that aren't as senior or experienced, or who may not even do much in the way of white-box testing?

What information there is on software security testing is also very dispersed and decentralized. It requires some digging to find, even if the testers know what to look for. Because software security even has its own jargon and terminology, locating information can take a lot of time and a lot of data mining.

All too often, in the course of this research, testers become lost — especially the more junior testers. What security testing do they need to do? There are a lot of vulnerabilities to choose from. Do they need to wade through the intricate details of each one to determine if they need to test for it? It's a time-consuming, daunting, and nearly overwhelming task. How do they go about designing test cases for it? How do they integrate this into their ongoing process and methodology? What is this threat-modeling process, and do they care?

There really aren't resources for those testers who want to learn more of a framework with which to approach security testing but are not yet assigned to a product; or for those testers in school or in a test certification program. There needs to be a consolidated resource available that will teach the basic software security concepts specifically to testers and that will start at a basic-enough level to be truly useful to them.

The view in the software industry is already changing. The idea that security testing is an arcane specialization that only a few testers practice is disappearing. The idea that security testing is the domain of only white-box testers is also disappearing. Software security is really everyone's problem and, more and more often, even entry-level testers are expected to be familiar with basic software security and include it as a standard part of their test practices.

Why Am I Writing This Book

I began my career in software testing as one of the people who didn't have a computer science degree but instead a business degree. Although I was very computer literate and had done some programming in school, when I entered the field of software testing I was blown away. The amount of digging and self-education I had to do in order to develop and improve my skills and the lengths I had to go to was just amazing. There just weren't a lot of resources out there geared specifically toward test.

I've always enjoyed both writing and teaching and, as I learned more, I took on the additional (self-appointed) task of writing short overview papers on various subjects of interest to testers and distributing them among my teammates and peers. My passion for process organization paid off when I began to teach some companywide classes after I had rewritten the papers into what I felt needed to be taught. (For future reference, saying a class is inadequate really translates to volunteering to rewrite the course materials and then teaching the class yourself — in case anyone wondered.)

Over the course of my career in testing, I developed an interest in software security. Because of that, I became the principal driver of security testing efforts and security awareness in several groups I worked in over the last decade. It started out as mere curiosity, but the more I learned, the more I wanted to know.

However, even as my own professional skills grew, I saw how my peers and our newer testers and interns continued to struggle, especially when it came to security testing. In an effort to help, I became a mentor and taught test theory and functional test techniques as well as security test techniques to the more junior testers, both formally and informally.

I wrote my first short paper on a security topic for testers (SQL Injection Testing) in reaction to some testing my own group needed to do but about which the rest of the testers in the group had no real knowledge. I was surprised by the eager reception it received and how quickly it started showing up in other groups and test teams. Seeing this as a need to be filled, I started to make a list of the other topics I considered important for a tester new to security testing to know. After about two pages of notes, I decided that the only way to comprehensively explain a subject of this size was to write a book — this book.

Goals of This Book

The main goal of this book is to serve as a basic guide on how to approach the task of software security testing. The readers will take away the knowledge needed to begin testing software security for whatever project or product they are charged with testing. This book provides a foundation that includes information such as:

■ How to think about the process of security testing and the differences between it and traditional functional testing
■ What role threat-modeling plays and its pitfalls are
■ How to approach the creation of a security test plan
■ What the root problems are behind various types of vulnerabilities, especially those that have been exploited, and ideas on how to test for them

The goal of this book is *not* to make anyone into a security expert or a hacker. There are plenty of books and reference materials already available on that subject, and I've listed a few in the section on additional reading at the back of this book.

The word *security* encompasses a huge amount of territory, and not all of it could (or should) be covered in this book. Subjects such as physical security, network perimeter security, etc., may be mentioned in passing but will not be covered in great depth. In those cases where I have discovered a consistent knowledge gap in the testers I've mentored, I've included a background chapter for those subjects near the back of this book. This is simply a way to insure that a clear understanding exists before details are explored, not as a comprehensive work on those subjects.

Perhaps most uniquely, this book is not intended to be or sound like a thesis or academic work on software security. My personal experience has been that, if complex concepts can be explained in very simple and common terms, the chances of those concepts being understood and absorbed are much higher. My goal is to give a jump start to testers with the knowledge they need to start performing security testing, not to test my thesaurus or dictionary.

Intended Audience

The intended audience for this book is the beginning-to-intermediate software tester. Advanced or more senior testers may find the information of use as well, but they are not the primary audience for this material, and some of the subjects may be more simplified than they would prefer.

Although some of the information in this book uses Microsoft Windows® (Microsoft Corporation, Redmond, Washington) functionality as an example case, it is purely because that's what I'm most familiar with. Most classes of security vulnerabilities are not unique to a particular operating system, and the concepts introduced are not platform or operating-system dependent. In the cases of the few that are unique or specific, I have noted that in their section.

How This Book Is Organized

This book consists of four main sections. The first section is the one that deals with the concepts and information that will give readers a basis on which to build their security knowledge.

The second main section focuses on the actual process of security test planning and the test pass.

The third section is comprised of information on various vulnerabilities and attacks that readers can review for ideas on whether their product may need to be tested to see if it is open to that particular vulnerability or attack. It also includes some real-life examples of that particular vulnerability or attack, and ideas on the testing techniques that can be used to look for it.

The last section is a collection of background overviews on subjects I have discovered many testers in my target audience are not familiar with. These are not intended to be a complete explanation or in-depth examination of those subjects but rather intended to be a way to gain a quick basic understanding that will get the reader started, and more information can be obtained if needed.

Chapter 2

Security Vocabulary

Virus or Attack Naming

The first thing I want to point out has to do with the names given to the various viruses, worms, and similar entities. As much as a name may be publicized or referred to, it's important to realize that there is no standardized naming convention that exists in the industry, and just about every anti-virus vendor will name a virus something different. For example, the CERT® (Carnegie Mellon University, Pittsburgh, Pennsylvania) Incident Report IN-99-02 is titled Happy99.exe Trojan Horse but lists the following as the various other names this Trojan is known by:

- SKA
- WSOCK32.SKA
- SKA.EXE
- I-Worm.Happy
- PE_SKA
- Trojan.Happy99
- Win32/SKA
- Happy99.Worm

As you can see, you really can't count on much in the way of consistency in any particular virus's names. This makes researching a particular virus not only a little more difficult, but seeing any relationships between multiple viruses or attacks becomes extremely difficult. So, never rely on the name of the virus to tell you much of anything about it.

Security Terminology

Software security and software security testing, like many other special-izations, comes with its own concepts and vocabulary. At first it can seem somewhat like attempting to decipher the Rosetta Stone; so, I have made a list of some of the most common terms and their meanings to make it easier for you to be able to get the most from this book. Remember that this is not a complete list but only a basic one.

Access Control List (ACL): A data structure or list that is maintained to track what users or groups have permissions to perform what actions. This is a Windows term.

Attack: A particular instance of an attempted introduction of one or more exploits to a system.

Attacker: Someone who is trying to bypass the security of one or more pieces of software to carry out his or her own agenda.

Back Door: A piece of malicious software that is installed and left running to provide a way for an attacker to regain system access at a later time.

Cracker: Someone who "cracks" through software security, particularly licensing and copy protection. It's thought to have its roots in "safe cracker." This term isn't often used, in part because it's more narrowly focused and in part because it's just not as widely known, and the differentiation between a hacker and a cracker is not clear.

Cracking: The act of circumventing the copy protection, licensing, or registration functionality of software.

Daemon: A piece of software running in the background, usually as a process. Sometimes used interchangeably with "demon." This is a Unix® (The Open Group, San Francisco, California) term.

Denial of Service (DoS): Where legitimate users are prevented from accessing services or resources they would normally be able to access.

Distributed Denial of Service (DDoS): Where legitimate users are pre-vented from accessing services or resources by a coordinated attack from multiple sources.

Escalation of Privilege: When attackers illegitimately gain more func-tionality or access than they are authorized to have.

Ethical Hacker: One that performs penetration tests. Sometimes ethical hackers are also called "white hats."

Exploit: A code, technique, or program that takes advantage of a vulner-ability to access an asset.

Firewall: An application or hardware appliance designed to diminish the chances of an attack by limiting specific types of information that can pass into or out of a system or network. It's a piece of perimeter security.

Hacker: Someone who "hacks" together programs, i.e., writes them in a particularly haphazard or unorganized manner. This wasn't originally a term that was specific to attackers, but in the last few years it has become an often-used synonym for attackers, especially in the press.

Hijacking: A situation when an attacker takes over control of one side of a two-sided conversation or connection.

Hub: A networking device that repeats the network packets on the physical network layer among many devices.

Information Disclosure: A situation when an attacker is able to access information he or she shouldn't be able to.

Intrusion Detection System: An application that monitors a system or network and reports if it recognizes that the signs of an attack are present.

Leetspeek: The stereotypical sign of a script kiddie where text is written with numbers substituted for letters. The name comes from "elite." For example, "leet" is often written as "1337" or "l33t." It's also seen a lot in gaming communities.

Media Access Control (MAC) Address: Also called the Physical Address, it is physically embedded in every network interface card (NIC) during the manufacturing process. MAC addresses are often treated as unique, although that is not actually guaranteed.

OSI Network Model/OSI Seven Layer Model: The Open Systems Interconnection Reference Model. This is commonly used to explain at what point certain processes are taking place and how information travels.

Personally Identifiable Information (PII): Information that is private to the user or machine. Disclosing PII is a violation of user privacy and can be a part of identity theft problems.

Phishing: Social engineering on a large scale, usually to obtain things like login information, credit card numbers, etc.

Protocal Stack: A system that implements protocol behavior based on a series of the OSI Network Model.

Reverse Engineering: The act of wholly or partially recreating the algorithms or designs used in software. This is usually done without source-code access.

Rootkit or Root Kit: A set of tools and scripts that an attacker installs after successfully compromising a system. These are designed to automate additional tasks including installing additional programs like key loggers, remote administration tools, packet sniffers, backdoors, etc. Kernel Rootkits are rootkits that hide themselves within the operating system's kernel, making them a lot more difficult to detect.

Router: A hardware device that routes traffic between two networks. It can also disguise the traffic from the network behind it to make it appear as if all traffic comes from a single system.

Script kiddie: The somewhat derogatory term for an attacker who primarily downloads and uses exploit code designed and written by others. "Script kiddie" tends to be used to signify a copy-cat type of attacker that is not particularly skilled or creative on his or her own. A script kiddie is also considered to be young, cocky, and brash.

Social Engineering: The process of tricking or convincing a user into volunteering information the hacker can later use. This is often focused on things that are either finance related or material for identity theft.

Spoofing: Impersonating someone or something else — such as another user or machine — in order to trick software security checks or users.

Switch: A hardware device similar to a hub but which knows the hardware (MAC) addresses of each machine connected to it. This is so it can transmit packets only to the individual machine it is addressed to. This has the positive side effect of reducing network traffic and noise.

Threat: A possible path to illegitimate access of an asset.

Trojan Horse: A piece of malicious software designed to deceive the victims by appearing to be a benign program that they may wish to use and thus are willing to download or install.

Virus: A piece of malicious software that is capable of spreading itself, typically as part of a piece of software or a file that is shared between users.

Vulnerability: A bug in the software that would allow an attacker to make use of a threat to illegitimately access an asset. All vulnerabilities are threats, but only unmitigated threats are vulnerabilities.

Zero-Day Exploit: A vulnerability that is exploited immediately after its discovery, often before the software company or the security community is aware of the vulnerability.

Chapter 3

Software Testing and Changes in the Security Landscape

Software Testing as a Discipline

The idea of performing basic tests on code to ensure it works isn't new. At first it was an informal process, and typically done by developers while they were writing the code. Software testing as a distinct and separate discipline has only really come into its own in the last ten to twelve years or so.

There really wasn't a formal curriculum with which to teach software testing, especially at first. Some debugging skills were taught in computer science classes, but being a software tester required and continues to require more than just debugging skills. To be a good tester, you really need to have an inquisitive mindset, with the ability to learn as you go. Testers would exchange tools and ideas between themselves, and most testers developed their own methodologies and approaches. It was definitely an art more than a science.

Where software testers fit into the corporate or engineering world was (and still is) widely varied. In some cases they were part of the development teams and worked alongside the developers and designers or architects, and in other cases they were part of a quality assurance department or team that worked independently from the team that produced the software. There were benefits as well as drawbacks to each of these, but there just wasn't any real consistency. If you moved to a new company, you could end up in a completely different part of the organization than you had been in at your last company. Even staying with the same company wasn't an assurance against this kind of change as companies tried to determine the best part of their organizations in which to place these new software testers.

In the late 1990s, there was a huge shift in the software industry as attempts were made to improve the quality of the software being released by investing in the creation of dedicated software test teams. Many companies saw the huge jump in the complexity of the software being released and the number of major issues it was being released with. Those defects ended up causing damage — both to their customers and, as a result of that, to their own reputations. The cost of fixing those defects was enormous, and there was a realization that, if they had been found earlier in the software development process, the cost to have fixed them at that point would have been a fraction of what it had cost to issue patches. It only made sense to look for the issues earlier and more carefully.

Suddenly, there was a huge demand for software testers, and it became an applicant's market. The number of job openings far outstripped the number of people with experience in software testing. A lot of people were hired on the basis of potential — they appeared to have talent and aptitude for testing software, but they may not have had any real exposure to the basic techniques or training that would allow them to be successful in this new field. This wave of hiring included people with software development, design and IT experience, as well as those who had no experience beyond being computer literate and insatiably curious. It really was a time when the industry was trying to solve the problem of software quality by throwing bodies at it.

Some of the entry-level testers hired at this time were able to find their own resources and training materials and become very successful as software testers. However, it was an uphill battle between the ever-changing landscape of technology and the training they had access to. Books were being published that were actually intended for this audience of new and largely self-taught software testers. More and more classes became available as continuing education. Some professional conventions sprang up that were dedicated to software testing and software quality assurance. Even a few software test certification programs were put into place by colleges and universities.

At the same time that these new resources were popping up, there was an industrywide rethinking of what the process of software testing should consist of. The first attempt at solving the problem of poor software quality by throwing more and more people at it had been showing its weak points, including the fact that it wasn't really scalable.

Now the goal became to "work smarter, not harder." Test automation became the "magic bullet," and huge efforts were begun to automate everything possible. The accepted wisdom was that this would reduce the costs associated with software testing by reducing the number of people needed to achieve the same or better level of test coverage.

A side effect of this movement was that, to be considered for a position as a software tester, many employers now wanted considerable coding and programming skills. If anything, coding skills were considered more important than test skills. More developers moved into software testing who already had the programming skills but needed to learn to test. There were more resources available to testers by this time, but they were still focused mostly on development and program management instead of skills specific to testing.

By now, new test methodologies were being introduced and championed by various segments of the industry. Testers were being inundated with theories, opinions, and tools. Probably the biggest challenge as testers at this time was figuring out how to stay informed and sift through all the changing technologies and automation requirements for things they may be able to use on their projects. Then they had to figure out which to integrate into their ongoing professional repertoire so they could do the best job of testing possible with the least amount of overhead.

At this point the pendulum had swung back a bit, and automation was no longer perceived as the be-all end-all cure for the expenses of software testing. However, software testers were still left with the problem of trying to integrate knowledge and skills that are not produced with an eye to software testing into something they can use to improve their test efforts. This was especially difficult for those testers performing black-box testing where the lack of visibility into the code makes it more difficult to use the code-level techniques.

A whole new challenge has now arisen. Testers are now being told to integrate security testing into their test passes or to switch entirely from functional testing to security testing. It sounds simple — if you are not the tester being told to change your entire mindset about testing and to do it now, if not sooner.

Security Has Become More of a Priority

Many factors have converged in the last few years and made software security one of the largest concerns of both businesses and consumers.

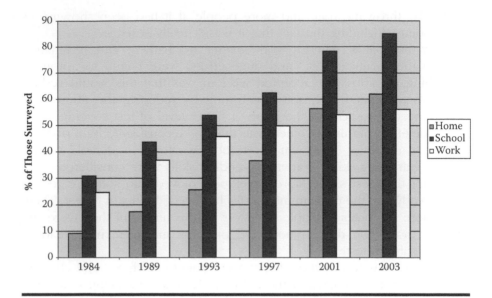

Figure 3.1 Computer use in the United States: 1984 through 2003.

The Number of Computers Has Increased

More people have computers now than ever before — at home, at school, and at work. The U.S. Census Bureau has been performing periodic surveys on computer and Internet usage since 1984, with the latest published results being those for 2003. Figure 3.1 shows the trend between 1984 and 2003 in the percentages of people surveyed who report that they use computers.

As you can see, the percentage of people reporting that they have a computer at home has grown from under 10 percent in 1984 to almost 62 percent in 2003 and is only higher now. One implication of this is that there are now more potential attack victims, both direct and indirect, than ever before, and this pool of potential victims is only continuing to grow. Along with the increase in the number of potential victims is an increase in both potential attackers and potential sources for attacks to be spread by.

The Use of the Internet Has Increased

Another interesting statistic reported by the U.S. Census Bureau is the percentage of users who have access to and use the Internet. Figure 3.2 shows another upward trend in just the three years between 1997 and 2003.

The very fact that so many more people were connecting to and actively using the Internet means that any malicious code that can be

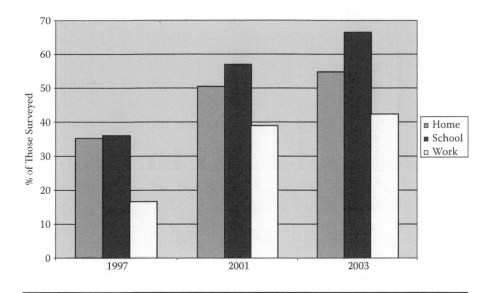

Figure 3.2   Internet use in the United States: 1997 and 2003.

transmitted by a vector that uses the Internet or electronic communications has a better chance of being able to reach a large number of potential victims quickly.

More Activities Are Performed Online

The types of activities performed online have also changed over the years. The prevalence of various methods of electronic communication such as e-mail and instant messenger programs has increased significantly, and new activities have emerged as the infrastructures have been developed to allow them to be conducted over the Internet. This is especially true in activities such as online banking and E-commerce, and is shown in Figure 3.3.

The percentage of people using the Internet to obtain information on news, weather, and sports went up from 7 percent in 1997 to over 40 percent in 2003. The percentage of adults using the Internet to obtain information on government and health services almost tripled from 12 percent in 1997 to 33 percent in 2003.

Communication has changed as well. More than half of all adults use e-mail in 2003 as opposed to 12 percent of adults in 1997. Instead of being an oddity with a user-base that is more technically savvy, e-mail is now a major method of communication for people with all levels of expertise.

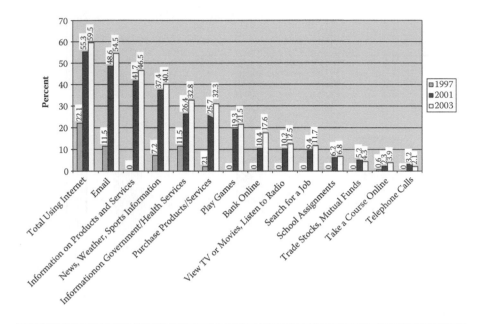

Figure 3.3   Population 18 years and older using the Internet for a specific task: 1997, 2001, and 2003.

The way people deal with personal finances has changed. In 1997, online banking wasn't even reported, but by 2003 18 percent of adults used online banking.

Even shopping habits have changed. The percentage of adults who used the Internet to research purchases and products was also not measured in 1997, but in 2003 it was at 46.5. The percentage who actually bought something online rose from 2 in 1997 to 32.3 in 2003.

The expansion and migration of all these activities from their prior methods such as in person (sometimes called brick and mortar), catalog, or mail to being performed online have the following multiple impacts when it comes to security:

▪ Users are visiting the Internet and making use of more and more online resources; thus more potential victims are being exposed to more potentially malicious software.
▪ As users become more and more used to carrying out tasks that involve their most sensitive information online, they naturally have a tendency to become more trusting and less likely to continually exercise sufficient caution when disclosing personal data. This makes their vulnerability to some attacks increase significantly.

- The rapid growth of online communications creates a pool of potential victims for phishing and other social engineering efforts. This growth also makes it easier for exploits, spread via online communications, to proliferate.
- The data created and maintained during online activity, both stored and transient, is an attractive target. This includes everything from a user's personal bank information to the credit card information saved during online transactions, and even the social security numbers by which almost all medical and insurance records used to be identified.

Security Efforts Have Become More Visible

It's never been news to anyone that software ships with bugs, and the more complex the software, the more bugs are likely to exist. For many years, this was just an accepted part of choosing to computerize your home or business. It just "was," and it was not overly questioned. In a way, it's similar to how the dangers of automobile travel were just accepted for many years. It was merely a risk you took if you wanted to use a car. Eventually, the need for safety testing and safety systems were realized and acted upon.

Then, a chain of several events occurred that changed the view of software security risks from that of accepted and normal to being challenged, questioned, and publicized as well.

Introduction of the Trustworthy Computing Security Development Lifecycle

In 2002, a spotlight was cast on the issue by the launch of the Trustworthy Computing Security Development Lifecycle. This movement, pioneered by Microsoft and IBM® (International Business Machines, Armonk, New York) among others, sought to push security awareness into all aspects of software development. The introduction of this initiative had the most immediate impact on those products with quick ship cycles such as E-commerce applications, but it wasn't long until it sparked off an industrywide drive.

Although it did serve to drive up security awareness in the software industry, it also served to bring the importance of security to the attention of consumers of software. Now the security testing and development methodologies used during the development of any particular piece of software were of intense interest to end users. The new security awareness of the consumers became yet another factor.

In its own way, it was akin to publishing studies of the way safety restraints can be built into automobiles to save lives. Once there was a push that made the issues known and indicated that there were steps that could be taken to alleviate or eliminate them, the ability to merely accept or ignore the issues or their consequences was no longer as viable of an option.

The Enormous Costs of Security Exploits Recognized

For many years, the costs incurred because of the bugs shipped with software were also accepted and not really called out specifically. Now, attention is being paid to them, and those costs are being estimated and not only recognized but also publicized. The combination of this new consumer security awareness and the newly publicized statistics of the estimated costs of security defects to businesses created a change in how businesses in particular went about selecting the software they would adopt. Businesses began to track and consider the costs associated with software that go beyond just that to purchase and deploy new software.

Total cost of ownership now became, next to functionality, one of the main factors in software decisions for businesses. More costs were taken into account, especially those associated with security exploits such as:

- Potential downtime
  - What will be the impact in dollars of downtime on the business if this software is adopted?
  - What other systems will be affected by this software going down? What is the cost associated with that?
- Data theft
  - What data does this system collect?
  - What data does this system store?
  - What is the cost associated with the theft of that data?
  - What is the cost associated with the destruction of that data?
  - What is the cost associated with the publication or spread of that data?
- Cyber-vandalism
  - What is the impact of possible vandalism or destruction of this software or its data?

In addition to the basic monetary cost to the company of some of these factors, there emerged an awareness of other costs that were either not immediately monetary or wholly nonmonetary. These included things such as:

- Theft or destruction of user data
- Violation of regulatory rules on security or privacy
- Loss of customer faith and loyalty

Companies now became interested in just how the software manufacturers conducted security reviews, how much security testing was actually done, and even how well-trained the software engineers were in security and privacy practices. Answers to all of these questions have become significant factors in the decision whether a company will choose to go with one software application over another.

In-House Software Is No Longer Immune

After an initial focus on commercially made software, this new awareness spread (and continues to spread) to software that is developed in-house for use in-house. Such software has always been rather hit-and-miss because the general view has been that, because the software is for use only within the company that made it, it doesn't need to be as secure (or carefully tested) as software that is being sold or released outside the company.

The new security emphasis has also brought to light that even in-house software has the potential to be used as an attack vector or to be otherwise exploited by attackers. It's especially vulnerable to insider exploitation by current or former users. Some of these in-house projects later go on to become commercial projects, often with their initial security vulnerabilities intact. Secure design and security testing has a definite place in these projects as well.

Perimeter Security Just Isn't Enough

There is an established reliance on perimeter security, usually the perimeter of networks. People have tried, and continue to try, to solve their security problems by installing firewalls and proxy servers. They are using a theory akin to the defense of the castles of ages ago — namely, that you are to build walls and hide behind them, and you'll be safe as long as you don't let anyone in. The tall walls, strong doors, and commanding view all further the purpose of defense, and you might have a single building or a compound inside those walls. This would translate to a single system or a network being inside the firewalls.

Unfortunately, not letting anyone at all into your castle leads to situations such as starvation — you get no resources if you don't let anyone in. So, often you will choose to let a few people in through a merchant's door. These people at least claim to be merchants or to bring news, and you decide to trust a few and open the door for them.

In computers, if you want to be able to let in some information, you generally open a port for communication to pass through. However, unlike a guard at the merchant's door, a firewall can't tell if the traffic it is receiving is legitimate traffic or an attack being attempted. So, when a port or door is opened for communication, the only real checks a firewall can do is to make sure the packets are speaking the correct language and that they conform to the network protocol. It follows a policy of "if it looks like a duck and quacks like a duck, it must be a duck."

There are some additional checks the proxy can perform beyond those that a firewall can do. The proxy can provide better checks for malicious use, but proxies are usually specialized to protect custom applications and are unreliable, inadequate, and tend to lead to system performance problems. In our castle analogy, this would be akin to putting people by the door and having them make a decision about whether or not to admit a person on a case-by-case basis. They could allow someone in who is dressed as a baker but who is hiding a sword under his apron, or, someone in armor might be able to sneak by if the proxy looks away for a while. Certainly, it would take longer than letting people in without examination.

This is only the legitimate "way in." There are certainly illegitimate ones that are possible as well. In a castle, an attack can take place by going over the walls, digging under them, climbing in through the sewers, etc. Because all the defenses are geared toward keeping attackers out, once those defenses are breached, everything inside the castle is pretty much defenseless — they do not try to protect themselves or their own resources. This is one of the problems to not having defense in depth.

This scenario is similar to the situation with networks and systems. All trust and any efforts at defense are geared toward keeping the attackers out of the system or network. However, if that is penetrated, and the perimeter wall is breached, there is little to no effort by the applications running within it to protect themselves.

Although this is ineffective in practice, there is a tendency during software design to trust firewalls and proxies to keep attackers away. So, there isn't as much of an incentive to put significant effort into making the software secure. Many incidents in the recent past have shown (in painful clarity) the flaws in this perimeter approach, and securing operating systems and applications as well as networks is becoming more and more common as well as important. Thus, security testing for all of these is becoming more and more important.

Bibliography

Computer Use in the United States: October 1984. United States Census Bureau. Available from http://www.census.gov/population/www/socdemo/computer/p23-155.html.

Computer Use in the United States: October 1989. United States Census Bureau. Available from http://www.census.gov/population/www/socdemo/computer/p23-171.html.

Computer Use in the United States: October 1993. United States Census Bureau. Available from http://www.census.gov/population/www/socdemo/computer/computer93.html.

Computer Use in the United States: 1997. United States Census Bureau. Available from http://www.census.gov/population/www/socdemo/computer/97tabs.html.

Computer and Internet Use in the United States: September 2001. United States Census Bureau. Available from http://www.census.gov/population/www/socdemo/computer/ppl-175.html.

Computer and Internet Use in the United States: October 2003. United States Census Bureau. Available from http://www.census.gov/population/www/socdemo/computer/2003.html.

Computer and Internet Use in the United States: October 2003 Special Studies. United States Census Bureau. Available from http://www.census.gov/prod/2005pubs/p23-208.pdf.

Howard, M. and Lipner, S. The Trustworthy Computing Security Development Lifecycle. March 2005, Microsoft Corporation. Available from http://msdn.microsoft.com/library/default.asp?url=/library/en-us/dnsecur e/html/sdl.asp.

Chapter 4

All Trust Is Misplaced

I consider the analyzing and questioning of both the giving and accepting of trust in any form as the key to security testing. When I read my first book focused on software security, *Writing Secure Code* by Michael Howard and David LeBlanc (Microsoft Press, 2001), I was intrigued by the stress put on one of its core concepts — "All input is evil." After quite a few years of security testing and self-education, I've decided that, though it's a valuable and very true concept, it really doesn't go far enough.

When carefully examined, most security exploits occur because of trust. Quite often this takes the form of a security vulnerability where trust is granted inappropriately. This can apply to cases of explicit trust where, for example, a source is verified; then anything coming from (or believed to be coming from) that specific source is trusted. It can also be cases of implicit trust where, for example, incoming information is trusted because it uses a particular protocol and the correct port.

All trust is misplaced. You'll find that these words appear a lot throughout the rest of this book as I point out trust issues to consider. This is also the key statement to remember when understanding the mindset differences between functional and security testing.

As software is designed and developed, a number of things are taken for granted that are outside the direct control of the software that is relying on them. Because software is written to specifically solve one or more problems, the focus during the design and development process is on how it will solve the target problem or problems for the intended customers in the easiest, most effective, and least expensive way possible.

However, because the attention of the software engineering team is on how the software fulfills its intended purpose for its intended audience, many security issues are overlooked, and many assumptions are made. The worst part of this is that they are hidden or unconscious decisions, which makes them much harder to isolate and question. One of the most important (and time-consuming) tasks of security testing is to find and document all the places where trust is granted without appropriate checks being done. At these points, validation of input must be done to protect the software being tested, and validation of output must be done to protect anything the project being tested interacts with and provides data or services to.

Some common examples of misplaced trust:

- Users are trusted to be trying to use the software as it was intended to be used and for its intended purpose.
  - Requirements and designs are made with an eye primarily toward the intended user — the software's target customer. The customer is trusted to be using the software only for its intended purpose, not using it as a way to compromise a system.
  - Because of this trust, there is generally little thought given to preventing misuse of the software. Even some possible unintentional misuses can be overlooked as environments change, customer needs change, and even the capabilities of other software or hardware change.
- Information is trusted to be intended as valid and correct.
  - Users are trusted to provide information and data that conform to what the software expects to receive. If the software expects to have a filename input, the user is trusted to input a real filename in the correct format, not a string crafted to cause a stack overflow. If a date is requested, the user is trusted to provide a real date, not one from before the Neolithic age that is crafted to cause an integer overflow.
  - Data passed into an API from another application is trusted to be correct, valid, and appropriate for the API being called. If the API expects a username to be passed, the call to the API is trusted to contain a real username in the proper format, not data intended to cause a heap overrun.
  - Strings passed into a search function are trusted to be strings that are actually what the user is attempting to search for. If a Web page expects a search string to be entered, the user is trusted to input a searchable text string, not a string crafted to exploit an SQL injection vulnerability.

In all these cases, assumptions were made, and trust was granted based on those assumptions. But trust that is issued based on assumption is inherently dangerous.

Chapter 5

Security Testing Considerations

Security Testing Versus Functional Testing

The primary job of a software tester has been stated in many ways by many authors and speakers over the years, but like the others, I also have my own take on it. Being a tester really boils down to the job of designing and executing tests to determine the quality of the product to enable management to make informed decisions about its readiness to ship. If you look at just that description, it's pretty clear that both security testing and functional testing fall within the umbrella job description of "software testing."

It's not the primary job of a tester to find all the bugs in a product. Unless you have an extremely small product that runs on a very limited system, you won't be able to find all the bugs unless you don't plan on releasing the product for a very long time.

The primary job of a tester is not to get all bugs fixed either. There are always bugs that will remain unfixed as a conscious decision. Testers also do not generally make decisions on which bugs get fixed and which ones are deferred to a later date, or even those that there are no plans to fix.

The primary job of a tester is also not to decide when to ship a product. Although you can relay the state of the product to the company, the decision to release the product is typically made by the company or a team within the product group.

However, there are some significant differences between security testing and functional testing that really require some fundamental shifts in how you think about testing. You have to step back and reassess some of the "rules of thumb" and "tribal knowledge" of software testing that you've learned over time.

Change Your Focus

Functional testing is testing that is performed on behalf of a legitimate user of the product who is attempting to use it in the way it was intended to be used and for its intended purpose. This is who the functional tester is really the advocate for; thus, the majority of functional testing is done from the viewpoint of a customer.

It's important to realize that testing from only this viewpoint will cause you to bypass a large percentage of security tests. Most security vulnerabilities, although they have a chance of being discovered (mostly accidentally) by the intended customers, are unlikely to be exploited by them. Instead, the customer may call technical support to report the bug or maybe just grumble about it to friends or acquaintances. It's unlikely that many of the intended customers will even recognize that bug as more than a nuisance or sign of poor quality, let alone correctly see it as a security risk.

The attention of functional testing is much more focused on how to enable the customers to perform their tasks in the easiest and most convenient way possible while providing enough checks and safety measures so that they can't cause inadvertent harm too easily. It's a sort of "protect them from themselves" mentality. If any security testing is done, it tends to focus on things such as permissions and privileges but, again, only based around the assumption that the customer is using something like the login functionality as intended.

In essence, because you are performing tests on behalf of a customer, you are trusting that all people using the software you are testing are customers and not merely consumers.

All trust is misplaced. Don't trust that everyone who uses all or part of your project will do so as it was designed to be used or for its intended purpose. It is far more realistic to recognize that a subset of people will intentionally attempt to misuse all or part of your product.

All Consumers Are Not Customers

The first step to take in order to move to more of a security mindset is to stop thinking of the users of your project as "customers" and start thinking of them as "consumers." This provides a way to differentiate the set of users your product is designed for from the set of users who may also include people your product was not designed for.

Customers are the people or organizations that your software is intentionally written to solve a problem or problems for. They have been the main focus throughout the entire development cycle, from the gathering of requirements through the implementation, and that then provides the basis for functional testing. For example, the customers for a software program designed to streamline writing a novel are the novelists. Those are the people that the specifications and requirements are written around and from whose point of view functional testing is done.

Consumers, on the other hand, are those people or organizations that might use your software in a way it was or was not intended and who are not included in your customers. Sometimes your product's consumer base grows because your product is able to perform some task as part of its normal repertoire, and that task is all that the consumer wishes to accomplish. Sometimes it is because your product interfaces with some other software or hardware, and the consumer wants to use that ability to interface to their own advantage or because they think it may be exploitable.

In the prior example of the novel-writing software, the product may have the ability to take a delimited text file and translate its information into the proprietary file format of a major scheduling software system. If consumers merely want to avoid having to use the scheduling software's UI (or even buying a copy of the scheduling software) before being able to share their calendar with others, they can just run their delimited file through the functionality of your software to convert the file, then share the file out.

Other consumers can use that same functionality to generate a specialized file for the scheduling software to consume that takes advantage of a security vulnerability in the scheduling software. Perhaps the scheduling software itself cannot generate a file that would exploit their security bug, but a file that included the exploit would be successfully consumed by the scheduling software and cause the vulnerability to be exploited.

All trust is misplaced. Don't trust all consumers of your software to be actual customers. All customers are consumers (or potential consumers), but not all consumers are customers. Further, there are several classes of noncustomer consumers, ranging from convenient consumers to those who are intending to take malicious actions against your product or using your product's functionality to attack something else.

The Intent of Security Testing Versus Functional Testing

The most basic premise behind traditional functional testing is that it is meant to validate that the software you are testing fulfills its requirements and it functions as intended. In other words, it does what it's supposed to. There are usually some basic security tests included in functional testing, typically around items such as passwords and permissions, and whatever login or authentication method is in use. Even these are intended to test within the system's expectations — permissions testing only tends to test items such as insuring that if you are not logged in as an administrator, you cannot carry out administrative functions. It does not, however, focus on items such as how to obtain administrative privileges outside of the user login.

Although "security" is often presented as merely an aspect of functional testing, it really needs to be considered and planned separately. It may take place alongside functional testing, but it has almost an opposite focus.

"Positive" Versus "Negative" Testing

Positive and negative testing are terms that are used periodically in software testing to differentiate between the base intent of the testing being done. Although these terms are used regularly, their exact definitions are often in doubt because there are easily as many interpretations of the terms as there are testers.

My personal opinion is that, especially in the context of security testing, the concept of "positive" versus "negative" testing is so arbitrary as to be pretty much useless. All testers can, of course, think about their testing as they wish, but these terms won't be used in this book.

Although quite a few authors and instructors stress the concept of whether testing is "positive" or "negative," I rarely refer to or think of any of my day-to-day testing as either. Personally, I think that it's much more useful to think of testing in terms of atomic statements of behavior that can then be tested to determine a pass or fail for these very nonambiguous statements. I don't particularly think this is a bad or wrong way to view testing or to include in your test process, but I don't personally use it or consider it meaningful for security testing. I have a lot more information on this in Chapter 28, which focuses on the process of Test Case Outlining.

Test Overlap and Streamlining

The distinct mindsets of functional and security testing serve different purposes, and each one tends to compensate for some failures or blind spots in the other. Functional bugs are found while running security tests and *vice versa*. Sometimes tests for both aspects are intermingled and run concurrently, though the results have to be evaluated separately.

That being said, despite the common wisdom of reducing test time and expense by eliminating redundant test cases, I strongly feel that there should be overlap between purely functional test cases and security test cases. This is because the pass or fail criteria for the two types of tests can be so different. I've found that more bugs are missed when assessing the results of a test case if the tester is attempting to assess both functional and security criteria at the same time. The mindset is different as well as the validation and verification, and it's far too easy to not be 100 percent thorough with both.

As an example, if I am running boundary tests on my software's sign-up function, and specifically on the username field, it would be a typical functional test for me to try employing a username that is the length of the username field +1 long. If I was running a black-box security test on that field, I would try a very long username and construct it with a specific set of characters that I could recognize if it came up in an error dialogue or in a tool I may be using to examine the contents of memory, the registry, etc. Although these are both overly long entry tests, they are not equivalent and should really not be combined into a single test.

Most of the time, the steps required to set up and run a security case aren't well suited to a functional case, and combining them isn't attempted, but if the question comes up, think carefully before that type of test case consolidation is attempted.

That said, I have had the experience, while running one type of test, of getting ideas for another type of test, and those flashes of intuition should not be ignored. I advocate always keeping a notepad at hand.

Changing Your Prioritizations

In most types of testing there are some universal "truths" or guiding principals that are used to help estimate how much time it will take to test the project in question and how much attention and test effort to apply to what sections of the product. These principles apply to most types of testing, but if you are performing security testing, they require some revisiting and, in some cases, reversals.

Code Maturity

Traditionally, the guideline for testing existing code is that the more mature the code is, the smaller the percentage of bugs that will be found in that code. This is based on the fact that bugs are often found by users and through prior test passes, so there are fewer and more esoteric functional bugs left to find as time goes on. This "stable" code is often only given a cursory once-over during a functional test pass. When it comes to security testing, this becomes quite a bit more complex and convoluted — almost to the point of it being reversed from the mindset of functional testing.

If dedicated security testing has only recently begun on your project, it's actually more likely for the older code to contain a greater percentage of security defects than the newer code for several reasons:

- More security vulnerabilities and attack vectors are found all the time, so code that was written before those came to light may still contain them.
- More ways are found to exploit security vulnerabilities previously deemed to be unexploitable every day, so code that was written prior to those exploits is more likely to still contain those vulnerabilities.
- More tools are being created and distributed that allow exploits to be created and attacks carried out by a greater number of people who have far less technical knowledge than ever before. This increases the odds that any security vulnerabilities already present in existing code will be found and exploited, and having these vulnerabilities in existence and exploitable for longer periods of time gives these tools and attackers longer to discover and craft exploits for them.
- Developers (and testers) have become more security conscious over time and are less likely to make the same mistakes today that they might have made previously. This is partly due to receiving more security training and partly due to self-education, as vulnerability exploits hit the news.

Code Complexity

The rule of thumb for testing when it comes to code complexity remains basically the same. The more complex the code in the project, the more likely it has to have functional bugs. The more complex the code, the more likely it is to have security vulnerabilities as well.

Code Coverage

This speaks more about how much prior testing the code has received but specifically about how much prior security testing. If the code has received extensive security testing previously via code analysis (code reviews or security test tools), it's less likely to contain security vulnerabilities than code that has never been examined before.

You should know that it's very difficult to use automated code coverage tools to provide meaningful data on security testing. The standard of measurement for code coverage metrics is the percentage of code touched during a test pass, but this isn't terribly meaningful for security test efforts. Although it's common (and wise) for white-box testers to walk through all the code in search of security vulnerabilities, the actual percentage of code that is touched by testing is really most meaningful to functional testing.

Discovery of Software Vulnerabilities

It's helpful to keep in mind the various ways in which security vulnerabilities (and bugs in general) are found. I'm sure there are a few other methods of discovery that I haven't listed, but most will fit into one of these main categories. Nevertheless, no matter how the vulnerabilities are discovered, the bottom line is that there are very good odds that they *will* be found.

You should also realize that the time between security vulnerabilities being found outside the product team and when they are reported or exploited may vary greatly. Although there are more and more instances of zero-day exploits (vulnerabilities that are exploited the day they are discovered or whose exploit is the first indication of their discovery), there is really no timeline in which you may find out about security vulnerabilities that are discovered outside the product team. If the information about a security vulnerability can be used for malicious purposes, there is no reason for attackers who think they may be able to exploit that vulnerability to want to tip off anyone about the risk.

The lack of predictability of these external reports can sometimes lull companies and teams into a false sense of security and lead to some rather optimistic decisions when deciding what vulnerabilities need to be mitigated next. Just because a serious vulnerability that was introduced into your product three releases ago has not been exploited, there is no guarantee that (1) it isn't known to attackers and (2) it isn't being exploited at that very moment.

The major methods of discovery are now examined.

Accidental Discovery

Almost everyone I've talked to has discovered some bug or undocumented feature in software by accident. These can be very minor things, or sometimes a major bug turns up this way. I still remember that, during a class I took on a popular spreadsheet program, the instructor taught us a particularly useful but undocumented command. He only knew the command because his cat had activated it accidentally while walking on his keyboard, and he had taken the time to reverse engineer the steps the cat had taken on the keys in order to isolate how to activate the same function.

Never underestimate what people can find totally by accident. No matter how unlikely it may seem, someone will manage to stumble across it eventually.

Insider Information

It's not at all unusual for current or former employees to leak information about security vulnerabilities — both specific vulnerabilities and more general areas of possible vulnerabilities. This also goes for employees of companies doing contract or subcontract work in either software production or technical and product support. Because these people are in positions where they have access to everything from lists of known security vulnerabilities to source code, they can do considerable damage — both to the software company as well as the customers and consumers using the software.

Some insider information isn't as deliberately harmful, but with enough pieces of this information (not harmful in and of themselves), attackers may be able to connect the dots and get lucky enough to find an exploitable vulnerability. Just consider how long it would take for one of the old "Easter eggs" to be found after a product is released, and you will get an idea of how fast what most likely started out as a hint or two on how to access the Easter egg became a full-fledged set of instructions and then became common knowledge.

The reason or reasons for the deliberately malicious leak varies greatly, but the most common reasons are revenge, vanity, or greed.

Deliberate Search Efforts

There is also an entire network of people who try to obtain various pieces of software, especially beta or prerelease versions and the latest versions of released software as soon as they hit the streets. They then take the software and carefully start exploring it to see just what it's doing and how, even to the point of disassembly and reverse engineering. They have access to a lot of tools and information and a lot of time to dedicate to the task.

Such a network could contain several sets of people, however — from the malicious attackers (often referred to as blackhats) to the so-called ethical hackers (often called grayhats) and the security professionals (often called whitehats).

Assume Attackers Know Everything You Do

In a way, the attitude that attackers do not know everything goes back to the whole "ostrich" belief that is still rife throughout the computer industry. Although it's been disproved again and again, there is still a persistent belief that if something is hidden or not clearly and overtly exposed, it is somehow protected. This can be one of the most harmful fallacies in the field of software security. It imparts a false sense of security that can lead to riskier behavior and less comprehensive testing than needed. It can also lead to using the same ineffective "hide it" approach to future sensitive items instead of developing the solution that would improve security.

They really *are* out to get you, and being "paranoid" in performing risk assessments and security testing is a good thing, really.

All trust is misplaced: Never trust that the attackers don't know everything you do. If you believe they are in the dark, you will be wrong in the long term. If they really don't know it now, it's merely a matter of how long it takes them to discover the hidden information.

Source Code Compromise Is Common

There are a multitude of cases where source code details have been revealed — sometimes small sections but frequently huge blocks of the source code. In some cases, these have been revealed by people working on the project. Occasionally, they have been revealed by people who are employees of a contractor or subcontractor company or even an employee at the software company who is not actually involved in that project itself but still has access to the source.

Another method of source code compromise is if attackers successfully penetrate the physical or software security of the software maker and are able to steal the source code to use it themselves or distribute it.

Tools Are Readily Available

There are a huge number of tools available, running the gamut from commercial to home-grown, and from requiring purchase to shareware to freeware, and to those for trade, that are designed to allow an attacker to perform a huge number of information-gathering tasks.

Such tasks include those of monitoring everything happening in a particular system so that data can be gathered on exactly what parts of the system are being touched, what appears in memory when a program is run, what registry entries are made or modified, etc.

There are tools available to watch the network activity in and out of a system or a network device. Then there are tools that allow compiled code to be decompiled and returned to reasonably understandable source code. There are also tools available to automate the testing of suspected security vulnerabilities. It's far easier to write a small amount of code to pound at a suspected vulnerability than sit there and press keys manually.

In general, if you ever find yourself wishing for a tool to do some task for you, there are very good odds that one exists somewhere because you are almost certain to not be alone in your need to perform that task.

Secrecy Is Not Security

I really don't think this can be emphasized enough, so it's no accident that I continue to push it forward as an example. I am not advocating that there should be full disclosure of all details of the system under test because obscurity can be a useful part of an overall security plan, but only as a way to make it a little harder to discover the information.

One excellent example is, again, how quickly any one of the (now discouraged) software Easter eggs are discovered. If they were truly secret and secrecy meant security, should they have been discovered as quickly as they were, if at all? I will admit that my own suspicions are that many of these discoveries are courtesy of insider information or hints, but that is only a suspicion that I have, with no facts to back up. Either way, there wasn't much of a delay between the software arriving at retail and the Easter egg instructions being common knowledge.

Putting your trust in secrecy is the electronic equivalent to hiding an extra key to your home under a rock near the front door. Hiding a spare key is a relatively common behavior, and the number of places a key is likely to be hidden are relatively limited. So, you've already introduced a risk that wasn't there before; intruders may not actually have to break into the house at all if they just find the key. This would certainly make the intruders less likely to be detected as unauthorized intruders if they are seen using the key to enter your home.

Now, if you tell a friend or two and maybe a relative where your key is hidden, you've decreased the secrecy level as well. Once you are not the only person who knows a secret, you no longer have control of the knowledge. This key location is now susceptible to being discovered through a social engineering attack on one or more of the people you have told.

Perhaps a neighborhood dog digs in your flowerbed and knocks away the rock that covered the key. Now the key is lying out in the open for anyone to see and potentially use, or tell someone else about.

Vulnerabilities Are Quickly Exploited

The time between the initial public disclosure of a security vulnerability and an exploit being created for it has been shrinking, and will probably only continue to do so. A study by Symantec® (Symantec Corporation, Cupertino, California) in early 2005 showed that, in late 2003, there was an average of six months between disclosure and exploit creation. Yet, by the last six months of 2004, that time had shrunk to 6.4 days. That's only going to continue to shrink.

Such created exploits are quickly shared and spread — often via IRC channels or underground bulletin boards. An attacker can have an exploit out to a whole network of other attackers in a surprisingly short period of time.

There has also been a growing number of zero-day exploits. These are situations in which an exploit is created immediately after a vulnerability is discovered. It often means that the first hint of the vulnerability to the customers, the software company, and the security community is by way of an exploit making its way through the wild. One reason such exploits may have become more common and popular is because the time for security vulnerabilities to be addressed, once they are known, has been decreasing, and most security exploits are examined, the severity or risk assessed, and the appropriate mitigations taken very quickly. Another reason is that both users and IT professionals have become more dedicated to keeping patches and updates current on a regular and frequent basis. So, a zero-day exploit has a better chance of getting to the desired asset before it is patched or otherwise blocked.

Social Engineering Works All Over

Another matter to remember always is that even if your employees are the most dedicated and committed people around who would never willingly divulge a secret, social engineering is always a risk. There are definitely social engineering efforts that are aimed at the people who develop and maintain the software and networks, and even the most cautious and knowledgeable person can occasionally fall victim to a really clever social engineering attack.

Know Your Attackers

In order to successfully portray an attacker and be able to write correct and meaningful security test cases, you've got to have a good idea of just who these attackers are and what their skills and motivations are. A mix of the information is used as a backdrop to writing and running security test cases, and it can also be used to design security "personas" or "actors." These are covered in detail later in Chapter 7.

This is the scenario where you really have to look outside your box of "customers" and start to look at the broader pool of "consumers." There are three main parts to this formula: what, why, and who. Because you already know who your customers are, this exercise is a way to become aware of the potential attackers your security testing is helping to thwart.

What?

The first question is what the attackers may aim at. The answer is basically the list of assets that may be at risk and, if you are doing threat modeling, this list of assets and the one from the threat model should be in agreement. If they are not in agreement, the differences should be analyzed and resolved.

I deliberately look at this list of possible attack targets separately from any threat model because I seem to think of different assets when I am making a list for my own use instead of for a formalized process. After this list is made, I do reconcile it with the list used in the formal threat model (if one is being done).

A few ideas of assets that could serve as the goal of an attack are:

> *User Assets*
> - User login information
> - User permissions
> - User data
>
> *System Assets*
> - Availability of system and services
> - System processes
> - Data and information on system
> - System permissions
>
> *Network Assets*
> - Availability of network

- Data and information stored on other machines on the network
- Network information

Why?

Why would someone want to attack the asset? If there was no reason to attack it (i.e., it's not attractive in some way), then there would be no point in doing so. This is basically their motivation for the attack. The reasons can include:

Cyber-Terrorism
- Hacktivism
- Cyber-extortion
- Defamation

Personal or Group Recognition
- Cyber-tagging
- Headlines/press

Data
- Data theft
- Data destruction
- Data modification

Resources
- System resource theft
- Network resource theft

Who?

Who are the people that are performing the attack? There can be any number of them from both sides of the proverbial fence (malicious attackers and security researchers) and of all skill levels. These can include:

- Security researchers
- Script kiddies
- Talented individual hackers
- Organized crime
- Attacks for hire
- Disgruntled current or former employees
- Competitors

Create a Matrix

The easiest way I've found to clearly see the combinations that I believe are useful or valid for my project is to create a basic matrix and walk through it. I rate the various combinations according to how much of an issue I think they are for my project. To make life easier, I rate each line from 1 to 3, with 1 as the highest level of concern. This gives me the basic data for creating security personas, if I am using them, or later test cases. Table 5.1 shows what just a small sample of a matrix can look like.

Table 5.1   What, Why, and Who Security Matrix (Partial)

Priority	Asset	Motivation	Attacker
3	User login data	Hacktivism	Security researchers
2	User login data	Hacktivism	Script kiddies
2	User login data	Hacktivism	Individual hackers
3	User login data	Hacktivism	Organized crime
3	User login data	Hacktivism	Attacks for hire
2	User login data	Hacktivism	Insiders
3	User login data	Hacktivism	Competitors
3	User login data	Cyber-extortion	Security researchers
3	User login data	Cyber-extortion	Script kiddies
2	User login data	Cyber-extortion	Individual hackers
1	User login data	Cyber-extortion	Organized crime
2	User login data	Cyber-extortion	Attacks for hire
2	User login data	Cyber-extortion	Insiders
3	User login data	Cyber-extortion	Competitors
1	User login data	Defamation	Security researchers
3	User login data	Defamation	Script kiddies
2	User login data	Defamation	Individual hackers
2	User login data	Defamation	Organized crime
2	User login data	Defamation	Attacks for hire
3	User login data	Defamation	Insiders
1	User login data	Defamation	Competitors
3	User login data	Cyber-tagging	Security researchers
1	User login data	Cyber-tagging	Script kiddies
1	User login data	Cyber-tagging	Individual hackers
3	User login data	Cyber-tagging	Organized crime
3	User login data	Cyber-tagging	Attacks for hire
3	User login data	Cyber-tagging	Insiders
2	User login data	Cyber-tagging	Competitors
1	User login data	Headlines/press	Security researchers
2	User login data	Headlines/press	Script kiddies

Table 5.1 What, Why, and Who Security Matrix (Partial) (Continued)

Priority	Asset	Motivation	Attacker
2	User login data	Headlines/press	Individual hackers
3	User login data	Headlines/press	Organized crime
3	User login data	Headlines/press	Attacks for hire
3	User login data	Headlines/press	Insiders
2	User login data	Headlines/press	Competitors
3	User login data	Data Theft	Security researchers
2	User login data	Data theft	Script kiddies
2	User login data	Data theft	Individual hackers
1	User login data	Data theft	Organized crime
2	User login data	Data theft	Attacks for hire
2	User login data	Data theft	Insiders
3	User login data	Data theft	Competitors

Exploiting Software Vulnerabilities

Now that you've gathered information on the identity, goals, and motivations of potential attackers, you need to understand the various ways for software exploits to be delivered as an attack and some of the issues that surround those delivery mechanisms. The most clever and talented of attackers with an innovative exploit still have to find a way to get that exploit to the systems they wish to attack. Because these are only the delivery mechanisms, the actual content delivered varies greatly.

Trojan

A Trojan in software security means a seemingly attractive or innocuous program that hides malicious software inside.

This is named after the ancient Trojan horse of the Trojan wars where King Odysseus of the Greek state of Ithaca set a giant wooden horse before the gates of Troy that, instead of being a gift, hid Greek warriors. When the citizens of Troy dragged it inside, it allowed the Greek soldiers to come out of the horse and open the gates of Troy to let the army into the city.

Trojans aren't typically capable of spreading themselves, but instead they require a separate method of distribution, and that usually consists of the file containing the Trojan being transmitted to potential victims using methods like e-mail, instant messaging, IRC, ICQ, etc. When the potential victim opens the file, the Trojan is installed. Trojans can also be staged on download sites and disguised as utility programs, games, etc., and the victim is tricked into downloading them because they look like a useful program the victim might want to use.

Trojan Horse Virus

This is a hybrid between a Trojan and a virus. Most Trojan horse viruses infect like a Trojan in that they need to be run or executed by the victim (still typically by opening a file), and then the virus behavior takes over and the Trojan horse virus automatically spreads itself to other systems. So, it spreads like a biological virus. Sometimes it sends itself to your address book or your IM contact list, etc.

Virus

A computer virus is a program, typically malicious, that reproduces by adding itself to other programs, including those belonging to the operating system. It cannot run independently but needs a "host" program to be run in order to activate it.

The source of the name is a reference to biological viruses that are not considered alive in the usual sense and can't reproduce independently, but rather invades host cells and corrupts them into producing more viruses.

Boot Sector Viruses

A boot sector virus is one that infects the boot sector of hard disks, floppy disks, CDs, and DVDs. Despite the infection being located in the boot sector, these do not require that the victims boot their system from the infected media to infect it.

These viruses often stay resident in memory and infect floppies and other media when they are being written by the infected system. Once relatively common, such viruses are becoming ever more rare as the use of floppy disks continues to decrease.

Master Boot Record (MBR) Viruses

A master boot record virus behaves very similarly to the boot sector viruses, except that it infects the master boot record instead of the boot sector.

File Infector Viruses

The file infector viruses infect executable files such as .EXE and .COM files. Some of these viruses will stay resident in memory and carry on continuously infecting files, but others only infect the system when their host file is executed.

Macro Viruses

A macro virus uses some sort of scripting language, often Visual Basic™ (Microsoft Corporation, Redmond, Washington) or JavaScript™ (Sun Microsystems, Inc., Santa Clara, California), and infects types of datafiles from applications that support that scripting language. This is most well known from the incidents of infections among the various datafiles of Microsoft Office™ (Microsoft Corporation, Redmond, Washington) suite.

Multi-Partite Virus

This is simply a virus that exhibits the characteristics of more than one of the types of viruses.

Worm

A worm is a program that can copy a fully functional version of itself to other machines across a network without intervention. It doesn't usually require another program in order to run, but worms can, and do, sometimes hide behind other programs.

The source of the name is a derivative of "tapeworm," which is a parasitic organism that lives inside a host and saps the host's resources in order to maintain itself.

Logic Bomb

This is a piece of code that sits and waits for some piece of program logic to be activated and then activates the bomb's payload. Date bombs are the most common type of logic bomb, but the trigger could be anything from a message to the deletion of a file or directory, or a file size.

Logic bombs don't replicate themselves but instead have to be specifically targeted to the recipient. These are sometimes attached to a delivery mechanism that will install the logic bomb on a user's system.

Although this is really a trigger rather than a delivery mechanism or method of spreading, I've listed it here because it's generally delivered with one of the other listed delivery mechanisms.

The Role of Social Engineering

There are probably as many definitions of what "social engineering" is as there are security specialists, maybe more. My own favorite definition is that social engineering is a clever manipulation of the natural human tendency to trust in order to persuade people to do as the manipulator wishes them to.

All trust is misplaced.

It's a human tendency to grant trust far too easily, and that makes the human factor the weakest link in the chain of security. The goals of social engineering, as applied to software security, are similar to that of the various programs and tools — to gain unauthorized access to systems or information to commit data theft, disruption, industrial espionage, etc.

Social engineering plays a huge role in many security exploits, often as the initial attack vector. There are multiple psychological reasons why social engineering is so successful and most of them simply boil down to aspects of human nature. The quandary with social engineering is that user education only goes so far, and you can't issue a patch for people to insure they cease whatever risky behaviors they have been exhibiting or to increase their skepticism.

At its core, social engineering is really a confidence (con) game. It's an age-old criminal approach that has now moved into the electronic age with a vengeance and at great benefit to the con artist. The costs to run the con game are far less. The chances of the con artists getting caught are much less because the victims and potential victims don't actually meet the con artists face to face. In fact, they may not even be in the same country as their victims. There is a much larger pool of potential victims that are far easier to approach, and it only takes one or two potential victims to fall for the con to make it all worthwhile.

Social engineering attacks (and, really, all security attacks) are not usually a single event that strikes like a bolt from the blue. The attack pattern may include a succession of more and more complex attacks that serve to gather information or probe for weaknesses and lead up to the culminating major attack. If you think of social engineering in particular, you can see that even the release of minor amounts of information that are not seemingly of much use on their own could be used later to form and carry out other information gathering attacks or even damaging attacks.

Imagine that someone persuades you to give him or her the last four digits of your social security number to "verify your identity," and then you get a call from a very convincing man who says he is from your bank and who tells you that the bank has intercepted a case of suspected identity theft using the social security number it has on file for you. He tells you the last four digits and then asks you to repeat the entire number so he can verify that your number is indeed the one being used and the bank can take action. By the end of the call, if you've fallen for the con game, the con man has your entire social security number and certainly already has your name, address, and phone number. Now the con man has a set of data that can result in identity theft.

There are two basic types of social engineering — active and passive.

Active Attacks

In active social engineering, the con artist has direct contact with the potential victim. This could take the form of telephoning the victims to talk them into revealing a password or other private information, and in many ways this resembles one of the more classic telephone scams.

This could also be an in-person attack where the con artist shows up at the office door and pretends to be a representative of your company's software vendor, and needs to install an emergency patch on your system.

Almost all active attacks depend on one or more of the following methods to gain the information and access the con artist needs:

- Authority — We are all taught to respect and bow to authority.
- Befriending — It's human nature to want to trust, and especially to trust those we feel are, or are becoming, friends.
- Blackmail — We've all done wrong or an impression can be created that we've done wrong, even if it's not actually true.
- Deception — Flat out lying is always a staple.
- Flattery — Who doesn't want to think they are special or somehow better?
- Impersonation — Most often combined with another method, especially authority. Just pretending to be someone they aren't or to represent someone they don't.
- Intimidation — When in doubt, play on people's fears by intimidating them.
- Pressure — Don't want to give you any time to think so you're less likely to see through the con.
- Sympathy — This applies to both seeking and giving sympathy. Who doesn't want to help someone who is in need or in trouble?

Who doesn't soften toward someone who seems to sympathize with our own predicament?

Passive Attacks

Passive attacks attempt to obtain information with stealth. They tend to be carried out in bulk so as to maximize the return. After all, why send one or two e-mails (or even fifteen or twenty) when you can send tens of thousands for not much more of an investment? This is true especially if you are using someone else's e-mail server or account.

These passive attacks use some of the same methods as the active attacks but aren't nearly as specific as the latter. They don't have as high a percentage of success, but with the quantity involved and the relative inexpensiveness, only a few successes are needed for them to pay off. They are also more anonymous than the active attacks.

Phishing

Passive attacks include items like phishing, where many thousands of e-mails are sent to potential victims claiming that the person needs to change a password or verify a credit card number, and includes a helpful link to click on to do so. This link typically leads to a look-alike site, many of which are quite cleverly done, but entering data on these look-alike sites is the equivalent to handing the attacker your information.

A lot of these links are titled in a way intended to conceal the truth of their origin or exact nature. The hyperlink title may be "eBay Password Change," but if the potential victim hovers over the text to see the URL, they may be able to tell that it doesn't even have a similarity to eBay. Some of the URLs themselves are designed to deceive. A phisher may use a domain very similar to that of the legitimate entity they are masquerading as (for example "www.ebaysecurity.com") These links are, however, similar enough to deceive the potential victim who only gives it a quick glance.

Lately, I've even seen some look-alike sites place a false "lock" symbol on their web page to pretend to be an HTTPS site. Because users are taught to look for this lock symbol as a sign that a site is safe, they may see that lock and never even look at the address and see it's not an HTTPS site at all, but rather an HTTP site using a bitmap to deceive them.

There is also a play on trust if the e-mail you get happens to claim to be from a company or entity you already use. Most of the time, that is merely a random event because phishing e-mails tend to be "blanket" mails rather than specifically targeted e-mails.

E-mail headers are notoriously easy to spoof, but despite that fact being rather well known, many people still believe that the e-mail they receive is indeed from who it claims to be from.

These passive attacks can also include pop-ups and redirects that the potential victim can't verify the source of and which may lead them to believe that they need to enter their name and password again, but that information is really being sent to the phisher instead.

Urban Legends

Although not technically a security risk, a look at how urban legends begin and are subsequently spread is an interesting study in some of the aspects of social engineering.

Urban legends are cautionary tales couched as tales of actual events that always seem to happen to someone only slightly removed from the alleged writer. Some are true and some are fictitious, but they all share the fact that they play on human fears. Most urban legends are also modern tales — supposedly taking place relatively recently.

These are often spread in e-mail and are typically forwarded to us by a friend, family member, coworker, or online acquaintance. I often see them spread in newsgroups and e-mail lists as well. Although many of these tales seem dubious at best, a surprising number of people will look at the e-mail and immediately begin forwarding them to their friends and e-mail lists without ever attempting to verify the information they contain.

When these people are confronted with information that the e-mail they forwarded is an urban legend and that they should check their information before passing it on, they almost inevitably became defensive. They immediately claim that it *has* to be true because it came from so-and-so who would never send them something that isn't true. Their defensiveness seems to be dual edged — part "how dare I cast doubt on the integrity of so-and-so" and part feeling embarrassed that they fell for the story and didn't ask questions.

However, the point doesn't seem to get through that I am not casting doubt on so-and-so's integrity. I'm sure that the people who forwarded that mail, all the way up the line to whoever first received it from the original author, sincerely believed that it was true and the cautionary tale, picture, warning, etc., should be passed on to their friends and relatives. Each person in the chain trusted the information's source. The motives of the original author, however, are often a different matter.

All trust is misplaced. Just because someone you know forwards an e-mail to you, never trust that the e-mail is true.

Nigerian (419) Scams

Another case study in social engineering is that of the Nigerian Scam — also called the 419 Scam or the Nigerian Advance Fee Fraud. (The 419 refers to a section of the Nigerian penal code that applies to these types of cases.) Various sources claim different dates for the start of this fraud — ranging form the late 1970s to the early 1990s. They do agree that it began with paper mail and fax but migrated to e-mail and the Internet relatively quickly. It is now sent almost exclusively by e-mail with occasional cases of instant messenger transmissions.

This well-known and well-publicized con game typically claims that it is from a person or a representative of a person who needs help to transfer large sums of money out of the country or to claim inheritances. There are numerous variations that have different stories such as being the beneficiary of an estate or needing help to claim an unclaimed estate. These are also not at all limited to Nigeria anymore.

If the potential victim asks questions, the con artist always has an answer, typically very apologetic and heartfelt. The con artist will continue to string the potential victim along with a variety of ploys until the potential victim either says no or gives in. Once the victim agrees to whatever deal that particular con artist is trying to pull off, the victim is sent official-looking documents or e-mails, then delays are claimed, and the perpetrators begin to request a transfer of a relatively small amount of money (in comparison to the promised payoff) to do things like bribe officials, set up an appropriate bank account in the local country, etc. As long as the victim pays, the delays and more additional costs are added while the perpetrators keep the carrot of the large payoff in sight. However, the promised payoff will never happen because the funds just do not exist.

All trust is misplaced. If a deal appears to be too good to be true, never trust the sincerity or honesty of the person brokering the deal. The entire 419 scam is a con game — a social engineering scam at its purest.

Lost in the Cracks

A prime place to look for security bugs is in all the "cracks" in and around your product. I consider a crack to be anywhere that control is passed or data is moved between separate functions, modules, applications, or even hardware. You'll see that this is also an area that is focused on in the section on threat modeling.

In a way this also goes back to trust. If data has been brought into the system somehow, an implicit trust exists that this data has been validated somehow by whatever brought it into the system in the first place.

All trust is misplaced. Data being passed, even between subsystems of the same project, is not inherently trustworthy.

This is especially true as programs, operating systems, and even accessories become more and more interconnected. There may or may not actually be any way to tell how any piece of data entered the system.

Vulnerabilities are also found in between areas of functionality in the same application or product. One module may take data from the UI and pass it to an application programming interface (API) to process. The API doesn't check the incoming data before using it because it trusts that the UI has validated the data and only passed it on to the API after validation.

However, if the data was sent to the API by a method other than the UI, that data may be untrustworthy for multiple reasons, including:

- Business logic rules violated
- Data boundaries not enforced
- Unexpected data passed through
- Source may be spoofed or otherwise untrustworthy

Vulnerabilities are often found in areas of interface between different applications, products, or hardware. One system may take direct user input and save it in a file that is then consumed by another system. In this case the secondary system may not check the file before using it because the first system has been trusted to produce only valid and usable files.

However, the file that was consumed by the second system may be untrustworthy for multiple reasons both inside and outside of the control of the first system. Some examples are:

- Formats not respected
- File crafted with malicious code
- Version changes
- File modified before use
- Generator of file unknown

Common Security Hindering Phrases

"That's not a user scenario."

This is really a holdover from functional testing. In functional testing, the emphasis is on testing the software from the viewpoint of an intended customer who is using the software as intended for its intended purpose. If you hear this reaction to your security bugs a lot, it might be worthwhile to take extra care in your bug reports to explain the risks and possible costs if this vulnerability is exploited or if it contributes to an exploit.

I've heard this response in reaction to security bugs I've filed, but my answer is always the same — it may not be a user scenario but it's an attacker scenario.

All trust is misplaced. Never trust the intentions of the consumers of your product. Pessimism is rarely misplaced.

"It's hidden. The user can't even see it."

The most repeated tenet of software security is, "Obscurity is not security." No matter how counterintuitive or unlikely it may seem that something carefully hidden will be found by an attacker, you need to remember that hiding something really only works, even some of the time, when no one is actively looking for it. But even if it's not being actively sought out, hidden data is often discovered purely by accident. The fact that the items are hidden is being trusted to protect them.

All trust is misplaced. Never trust that something you've concealed will stay concealed, even for a short period of time.

"No one is interested in trying to hack this product."

Often, the person making this statement is only considering the actual product as an isolated system and taking into account only what the product is designed to do. After all, who would want to hack into a solitaire game, for example?

Many exploits, however, that utilize a particular program as their attack vector are not focused on that program as the end goal of the exploit. Instead, the program with the vulnerability being exploited is just a doorway to another step in the attack or another piece of software that is the true target. Although the capabilities of the program being tested are in line with its intended use, the assumption that your program is not a target because its capabilities are not useful goes out the window unless the program interacts with nothing else, not even an operating system.

All trust is misplaced. Never trust your program to be so insignificant that it will never be of interest to an attacker.

"Our developers have a security focus."

This is often seen as a defense or a reason to not carry out extensive security testing. While having a security focus is a great head start to a more secure product, it never means there isn't a need for security testing. Even the most dedicated and security-aware developer will miss things that a security tester performing a comprehensive review and test pass may be able to catch.

There is also the issue that, although many developers may have a security focus, they may not have a great deal of security training to go with it.

All trust is misplaced. Never trust the use of secure coding practices or standards to be the sole source of your product's security.

"The UI prevents that."

Any time the UI is relied upon to limit input lengths, perform business logic, or validate access, there is an immediate potential for problems. If the UI can be bypassed in any way, those things that the UI was protecting are immediately vulnerable. Because UIs are often easily bypassed, security testing must be done while bypassing the UI to have reasonable confidence in the security of the product.

Sometimes refactoring is done to improve product performance or functionality, or a deliberate decision is made to expose an API that was previously restricted. Suddenly, the issues previously hidden behind the UI come to light, and those almost always include security risks. In this case, the UI was being trusted to protect the product.

All trust is misplaced. Never trust a UI to mitigate security vulnerabilities.

"It can't get to the back end."

This is another assumption made because of the preconceptions of the limits of how a backend is actually reachable. This statement places its trust in several complex expectations:

- That the consumer will use the product only as intended
- That the system has no undue or unexpected influences
- That everything the system is designed to interface or interact with is working as designed and expected by the system you are testing, 100 percent of the time

It's obvious that placing trust in all three of these statements being true all the time is a long shot at best.

All trust is misplaced. Never trust that the backend is unreachable.

"I got an error when I tested it. That means it's secure."

This is another holdout from functional test expectations and trusting the consumer. If a customer gets an error, they will generally try to avoid doing whatever caused the error the first time or, if forced to do so, report the error and try to find a way to accomplish their tasks without triggering the error again.

However, if an attacker gets an error, it can provide valuable information to the attacker on vulnerabilities, software in use, etc. It will most likely spur a minimum of more investigation on the part of the attacker to see if the path that generated that error is useful in any way.

All errors and error behaviors need to be carefully examined to see if the error being generated is the right error for the user to receive, if it is being generated at the correct place in the code, and that it does not reveal information that may be useful to an attacker.

All trust is misplaced. Never trust that receiving an error is a sure sign that a possible vulnerability is mitigated.

Software Development Life Cycle Versus Security-Testing Life Cycle

I want to make it clear that implementation of the security-testing lifecycle is not a requirement to conducting security testing. It is very useful when beginning a security drive encompassing the entire product team, but if that is not something happening at your company or in your group yet, reviewing and comparing these two life cycles on your own is a good idea. It will let you see the differences and overlaps and give you a start on the development of your own security testing methodologies that will work with the environment you are testing in.

The Generally Accepted Software Development Life Cycle

The software development life cycle (often called the Waterfall Method) is a fairly consistently documented and taught illustration of the process flow involved in designing, developing, testing, release, and maintenance of software.

Figure 5.1 shows the classic waterfall life cycle, although more and more often, to better utilize time and increase both efficiency and effectiveness, the stages actually overlap quite a bit. For example, test plans and cases are usually being written quite a bit earlier in the life cycle than the verification phase.

The following is a very brief overview of the stages in this life cycle.

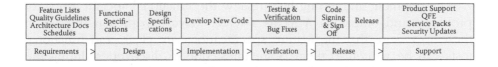

Figure 5.1 Software development life cycle (waterfall method).

Requirements Phase

The first task at this stage is to gather information on:

■ Requested new features and feature/design changes
■ Quality guidelines and release criteria
■ Upstream and downstream dependency schedules and requirements
■ Expected release timeframes
■ Schedule estimates from design, development, and test for each proposed feature

Once gathered, this information must be combed through and some decisions made on what features and requirements can be included in this release given the expected release timeframe and any dependency schedules and requirements that exist. It's a process of narrowing down candidates by priority, need, and time needed.

The quality guidelines and release criteria also need to be set. All disciplines generally have input into this stage, and testers have a particular interest in and input into the quality guidelines.

At the end of the requirement phase, the following should be determined and documented for the entire team:

■ A prioritized feature list
■ A draft schedule with the dates for the rest of the life-cycle stages
■ A set of release criteria for this particular release
■ A set of quality guidelines

Design Phase

This phase is the one during which the prioritized feature list from the requirements phase is taken, broken down into logical areas or categories, and then functional specifications are written. The functional specifications document what the system is going to do.

Development and testing help review the functional specifications for problems and omissions. You, as a tester, have a particular interest in these to ensure that the feature specifications are clear, and functional tests can be written to them. Sometimes, due to discoveries during the process of writing these functional specifications, features are trimmed back, timelines are adjusted, or features may even be cut entirely.

After the functional specifications are completed, they are handed off (usually to the development team) so that they can be turned into design specifications. Design specifications are items that state how the system will implement what the functional specifications describe.

You need to review the design specifications, again looking for errors, omissions, and obvious violations of standards. Another key item for testers is to start determining *how* you will test these features and changes. This is the time to have testability and test access built into the features that will make it possible to test them.

Although it's not technically included at this stage of the life cycle, you should already be starting to draft test plans and test cases as soon as functional specifications are at a complete enough stage to permit it. Such test plans and cases should be revised and updated as functional specifications are finalized, and then again with the data included in the design specifications as those are written and finalized.

Part of the reason for this is simply to maximize time and clarify the behaviors you will later be required to test, but it also means that if you find areas that are not testable, given the techniques or tools you have, you can point that out as early as possible.

Remember that if you can catch problems before the code is even written, it's very inexpensive to fix the problem. The rule of thumb is always "the earlier the better."

Implementation Phase

Once the design specifications are complete, the implementation phase begins. The whole focus of this phase is to write the code to implement the design specifications that were produced in the prior stage. Sometimes, as design specifications are completed and reviewed, developers will begin writing the code for them even as other design specifications are still being completed and reviewed.

Peer code reviews and formal code reviews are also a typical part of this phase.

Again, although it's not traditionally included in this phase, as soon as the code for any particular area is at all testable, you should start to test it. This will help the goal of finding bugs as early as possible and also compress the time needed to test the release.

I also advise you to attend any formal code reviews you can, even if you aren't a hugely technical tester or you are doing purely black-box testing. I constantly pick up useful information and a better understanding of the system by attending code reviews.

The other point I want to stress is that you should be talking to the members of the other disciplines all throughout the software life cycle. I realize that there are some authors and speakers who seem to treat software testing as a discipline that operates almost in a vacuum and doesn't really speak or work closely with any other disciplines, but I feel that this is one of the worst messages that can be given to any new tester. I strongly believe that consistent communication with the other disciplines, especially with your developers, is a key ingredient in an excellent test effort. So, not only should you attend code reviews but you should also ask questions — lots and lots of questions.

Verification Phase

This is the traditional phase for the majority of testing to be done in. During this phase, the code written in the implementation phase and any other code in the system that is carried forward is tested to verify that it meets its specifications. It includes functional testing as well as security and other types of testing, although they are not being done against the standard of the functional and design specifications but rather against other criteria or standards.

During the verification phase, the focus is on the bugs. The process of finding bugs, filing them, fixes being made to resolve them, and then those fixes being verified is called a "find/fix cycle," and there are typically several of these in the verification phase of each release.

If the product needs a beta release to a larger audience than the product team, the system can be released one or more times during this phase, and the beta testers will also be able to contribute bugs they find. As these bugs are reported, they are usually given to one or more testers. The testers then take the beta bugs and perform a number of steps on them before they are passed into the regular bug process:

- Verify that this really is a bug.
- Verify that this bug isn't already known.
- Determine a reliable set of steps to reproduce the bug.
- Document any additional information that will help the bug be addressed.

It is possible to have more than one beta release, and each one would follow the same cycle. The number of beta releases is usually determined as a part of the initial phase of the life cycle and included in the release criteria.

At the very end of this phase, there is typically a formal regression pass where all bugs fixed in this release (and sometimes the high-priority bugs from prior releases) are verified again to make sure that none of them has returned (regressed) before the product is released as complete.

Release Phase

Once the verification phase has been completed, the code is checked to see that all release criteria have been met, then approved or signed off on for release (typically by a representative of each discipline), and then the code signed, if necessary.

The code is then released to whatever method of delivery is appropriate to the type of system it is meant for. This is typically called RTM (released to manufacturing) or RTW (released to Web) at this stage.

Support Phase

The released system now is in the support phase, and product support (or technical assistance) takes over the daily work by assisting customers and researching any bugs or feature requests that are submitted by the system's customers.

Any bugs that must be fixed before the next product release is planned are often assigned to a QFE (quick fix engineering) or OE (ongoing engineering) team to be fixed. The fixes are then grouped and pushed out to the system's customers as service packs as well as integrated into the system code to insure that the fix is included in the next version of the system. The urgency and severity of the issue determines if the fix must also be released as a patch or "hot fix."

Security updates, on the other hand, are generally issued as patches and released for download immediately rather than holding them for release until enough other code fixes are accumulated. This is because most security fixes made between releases are urgent.

The Trustworthy Computing Security Development Lifecycle (SDL)

This is a process that was publicized in 2002 by Microsoft and IBM as a way to make security issues a priority during every stage of the software development process. The SDL rolls together a variety of techniques such as threat modeling, use of static analysis tools, code reviews, and a final security review into a structured process that can reduce the number of security vulnerabilities found after system shipment. There are four main high-level principles in the SDL.

Secure by Design

The system has to be designed from the start to protect both itself and any information it processes, as well as to be resistant to attacks. This design has to be carried out through implementation as well.

Secure by Default

The default state of the system should minimize the possible risks when attacks (successful or unsuccessful) take place. This includes items such as running at least access, turning off features not needed by the majority of users, etc.

Secure in Deployment

The software needs to be shipped with documentation and manuals that will help both the end users and administrators install and use the software securely. Any updates must also be easy to install.

Communications

There must be open and responsible communication with consumers when product vulnerabilities are found, in order to keep the end users and administrators aware of how to take proactive measures to protect themselves.

In addition to the preceding four main principles, the SDL lays out the security tasks that need to take place at each step in the traditional software development life cycle.

Probably, the key aspect to the success of any attempt to adopt SDL is education — a lot of education. Most people (in all disciplines) do not come to a project already completely educated on what they need to do to insure an effective and comprehensive job of implementing SDL. An educational effort needs to be put in place, both at the beginning of SDL adoption and on an ongoing basis. This can be an in-house or a contract effort, or even a mix, depending on the size of the organization and its needs. Figure 5.2 shows a graphical representation of SDL.

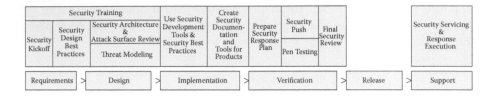

Figure 5.2   Security development life cycle.

Requirements Phase

The first thing to be done at this stage is to determine a person who will serve as the point of contact, advisor, and resource as the release goes through the stages of SDL to release. This person must have the training and experience sufficient enough to lead and guide the project and its team. Such a person is the Security Advisor (SA), who also assists in reviewing plans, making recommendations, and insuring any required resources or training are received by the team.

During the requirements phase, the following decisions are made:

- How will security be integrated into the development process?
- What are the key security objectives?
- How can security be maximized with disruption remaining minimized?
- What software is likely to be used with the system under development, and how will the security features integrate with that other software?
- What security feature requirements are needed for the system under development? Though some of these are discovered later (when threat analysis is done), this is the time when the features determined by customer request, certification requirements, or regulatory requirements are considered.

All of the preceding steps should be taken into account and addressed at the same time the new feature and other requirements are being collected.

Design Phase

During this phase in the software development life cycle, the overall plan and architecture for the system is created. As the project goes through this stage, the SDL focus is:

■ Define the security architecture and design guidelines. It includes determining what functions are integral to security as well as what design techniques apply to the project globally. Basically it involves the creation of an overall security design.

■ Document the elements of the software attack surface. What features must be exposed to all users by default? What is the minimum level of privilege that is feasible for these features? It's important to find any place where the attack surface is increased and question it every time.

■ Conduct threat modeling. This should be done at a component level. There are several methods of threat modeling that can be used, each with its own focus and take on the process, but the intent is still to come away with a prioritized list of threats that must be mitigated, as well as areas that should receive careful examination to insure that those areas function properly. There are more details on threat modeling in Chapter 6.

■ Define Supplemental Ship Criteria. This can include criteria such as the beta testing being security bug-free or having passed a security bug bash.

Implementation Phase

During this phase, coding and integration are performed. Note that, in the Microsoft version of the SDL, this is when the formal testing is conducted, but testing should (and usually does) continue all the way through until the system is actually shipped. Any steps that can be taken in this phase to prevent or remove security flaws are very inexpensive, and they significantly reduce the chance that these flaws will make their way into the final version of the system. In the SDL, the following steps are implemented:

■ Apply coding and testing standards.

■ Apply security-testing tools including fuzzing tools. There is more information on this is in Chapter 22 — Fuzz Testing, later in this book.

■ Apply static-analysis code-scanning tools.

■ Conduct code reviews.

Verification Phase

This is the phase in which the features are code complete and testing (include beta testing) is being conducted. In the SDL, this is the time that more focused code reviews and a specific security test pass are conducted. It allows review and testing of not only the new or modified code but also the legacy code that was not modified during the release phase.

Release Phase

The release phase in the SDL is when the system is put through a final security review (FSR). This review is designed to answer the question of whether the system is now ready to be released to the customers from a security standpoint. The stated ideal is to have the FSR conducted two to six months before the system is to be released, both to insure that the FSR is conducted on code that is as mature as possible and as least likely to be changed. Of course, this depends heavily on the release schedule of the system, and the move to faster and more nimble release schedules makes this timeline an almost unattainable goal in many cases.

The FSR is intended to be conducted by an independent team, and sometimes even by outside security review consultants. This is to try to isolate the FSR from preconceptions and biases that exist on the product design team as much as possible.

Support and Servicing

There is no way to ship a system that is 100 percent bug free, so there has to be a way to respond to newly discovered vulnerabilities. This process includes a way to evaluate reports of new vulnerabilities and issue fixes as needed.

The other thing that needs to occur during this part of the SDL is a postmortem assessment and analysis of the security bugs found. How, where, and when they were found may indicate a need for process change, a need for tool updates or changes, etc.

Extreme Programming and Security Testing

Extreme Programming (XP), Agile Programming, and other development methodologies that are lumped under the umbrella of "test driven development" are ones that tend to encourage coding the system to pass predesigned tests. This is beneficial for functional tests and feature tests but doesn't work nearly as well for security tests. In XP, the code is the design, and the user stories and unit tests that drive that code aren't detailed enough to make design flaws sufficiently visible.

To be better able to address this, security issues should be moved to an earlier portion of the cycle, and "attack" or "abuse" stories should be added to the project to better address security issues.

Black-Box Versus White-Box Security Testing

These are common terms in software testing, and most definitions are relatively consistent, but, just to be clear, "black-box" testing is testing done without knowledge of the system's internal design and is called black box because you can't see what's going on inside the system. Anyhow, it's usually used to indicate testing that is being done without walking through the code.

On the other hand, "white-box" testing is a term used to indicate testing that is being done with explicit knowledge and access to the underlying code of the system. I've also heard it called "glass-box" testing to more closely conform to the idea of being able to see into the box.

Part of the challenge of being a software tester is to find creative ways to test your system. To most testers, it really is like a giant puzzle they take great delight in constantly challenging themselves with. You have to find ways to validate functionality and also ways to try to get around the checks and mitigations of the system. It's a satisfying feeling to discover a really ugly security vulnerability and boggle the developers with how you discovered or exploited it.

I have heard differing opinions voiced about whether or not black-box testing has any validity or place in security testing. Part of this goes back to the idea that security testing is an arcane art, and part of this is really just prejudice on the part of the person voicing the opinion. I strongly believe that there is a clear role for black-box efforts in the realm of security testing and, in fact, in has some definite benefits that are different from those in white-box testing.

Many Attacks Require Little Coding

One reason that there is a role for black-box testing in security is the simple fact that finding some security vulnerabilities doesn't require coding. Typing a particular string into one of the parameters of a Web page and hitting return requires no coding at all. Quite a few attackers do not have much in the way of coding skills either.

Security Testing Is a Part of All Testing Efforts

Black-box testers need to be as aware of security and as involved with security testing as white-box testers. Whether or not you read code, write code, or even see the code should never excuse you from being concerned and testing security.

Despite the differing opinions of just how security testing should be done and the relative effectiveness of the two main types of testing, they both have a role. Black-box testers are not immune from doing security testing, despite some statements I've heard to that effect.

The Differences Between Black-Box and White-Box Security Testing

Black-box testing has the advantage of a lack of bias on the part of the testers toward the code behind the system. They are better able to test purely what's happening before them, and the lack of assumptions can mean their tests are more random and contain more unexpected data. However, they are only able to test what they can get to and don't generally write automation (although this is starting to change with the introduction of more tools designed to allow testers to programmatically manipulate a system's User Interface [UI]). Black-box testing involves more of a focus on the customer and consumer points of view and may have better success with issues such as safe install questions.

White-box testers are better able to explore the code behind the system to look for security vulnerabilities. They may be able to write automation to perform some security tests. They do have a tendency to let their knowledge of the system's code bias the cases they choose to run and the inputs they choose to use. White-box testing tends to keep the customers and consumers a little more at a distance. The code itself provides a separation between the tester and the customer or consumer of the system.

There are certainly types of bugs that are easier to find using one methodology than the other. In each of the vulnerability case studies, I have tried to include both general tips and test ideas as well as ones specifically for white-box and black-box testing wherever possible.

Guard Your Own Gates

Another of the concepts that I can't stress enough is that of your system guarding its own gates.

Reliance Solely on Outside Protection Is False Security

As the software industry has been discovering over the last few years, reliance solely on any outside entity for security or protection is not sufficient, be it software or hardware solutions. Anytime that protection fails, it means that your system is exposed to unanticipated risk it probably has no defense against.

Firewalls are a great example of this. A common theory for a while was that placing security devices at the network perimeters (which is where firewalls are set up) would protect the systems inside the network so they did not need to worry about their own safety. Instead, what has been demonstrated is that this creates a single point of failure for the security of multiple systems. Once the perimeter security is breached, the attackers have little or no problem exploiting the systems inside the perimeter.

Now, anyone who deals with other types of security will realize that this is in direct conflict with the security tenet of "defense in depth," but, surprisingly, this perimeter security reliance is still fairly common — and risky.

Your Application Must Defend Itself

Because your system cannot afford to be exposed or exploited due to the failure or bypassing of outside security measures, it follows that the system has to be able to at least provide security for itself at some reasonable level.

This is where threat modeling and risk assessment processes come in, as well as security testing. The most important or valuable assets need to be protected, ideally with multiple levels of security. In a way it's similar to a brick and mortar business not putting its sole reliance on the security guard in the lobby to protect its assets but instead also having locked doors, card key access, and even its own private security guard to further secure its assets. If it has valuable items such as money or stocks, it may have those inside a safe as well. Multiple levels of security exist, and the more valuable the asset, the more security is provided.

Software systems need to have a similar theory of protecting themselves and their assets. While the external measures are useful and not to be just discarded, they should never be the only measures in place.

Don't Let Your Application Be the Achilles' Heel

The other side of the security coin is that your system can be used as a gateway in order to attack another system that has some sort of relationship with your own. This relationship can be as simple as running on the same piece of hardware, running on the same network, and where your system is designed to directly interact with another system or systems.

If your system has poor (or no) security, it is putting all the other interrelated systems at increased risk. Failing to find and fix security vulnerabilities has repercussions as well, even if you feel that your own system has no real assets to protect that would make any difference.

For example, my system is a little applet for amusement, written in C, which acts like a fortune cookie. It has a UI that takes a string as a question and returns a string that is your fortune. Now, say this ships with one or more large software packages as a "game"; there may be a lot of copies out there. It's also able to take the input via an API and return the string result. It sounds harmless, and there's not even anything to protect.

Now, what happens if I am calling the API and, instead of passing in a string that's a reasonable length (assuming I know what that is) for a question, I pass in a string that overflows the buffer? I have a buffer overrun vulnerability and any attacker owns the computer my system is installed on. This is akin to having a house with alarms and huge locks and thick strong doors — and leaving the front door standing open. The lack of a very simple security test for my system has now compromised every computer it is installed on.

Mitigation of Damages Must Be Considered

Even if your system has implemented security testing and put appropriate mitigation steps in place for high risk vulnerabilities, there is another aspect to security that needs to be addressed — detection and mitigation of actual damages. Although this is not typically a task for testers, I did want to point out this aspect in order to fill in one of the often neglected aspects of security.

For every important asset, there should be monitoring in place that can detect compromise, including unauthorized access, destruction, modification, etc. There needs to be some way to tell that bad things are happening. But what happens if security is breached and something bad does happen?

So, there needs to be a response plan. If a database is modified or destroyed, how will the system be recovered? Restore a copy? Go to an emergency failover copy? Who does this? If a database is accessed or known to be copied, who needs to be informed? What steps need to be taken with any other entity?

There Is No Perfect Security

Despite my continued encouragement and focus on improving and strengthening security, it's also important to realize that there is no perfect security that can coexist with reasonable functionality. I'm not even convinced that there's perfect security in any case, even without functionality entering into the equation.

Perhaps there could be perfect security if you have a system locked in a room that has no power, no connection to any other computer or network, has no input devices and no drives or ports, no printer or output devices. Of course, that would equate to a very expensive piece of unviewable modern industrial design, but it would be highly secure, but not perfectly — what if someone picks the door locks?

If there is sufficient motivation, time, and resources, any security can be broken. The key in instituting security is to create a situation where more motivation, time, or resources are needed to break into the system than the assets are worth. You want to make it so the assets are not worth the effort needed to find a way to them. Logic says that if you have very attractive assets of some sort, your security has to be strong enough to offset the attractiveness of these assets.

The Role of Security Testing

This section is really just to give you a bit of background on what the members of the different software disciplines tend to focus on and to provide some food for thought. I am perfectly well aware that these are generalizations and do not apply to every member of any of these disciplines. Don't bother to send me mail to tell me that. Take them as what they are intended to be — just to provoke thought.

What Developers Want

Developers are taught to strive for compact and elegant code that performs its required functions without extraneous code or functionality. This is often at odds with security because it can lead to taking unsafe shortcuts or not validating input as often as necessary in a drive to keep the coding elegant and compact. Developers do want their code to be secure — don't get me wrong — but their natural inclination is to be more trusting of input and data.

Developers also tend to be very focused on just the system or subsystem they are writing code for. Because of this, they can tend to have a little bit of tunnel vision when it comes to implicit interfaces with other systems.

Most developers I've worked with are also somewhat optimistic. When they write code, their first concern is to make it work and, often, once they get it to work, they don't test it themselves any further, and they retain an optimistic view that it won't break unduly.

What Program Managers Want

Program Managers or project managers (though the actual title may vary, based on your industry and company) are generally focused on the needs of the customers and trying to align those with the needs of the company producing the system.

The system has to fulfill the needs of the customers because, without customers, you have no income. However, the focus on this means that program managers tend to want to make thing as easy as possible for the customers, and this is sometimes at odds with good security practices.

Part of the desire to make things easier for customers has been the ever-increasing move toward tight integration of different systems with each other, allowing them to interact and share functionality and data with each other. This also involves a more expanded trust relationship with each other that creates additional security concerns as a by-product.

Adding security testing and processes such as threat modeling and risk assessment are also at odds with one of the primary functions of program management, which is to keep the projects as "lean and mean" as possible. They often require additional time and manpower to complete, and have a potential to increase costs and push the project schedule out.

What Management Wants

Management wants the company to prosper and make money. That's the only way that the company can continue to stay in business. Their focus is, therefore, on ways to increase sales; at the same time, they want to decrease costs.

Sometimes the reaction of upper management to security testing and software security drives is dependent upon the way in which the process is presented to it. To most effectively inform management of the factors it cares about, you have to be able to couch the security concerns in a way that makes sense to the bottom line it is responsible for.

What Testers Want

Software testers really want to find bugs before the customers or consumers do, and they consider their job to be acting as the advocate and stand-in for the customer. Their other main drive is to solve the puzzle of how to convince the system to do something it's not supposed to do, and this really translates to acting as the system's consumers.

Because there are always more tests to run, security testing often seems to add yet more cases to be fit into roughly the same amount of test time, so sometimes there is some resistance to adding more tasks without adding resources. However, I've never met a tester who didn't feel that more testing would be even better, including security testing. Security testing, with the appropriate resources and especially training, is usually an easy sale to testers.

Effectively Presenting Security Issues

One of the real issues faced by testers (and sometimes other members of the project team) when they have found a security vulnerability is how to get it fixed. Sometimes everyone is on the same page, especially if there is a formal security drive in place, and getting security issues approved for a fix is relatively easy.

However, what if you are not so lucky, and your bugs may be returned to you time and time again with some reason why they are not important or urgent enough to be fixed? Sometimes this means they are being pushed out for a possible fix in the future, and sometimes they are being permanently decided as a "won't fix."

It's relatively easy to explain the repercussions of not fixing a functional bug, and the process of prioritizing that fix is straightforward. Because it's a very customercentric view, it's simple to explain to program management or upper management. After all, the ramification of not fixing a "crashes when used" or "won't read files from prior version" are pretty easy to imagine.

Security vulnerabilities, on the other hand, are not nearly so easy for someone not familiar with security to understand and be able to assign an appropriate priority to. There are, however, a few steps you can take when you file these bugs that will give that bug the best chance of being correctly prioritized and to have an appropriate decision made on when to fix it. These are actually useful steps to take for all your bugs but are particularly good for security bugs.

Carefully Evaluate All Factors

Always begin by carefully looking at all the factors that will play a role in determining how urgent this bug fix is.

Risk

What asset is at risk because of this security bug?

Cost to Fix

What is the cost in time to fix and do any retesting of the revised code if this bug is fixed? You may not know the cost, but you can often get an idea by talking to one of the developers.

Cost if Exploited

What are the monetary and nonmonetary costs to the company if the bug is used in a security exploit? What are the costs to the customers?

Trickle-Down Effect to Dependents

What are the effects on systems that are dependent upon your system of the bug remaining? What are the effects on the dependent systems if the bug is fixed?

Trickle-Up Effect to Dependencies

What are the effects on systems your system is dependent upon if you leave the bug? What are the effects on these dependencies if the bug is fixed?

Think Outside the Box

The next thing to do is to see if you can think of any possible fixes and mitigations to suggest for this security bug. If you have any good ideas, they are always a valuable addition to any bug reports. These can either provide possible solutions that may not have been otherwise considered or spur brainstorming of other ideas.

Possible Solutions

These would be ways to eliminate the security bug completely, and may be possible if the bugs are pretty clear-cut code mistakes or oversights.

Possible Mitigations

Consisting of ways to mitigate the security bug, these can include additional validations, filtering, etc. They may not eliminate the bug but will mitigate or reduce the risks of its existence.

Pick Your Battles but Continue the War

One of the most important things to remember when trying to get bugs fixed is to always pick your battles. Nothing will make your bugs sink to the bottom of the list and not get the attention they deserve, faster than doing a professional imitation of a constant false alarm.

It's common and natural for testers to want to be sure all their bugs are fixed. After all, their job is to eliminate bugs; except, the decision of when to fix any particular bugs doesn't belong to the testers at all. It generally belongs to either a team of representatives from the various disciplines or to program management.

Testers generally decide on what they think the severity of the bug is — how badly it affects the system. The priority is how quickly the bug needs to be fixed, and although it may be given a suggested value by the tester, the final decision is usually up to the team of representatives or program management.

Make Bug Reports Accurate

For the correct decision to be made, your job is to accurately represent the bug, its severity, and the various factors that may play a role in the bug's eventual disposition.

One mistake that is often made by even seasoned testers is to try to influence the decision by artificially inflating the reported severity of the bug. Although it may work once or twice, you will quickly develop a reputation for overstating your bugs and, later, when you have true issues, no one will believe it can be as bad as you say. Just don't do it. The management and the product team need to be able to count on you to accurately and honestly report the bugs you find.

Include Appropriate Information

Another point that will greatly help the team in charge of assessing the bugs to make the correct decision regarding your bugs is to insure that your bug report contains all the information they need to know. This includes not only the core issue and steps to reproduce the behavior but also a brief overview of why you have given the bug the severity you did. Then include details of the various factors listed earlier and the possible solutions or mitigations that you would suggest.

If You Don't Agree with the Decision

There are always times when your assessment of what priority the bug should have is not in agreement with the decision made by those charged with determining the official bug priority for the team.

When that happens, I generally look at the bug again and compare it to any remarks or notes made by those processing the bug, and I try to determine why our opinions are at odds. Sometimes, usually from comments that have been made, I can tell that the reason is that the way I went about explaining some of the risk factors or side effects were not correctly understood. In the case of security bugs, this can be fairly common if the group prioritizing bugs doesn't have a strong software security background. In this case, if I believe the priority is really incorrect for the actual severity of the bug, I will revise the bug and add information or explain my case in another way and then resubmit it.

If I can see that the problem is that they do not see the bug as being as high a priority as I do, I will look at my point of view and try to compare it with the reasons given for the priority assigned. If I have no reasons, and I believe strongly in my own assessment, I will often try to speak to one or more of the team who assigned the priority and see if I can obtain some insight into their reasoning.

If our opinions are still at odds, I will look carefully at the bug and how bad it is, and decide whether I will try to fight this battle. If I think it's worth the battle, I will revise the bug report with more information to make my case and resubmit it to the team in charge of priorities.

At a certain point, all testers have to accept that they have done their job in making sure the bug was found, and all information about it and the associated risks and implications were reported. They have no control of the business decisions made about what to fix and when. You will just have to let it go, and I suggest doing so gracefully.

Don't Fight Every Decision

Just as artificially inflating the severity of your bugs will quickly cause people to believe your bugs are always listed as more severe than they really are, fighting every decision about the priority of your bugs that you do not agree with will gain you a reputation for being short-sighted and argumentative.

You really do want to pick and choose your battles and only fight those you feel are essential.

Foster a Security-Conscious Environment

Another way to help the system you test become safer and more secure is to proactively foster an environment that is security conscious. Even if you are new to security testing yourself, you can easily be a part, or even the driver, of positive changes in your team or even your company.

Be Persistent

Don't let a lack of immediate understanding or eagerness on the part of the other team members put you off. Software security is a complex and unfamiliar subject for many companies, and it can take time to really see some change taking place.

Share Knowledge

Any knowledge you can share with others on your product team, your division, or even your company can help keep attention on the subject of security and educate others at the same time. This can be as simple as passing around articles of interest and as complex as holding informal classes or meetings to review the basics of various security subjects.

Advertise Success and Failure

It's great publicity for your security efforts to blow your own horn, but be sure to advertise both the good and the bad. Periodic reports that outline the "state of security" of your system can gain important visibility for the security testing efforts at the level of both peers and management.

It is also a good idea to carry out a postmortem assessment of each release or stage of the product life cycle and track items such as the number of security bugs found and fixed, any new security concerns in the industry, what is being done to address them, etc. Even the number of security related tests, how often they are run, and the state of any threat modeling can be valuable information for informational reports or e-mails.

Bibliography

Alberts, C., Dorofee, A., Stevens, J., and Woody, C. Introduction to the OCTAVE® Approach. August 2003. Available from http://www.cert.org/octave/pubs. html.

Bernz. The Complete Social Engineering FAQ. August 17, 1999. Available from http://packetstormsecurity.org/docs/social-engineering/.

Granger, S. Social Engineering Fundamentals: Hacker Tactics. 2001. Available from http://www.securityfocus.com/infocus/1527.

Howard, M. and Lipner, S. The Trustworthy Computing Security Development Lifecycle. March 2005, Microsoft Corporation. Available from http://msdn. microsoft.com/library/default.asp?url=/library/en-us/dnsecure/html/sdl. asp.

McGraw, G. XP and Software Security?! You gotta be kidding. 2003. Cigital. Available from http://www.cigital.com/presentations/xpuniverse.

Nyman, J. Positive and Negative Testing. 2002. GlobalTester, TechQA. Available from http://www.sqatester.com/methodology/PositiveandNegativeTesting. htm.

Patch Management in Healthcare. March 29, 2005. Symantec Corporation. Available from http://enterprisesecurity.symantec.com/industry/healthcare/article.cfm? articleid=5502.

Chapter 6

Threat Modeling and Risk Assessment Processes

Threat modeling and risk assessment, as a formal process, may or may not be something that your product team or company practices. The formalization of the process into any particular specific format is not a requirement for security testing to take place, but it adds considerable benefit to the entire effort. You will find that if you do not have a formal process, reviewing some of the formats will help you know what you need to look at as an individual tester to improve your own security testing process.

Although threat modeling and risk assessment are generally a task done by a committee or a subgroup of the product team, I've covered the basics in this section with a fair amount of detail, but I haven't attempted to cut back this section into only the "tester's job" for several reasons. One of these reasons is that I believe it's important to understand what should happen and to discuss it as a part of this process. The second reason is that reviewing these types of issues may lead to some of those "flashes of tester intuition," and that can lead to security vulnerabilities being exposed. The third reason, however, is that even matters outside the realm of the software tester (such as physical security issues, etc.) may be those that have been overlooked in a threat model you are working with, and you will be aware of the fact that they should be considered and be able to question its absence. The more people who will constructively question software security vulnerabilities and mitigations, the better.

Threat modeling systems are basically specialized and structured ways of conducting risk assessment. There are quite a few threat modeling systems already out there, and new ones are often being developed. In addition, many companies, software teams, and even individual testers will, over time, either develop their own or modify one they have learned to best suit their processes, the software being tested, any regulations that need to be adhered to, and their own professional experiences.

At its core, threat modeling is a process by which the security risks of an application (or those associated with an application) are assessed and documented along with any mitigation of those risks. The development of threat modeling is a response to the need for a methodical and systematic process to analyze the security of a system. To fulfill this purpose, any threat modeling system needs to examine an application or system from the point of view of an attacker, and describe and examine attack goals and methods from that point of view.

There are three ingredients required for most threat modeling:

- An attacker — If no attacker exists, there is no attack.
- A method of communicating with and supplying data to the system — If there is no way to either directly invoke the functionality or to supply data to the system, the attacker can't affect the system.
- A goal (asset) — If the system doesn't have anything of value or interest to the attacker, there is no reason for the attacker to be attacking it.

Threat modeling starts with documenting any way the system being modeled has of being accessed (called "entry points"). Then, any functionality that can be accessed through those entry points is examined to determine which assets can be affected. Any way that an attacker can possibly affect an asset is termed a threat. If a threat is investigated and proven to be possible to realize, the threat then becomes a vulnerability.

The end goal of threat modeling is to produce a document (a threat model) that details the potential attackers, the possible targets, and any vulnerabilities that can be exploited. From this threat model, testing can be done and mitigations designed, but merely completing a threat model once is not enough. The model must be reviewed regularly and any new types of vulnerabilities and system changes accounted for.

I tend to use a spreadsheet program for threat modeling, but I've also seen databases used as well.

Threat Modeling Terms

Assets

An asset is any resource that the system must protect from attackers. These include:

- Physical assets such as paper files, computers, janitorial supplies, drinks, product inventory, etc.
- Abstract assets such as employee safety, company reputation, the availability of resources, etc.
- Electronic assets such as databases, servers, files on computers, etc.
- Transitive assets that act as a gateway to other assets. If the first component is accessible via an entry point and interacts with other components in the system, it can be a gateway to the functionality and assets of the components it interacts with. The assets of these other components are called transitive assets of the first component.

Attack Path

An attack path is the sequence of steps (often tracked in a threat tree) that must be traversed to achieve a threat. If this attack path has no mitigations, it is considered a vulnerability.

Condition

A condition is an action or weakness that must be present in the attack path for a threat to be a vulnerability (an unmitigated threat).

Entry Points

Entry points are places where the control or data crosses the boundary of the system being modeled. In an office, the obvious candidates would be the doors, windows, and elevators, but the not so obvious entry points are the drop ceiling panels, the telephone cables, the electric cables, the water supply, the airconditioning ducts, and the network cables.

All points of transition of either control or data into or out of the application must be considered. This includes any interaction with other applications, network data, network services, network time services, APIs, and administrative controls. Note also that:

- Infrastructure entry points can include data that is read from the file system or configuration stores such as the registry.
- Layered entry points are items such as Web pages where each Web page is not only a separate entry point but also every function carried out by every one of those Web pages is a separate entry point.

External Dependency

An external dependency is a dependency on another system that will affect the security of the system under test if it is not abided by.

Exit Points

Exit points share some aspects with the entry points but include items such as the garbage chute behind the building, the trash cans outside the office doors, the break room sink drain, the toilet and bathroom sink drains, etc. These are places where data or information leaves the system. They can also include log files.

Risk

Risk is the measurement or assessment of the real or potential danger of the threats, conditions, or vulnerabilities in the system.

System

A system is the set of functionalities is being modeled, which is characterized by having interactions outside its own control and having assets to protect.

Threat

A threat is what an attacker may attempt to do to a system. All threats against a system are compiled into a threat profile.

Threat Model

A threat model is the output document of threat modeling that details the system's threat profile, any background information, and an analysis of the system's mitigations and vulnerabilities in relation to that threat profile.

Threat Profile

A threat profile is a list of all threats for the system being profiled.

Trust Levels

Also called access categories, trust levels are the set of rights given to any entity based on what is known (or thought to be known) about that entity. Sometimes these correspond to user groups.

Use Scenario

How the system is intended (or not intended) to be used.

Vulnerability

A vulnerability is a threat that is unmitigated and therefore is a valid way for an attacker to be able to realize a threat.

Initial Modeling Of Threats

Most threat modeling I have participated in has been based on a data-flow process — following the various paths that can be taken by attackers through the system being modeled with careful attention to how the data and commands are parsed and acted on, as well as which assets are being touched or interacted with. Any action or transformation on behalf of the data could be susceptible to threats.

This approach has the benefit of being more structured and methodical to both prepare and walk through when compared to simple brainstorming. The downside is that if the initial preparation misses an entry point or asset, those missing items may not come up in threat modeling meetings because the focus is on what is already on the list, not what may be missing from the list.

It should be noted that there is a very formalized method of threat modeling, called OCTAVE® (Carnegie-Mellon University, Pittsburgh, Pennsylvania) that is detailed later in this chapter. It runs through similar basic steps in a different way and with different methods.

The first step in threat modeling is to detail and document what the attacker considers when attacking a system. These are discussed here.

Document Entry and Exit Points

Threat modeling starts with a list of all the entry points for the system being modeled, no matter what permissions are required to use them or what checks exist. An entry point is any place where data or control is transferred between the system being modeled and any other system. All entry points are places where an attacker can attack the system, and include items such as:

- Advanced programming interfaces (APIs)
- Sockets
- Web services
- Remote procedure call interfaces (RPCs)
- Data from the file system
- Registry data
- Network data
- Administrative controls

Once the entry points are all listed, they are cross-referenced with the trust levels that are supposed to be required to access them.

If you have entry points where the functionality used and even trust levels needed depend on the information included in a specific request, these are termed "layered entry points." They are most often Web pages, and they must be listed as if each was a separate entry point. APIs are also really layered threats, but they work well when modeled with a class or method layering scheme.

Even though the preceding is technically a list of entry points, exit points should be listed as well. Exit points are the places where data or control is moved from the system to external entities. Vulnerabilities in exit points are often those that result in information disclosure, and even if the information disclosed isn't overly damaging in itself, it can lead to other attacks or threats to other systems.

Entry points are usually mapped out by the designers and architects but, especially in the case of legacy code, you should track any interactions or entry and exit points you find in the course of testing and verify that all these entry and exit points are tracked in the threat model. If they are not, they need to be added to the model.

A sample and very simple entry point list (but which does include layered entry points) may look like Table 6.1.

Table 6.1   Sample Entry Point List

ID	Name	Description	Trust Levels
1	Web server listening port	All Web pages layered on this — the port that the Web server listens to	(1) Remote anonymous user (2) Remote registered user (3) Application administrator (4) Web site administrator
1.1	Login page	Page for existing users to log in to the system or request a redirection to the registration page	(1) Remote anonymous user (2) Remote registered user (3) Application administrator
1.1.1	*UserLogin* function	Compares user credentials entered on the Web page to those in the database's *Users* table and returns a session if the credentials match	(1) Remote anonymous user (2) Remote registered user (3) Administrator
1.2	Registration page	Page for new users to set up a login	(1) Remote anonymous user (2) Remote registered user (3) Administrator
1.2.1	*UserRegister* function	Creates a new entry in the database's *Users* table	(1) Remote anonymous user

Document Assets

Now a list is made of all the assets that an attacker might be interested in attacking. This includes assets that an attacker may want to steal as well as those the attacker may wish to damage or prevent others from legitimate access to. Remember that without a reason to attack the system, an attack wouldn't exist. Some of the assets are tangible assets such as:

- Process tokens
- Database contents
- User data
- Processes

Other assets may be more abstract, such as:

- Data consistency
- Company or software reputation
- Resource availability

Some assets are called "transitive" assets — they are accessible when a component acts as the gateway to the functionality and assets of the other components. An example of this is an ACL (Access Control Mechanism) that checks to see if a user has rights to a resource. The use of the ACL functionality means that the ACL has now become a transitive asset.

When I participate in a threat modeling process, I list all the assets I can come up with, and I don't take any asset off the list merely because someone does not feel that the asset would be interesting to an attacker. Instead, it remains until it's proven that even if that asset was compromised, there would be no repercussions or damage.

Once the assets are listed, they are cross-referenced with the trust levels that are supposed to be required in order to access them.

For each asset, a determination is made as to what damage an attacker could cause and what information could be gained if the attacker gains access or control of the asset. Although this is not technically a part of this stage of threat modeling, it pays to start thinking of it now. Later it becomes a part of the prioritization of mitigation and testing.

A sample and very simple asset list may look like the one shown in Table 6.2.

Notice that some of these assets are privacy concerns as well. In some systems, there may be regulations or restrictions made on the protection of PII (Personally Identifiable Information) or on any other data your system may collect and store. Stored data of this type must always be listed as an asset and specifically addressed — including the storage of backups or logs that may also contain this data.

Table 6.2 Sample Asset List

ID	Name	Description	Trust Level
1	User	All user assets	None
1.1	User's login data	Username and password	(2) Remote registered user (3) Application administrator
1.2	User's personal information	All user PII and billing information	(2) Remote registered user (3) Application administrator
2	Process	All process assets	N/A
2.1	Ability to execute code with the identity of the Web server	Web pages use Web server security tokens	(4) Web site administrator (5) Web server process identity

Document Trust Levels

A trust level is a way to indicate the level of access any user, process, or application has to the system. It is used to define what privileges one of the external entities should have in order to use each entry point (or the functionality at each entry point) and also to define what privileges any of the external entities should have in order to access or affect each asset.

Trust levels are granted explicitly and implicitly, and both must be taken into account when threat modeling is pursued. If your system utilizes a Web server, there is an implicit trust level of "remote anonymous access" for the network socket the Web server listens on.

A typical trust list might look like the one shown in Table 6.3.

Document Use Cases and Use Scenarios

Now use cases are created that demonstrate how the system being modeled is or is not intended to be used. The purpose of use cases is to show what threats were considered during system design. They also explain where security is dependent on correct configuration and what misconfigurations can put the security it is designed in at risk.

Table 6.3   Sample Trust List

ID	Name	Description
1	Remote anonymous user	A user connected to the Web site but who has not yet provided user credentials
2	Remote registered user	A user connected to the Web site and has created an account for which the user has entered valid login credentials
3	Application administrator	The application administrator has access to the application's administrative tools to configure and update application data
4	Web site administrator	The Web site administrator can configure and maintain the Web site
5	Web server process identity	The account the database server process runs as. The database process has all the privileges and access that correspond to the security token it runs under

Table 6.4 Sample Use Scenarios

ID	Description
1	The Web site will be installed on a Web server running Windows Server 2003 and IIS 6.0 that is secured in line with current industry and manufacturer guidelines and which has all security patches installed and kept current
2	The Web server and the database server will communicate over a private network
3	The Web server will be deployed behind a firewall with only the HTTP and HTTPS ports open to internet traffic

There will be some security risks that arise during the process of documenting use scenarios that simply cannot be addressed effectively by the system being modeled because they are outside its control. These should be noted as well.

The purpose of this documentation process is to create a limit to the scope of the threat analysis by indicating what situations will and will not be considered as part of the threat model.

Samples of some use scenarios are shown in Table 6.4.

Document External Dependencies

These are the requirements on the system being modeled that are outside its own control. They can include items such as protocol versioning compliance, algorithm consistency, file system path consistency, etc.

Although it's tempting to use external dependencies to mitigate threats, great care must be taken while doing this because you are then trusting something outside your control to enforce parts of your security for you.

All trust is misplaced. Do not trust an external system to enforce your security for you. Unless you have no way of mitigating threats yourself or it's extremely expensive, it's a good idea to at least have a way to doubly check the mitigation through another means.

A sample of an external dependency is shown in Table 6.5.

Table 6.5 Sample External Dependency

ID	Description
1	The Web site depends on the Web server or host's session management to be secure. If the session is not secure, an attacker may be able to hijack another user's session

Table 6.6   Sample Security Notes

ID	Description
1	The Web service only enforces that password length be greater than eight characters, but the users must choose passwords that are hard to guess or discover via brute force
2	If a user tries to log in unsuccessfully three times, the user will be blocked from logging in again for 1 hour. After 1 hour, the user may attempt to login again.

Document External Security Notes

Whereas external security dependencies are items the system being modeled depends upon, external security notes are pieces of information the system being modeled is documenting on behalf of its own users or other systems. This includes integration and usage/API information.

External security notes can be used to allow threat models for different systems to be integrated or cross-referenced. They can also be used to back up developer or user notes, if appropriate.

Table 6.6 demonstrates several samples of external security notes.

Document Internal Security Notes

These are notes internal to the threat model itself and include anything that may make it easier to read and understand the particular threat model. Such notes are used to explain the logic and rationale behind decisions of what to include or trade-off. Although very useful, they are not a replacement for clear threat model documentation.

Model the Application

Most applications I have modeled as part of a threat model were done via a Data Flow Diagram (DFD). These are visual representations of how the system processes data and have a focus on transformations and processes applied to data. This does not mean, however, that the modeling can only be done via a DFD. I've seen some done via UML, a few flow charts, and even a couple that were done via Client/Server diagrams. The only real constraint is that the modeling method chosen suits the type of system being modeled, and it helps increase understanding of how the system and its subsystems fit and work together.

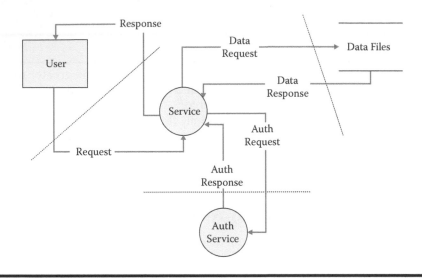

Figure 6.1   Sample data flow diagram.

DFDs do have an advantage in that they are naturally hierarchical and lend themselves to the task of modeling only the security-involved components.

There are quite a number of references available on how to create and use DFDs and what the individual symbols mean, so I won't go over that here. It's a good general rule to make a high level DFD of the entire system, then drill down into more granular documents only where needed to examine security concerns.

One thing that should always be included it these DFDs are the permission boundaries. Figure 6.1 shows a small sample of a data flow diagram with the boundaries marked on it.

Create Threat Profile

Create Attack Hypotheses

The next step is to use the data you have been gathering up until now to create hypotheses of how an attack might be realized. These are sometimes called Attack Stories. There are several ways of approaching the task of creating these attack hypotheses, depending on where you start the process.

If you start with a known vulnerability, you would then identify an asset that might be susceptible to that vulnerability and find a corresponding threat that would need to be realized. From there, you continue to work back toward the root asset and threat. Not all systems are alike. Starting from known vulnerabilities will limit the threat profile to known threats and will neglect threats that are very unique to the particular system being modeled. Although this approach will help jumpstart your threat model, it shouldn't be the only approach used.

Instead, you can start with the system's assets. First, you identify these and for each asset, the possible attack goals. Then for each goal, you figure out how it might be possible for the attacker to fulfill all or part of these attack goals against the assets. This approach is a little more versatile than the approach that starts with known vulnerabilities but still has the possibility of becoming a rote task. If this happens, it can suffer from loss of creative thinking.

Just listing threats will only provide a laundry list of those that may or may not exist. The threats have to be investigated to verify their validity, and steps should be taken to mitigate them.

Classify Threats

Threats are now categorized. This means that threats are grouped together according to one or more common criteria to make it easier to understand the threat as well as to determine priority.

One way to do this is through the STRIDE method, introduced in *Writing Secure Code, Second Edition* (Microsoft Press, 2003) by Michael Howard and David LeBlanc. The basics of STRIDE are explained at a high level later in this chapter.

Analyze Threats to Determine Vulnerabilities

Now all these threats need to be analyzed. The goal is to see if they are actually vulnerabilities (threats the system is susceptible to) or are mitigated. This is usually done using a "threat tree." The process of creating threat trees is also described later in this chapter.

All threats must have their mitigations documented in the threat model document. This becomes especially important to you because those mitigations need to be tested. All too often a mitigation that may have been designed into the system either isn't present, isn't functioning as designed, or has side effects that create other threats of its own.

At the end of this process, you will have a list of which threats are actually vulnerabilities. These are the items to focus on for the next step. Remember that threats always exist, but vulnerabilities can be mitigated to prevent the threat from being realized.

Prioritize Vulnerabilities

Now this list of vulnerabilities is prioritized to determine the order in which they must be addressed for attention and mitigation. There are several ways of doing this, but I tend to use a slightly modified version of the DREAD method, which is described in greater detail later. The end result of this prioritization is a list that's grouped into vulnerabilities of similar urgency and ready for mitigation.

Mitigate Vulnerabilities

Now these identified and grouped vulnerabilities must be mitigated or resolved in some way. Sometimes the core asset can be removed because it's a legacy item or not really necessary. Other times the vulnerability needs to be treated as any other bug, albeit usually with a fairly high priority, and a mitigation designed and implemented in order to resolve it.

Update Threat Model

All mitigations that are put into place must be added to the threat model to keep it up to date, but when mitigations are added, they also must be examined for any chance that they add another threat, a new attack path, or even a new vulnerability.

In addition, whenever the product changes, the threat model must be kept current so those changes are included and addressed. After being through several different processes to keep the system security up to date, I firmly believe that a review of the threat model needs to take place during the design phase of every release of the product, including major versions, minor versions, and patches or updates. If this model is revisited as a part of this process, the decisions made on new features, fixes, etc. can be done with security firmly in mind, and not require later changes to mitigate security vulnerabilities. It also makes it much easier to perform security testing.

Pitfalls of Threat Modeling

In my own experience, there are a number of pitfalls common to threat modeling and how threat modeling is used that should be kept in mind and guarded against. These will now be discussed in detail.

Blindness to Interactions with Downstream Dependents

Although most threat modeling is careful to take the entry points of the system being modeled into account, there is a tendency to not give sufficient attention to the exit points of that system — places where data or control moves from the system being modeled to external control or use. Almost all attention is paid to the system protecting itself, but attention should also be invested in not being the attack vector through which some other software is attacked instead.

There are plenty of examples of attacks where the initial exploit was made on a system that was unrelated to the asset being sought, other than it provided a vector for the attack. Lately, this has come up even more with issues like driver vulnerabilities garnering more and more attention. No one wants the software their company or team produces to become the Typhoid Mary of the industry.

All trust is misplaced. Never trust your downstream dependents to be able to deal with anything you throw at them. Your output to them should be in line with specification and standards.

Threat Model Tunnel Vision

There is also a tendency to rely solely on the threat model to determine actions needed, testing in particular. The items on the threat model are a great guide, but a threat model is not the be-all, end-all of security for the system. New vulnerabilities in those entities your system integrates with are being found all the time, and even new classes of vulnerabilities are being found. Existing classes of vulnerabilities that were once thought to be benign or unexploitable can become an increased concern, once someone figures out a way to exploit them.

There is always a place for "tester intuition" in any test effort. Most testers have moments of inspiration that give them ideas of possible places where bugs are lurking or possible ways around the system's security. These should always be followed up on, even if they are not listed on the threat model. All too often, these pay off — either in the discovery of a bug or vulnerability, or in the ability to demonstrate that a suspected vulnerability does not exist or is mitigated somehow.

All trust is misplaced. Do not trust any plan to have all the answers. Always look at hunches and consider multiple points of view.

Failing to Track Dependency Changes

A common blind spot in threat modeling is to trust that both the upstream and downstream dependencies remain static, even to the point of never investigating or documenting these dependencies at all. Almost all software is in some sort of flux; changes are made to accommodate new functionality or even to mitigate security vulnerabilities in the dependency.

Sometimes these changes are obvious because they break existing functionality, and the issue is quickly brought to light. But if the changes are not "breaking" changes, they may not come to light for quite a while.

There are some obvious cases where this could cause problems. If your system is expecting data to be passed in a certain format and with a certain length, and that length changes, you have a new issue. Now, hopefully, this is already mitigated by some functionality within your system, but it still needs to be documented and verified.

If you are sending data to another system, and that system suddenly implements a security review, and now checks to see that the data being sent is no smaller than x size — but your system has been relying on a workaround of only sending a subset of the data, and letting the system on the other end fill the rest out, because it isn't important to the transaction. Now that system is rejecting your data as malformed.

In addition to putting your own mitigations and checks into place, there needs to be a concerted effort made to watch upcoming changes in the software your system is designed to communicate with any changes in what these other systems expect from your system need to be updated in the threat model. Obviously, your first priority is to track changes in software (and hardware, if applicable) that your system is designed to interact with, rather than those items which are outside the design specifications for your system but which someone might force your system to interact with. For example, a system for outputting graphics would be less concerned over minor issues with output to a prototype product than output to established display software.

All trust is misplaced. Never trust that the dependencies (upstream and downstream) will not change requirements in a way that might break either your system's functionality or your system's security mitigations.

All Copies of Data Aren't Addressed as Assets

Data is a huge asset to protect and figures heavily in the threat modeling process, but all too often the copies of that data are neglected and exposed to unnecessary (and often unrecognized) threats.

During threat modeling, all asset lists must include "stored" data.

Temporary Files

Quite a few systems create one or more temporary files that are supposed to be deleted after their use is fulfilled. But personal experience has taught me that even without an intruder, these files aren't always deleted on schedule, and this fact is first discovered by the monitoring (if there is monitoring in place that can detect this) or when the disk fills up and processes start to fail.

Depending on what is contained in the temporary files, they can be as much of a target as any other source of data. This includes not only the ones that escaped deletion but ones in transition. If the file can be found and accessed, it can be copied or manipulated.

All trust is misplaced. Just because it's a temporary file, never trust it to be truly temporary and discount the times when it may be accessible.

Database Backups

This includes both online copies and those transferred onto other storage media for some reason. Data copies are often stored without the same attention to security and detail as that given to the "live" data. Offsite backup services keep copies, operations or IT teams keep copies, and there are often copies that are kept synched for live failover or hot swaps. These are all normal and expected to exist, but they need to also be listed as assets, and threats to them considered.

All trust is misplaced. Never trust that backup copies of valuable data are treated with the concern and security they deserve.

Log Files

A lot of data is logged for good reasons but it's not often listed as an asset on threat models, which can be a serious mistake. Sometimes this is transactional information within a database, but often information is logged to the system or application event logs on various machines. Even someone who hasn't been able to access the database itself may well manage to access log files and troll through them for any useful information.

The first question that should always be asked is why the data is being logged and if that level of logging is actually needed.

If the logging is needed, then all the log files (and any copies of them) must be added as assets and addressed in the threat model.

All trust is misplaced. Never trust that the only place valuable data exists is in the actual database tables.

Copies of Production Data Outside Production

The desire to have the most realistic data possible against which to test and validate behavior sometimes leads to teams taking the shortcut of deciding to just "make a copy" of the production data and use that to test against. This is a very dangerous shortcut to take. Here are further lapses I've seen:

- I've been casually handed a fully intact copy of production data to test against, and when I examined it, I found it was rife with information that I never should have had access to.
- I've seen some instances where copies of live data were sent to subcontracted companies who were hired to work on parts of the software development process.
- I've seen a copy of the live data checked into a source control program as a "resource."
- I've seen just about every developer on the project team have their own copy of the real data.

At the very least, this data should be sanitized, and it's not that difficult to generate completely bogus test data and avoid the problem all together. If the real data must be used, every instance of it must be listed as an asset and addressed in the threat model.

All trust is misplaced. Never trust sensitive data to be treated with appropriate care and security when used for testing or development purposes.

Failover Data

If a system is mission critical, there is often a requirement for full or partial redundancy of data, and this is sometimes addressed by utilizing one of two solutions: (1) an entire backup data center with constantly updated copies of all data so that if the primary data center goes down for any reason, the secondary data center can pick up the work without significant downtime to the customers, or (2) sometimes a separate data center is not needed but instead a separate database server is kept updated.

These failover systems also need to be listed as assets and addressed in the threat model.

All trust is misplaced. Never trust failover data to be safe merely because it isn't in active use or is not on the same servers.

Who Has Access or Control

Another issue all too often bypassed in threat modeling is to track who has been granted access to the production data and servers or devices within the project team. Unfortunately, one of the types of attackers that must be considered is that of disgruntled or opportunistic employees who may have access to sensitive information.

Consideration even needs to be given to employees or contractors who somehow fall victim to social engineering schemes and are tricked into disclosing information or maybe installing an exploit.

There was an interesting study done on whether a model could be created to teach organizations and their management to recognize and act on the precursors to insider threats. The resulting proof of concept is called MERIT™ (Carnegie-Mellon University, Pittsburgh, Pennsylvania) and there's more detail later in this chapter on the key items of interest from this paper. MERIT makes some very compelling arguments about employee access and the need to analyze who has access to what and whether they should, as well as some of the danger signs that management can watch for.

All trust is misplaced. Trusting everyone in a group, team, etc., with access to sensitive business information is a mistake. Access should be granted on a necessity basis and regularly reviewed so that access is removed when it is no longer necessary.

Physical Disks or Devices

This is a rarely discussed issue but just reading the news will demonstrate that it's one that needs to be considered, especially if there are multiple copies of your data in existence. Physical access to or possession of the data can be a big problem.

This could be anything from backup media to the actual hard drives that were used to store the system and its data. The more copies of the data that are in existence, the more opportunities there are for that data to be inappropriately treated or disposed of.

This becomes especially problematic if there are copies of the data on various desktop systems. Not a lot of thought is given to what happens to an older machine that is discarded when a user upgrades. Very few ways of destroying data on hard drives are even relatively successful, and there are many cases of people buying computers or just hard drives only to find the data on the drive was accessible and intact and often sensitive data at that. In most cases it was not even encrypted.

Another example of this is evident in a lot of news stories over the last year or so. The report that a laptop has been lost or stolen with copies of sensitive data on it is no longer even a surprise; it's relatively common. Sometimes this data is copied without permission, sometimes it's with permission, but almost always the data was sensitive and often not encrypted or encoded in any way.

The issue of physical copies of the data becomes more complex with the advent of easy access to CD and DVD burners, memory cards, and the very popular USB thumb drives.

All trust is misplaced. Off the desk is not the same as gone. Never trust the disposition of data storage devices once they have left your control.

Security Becomes Single Layered — No Defense in Depth

A very unfortunate, but all too common, temptation when threat modeling is to neglect to follow one of the most important tenets of all types of security — defense in depth. The rules for most threat modeling indicate that a vulnerability with even a single mitigation is no longer a vulnerability but is back to a mere threat. Although technically true, it's a mistake to take that simplistic an approach.

To have effective and robust security, you have to have defense in depth. There has to be more than one layer of mitigations because there are no mitigations that are 100 percent effective and 100 percent reliable. There will always be some way to go under or around a mitigation, even if the attacker can't go directly through it. If you have only a single layer of security, you are leaving yourself open to attacks.

For example, if you have paper financial records, you may keep them in your home. To prevent entry to your home, you lock the door. In case the door lock is defeated, you have an alarm system. In case the alarm system malfunctions, you have the records in a locked cabinet.

Or maybe you have a database that contains the credit card information of your customers. You have it on a system with the latest security patches, it has proper authorization rules and passwords. But in case those are circumvented, the data is encrypted. In case the encrypted data is obtained and decrypted, you don't store the CCV numbers of the credit cards to make the credit card data harder to use.

You should always ask the questions: "What if this mitigation doesn't work or is bypassed? How will I know this has happened? What are my secondary mitigations?"

All trust is misplaced. Never trust a mitigation to work all the time, and always have fallback mitigations or plans.

Vulnerabilities with Lower Priorities Are Ignored

Because one of the goals of the threat modeling process is to prioritize vulnerabilities so the most severe ones rise to the top of the pile, there is an inclination to address these top vulnerabilities first. Sometimes they are the only ones that get attention. This leaves the still existing, but not as severe, vulnerabilities unmitigated. But they are not necessarily unimportant just because they aren't at the top of the list.

The entire list of vulnerabilities should be reviewed with an eye to how much time is available, and how much time each vulnerability will take to mitigate or even eliminate. If several lower priority vulnerabilities can be mitigated by a change to a single stored procedure that will cost 15 min of a developer's time and an hour of a tester's time, it may be well worth doing if the time was available, even if the vulnerabilities aren't near the top of the list.

Perhaps a vulnerability near the bottom of the list is due to some legacy asset that is no longer used except for a single function that can easily be rolled into the newer code. This may be worth taking on as a work item because it not only mitigates a vulnerability, but it totally eliminates an asset from the list.

Modeling Becomes a Time Sink

It is incredibly easy to get sucked into the intricacies of threat modeling to the point that it incurs a much larger cost in hours and project delay than it should. You should always keep in mind the purpose and detail needed for the model and strive to provide what is needed without going overboard.

Usually it's a good idea to sit down with the other team members ahead of time to determine how complex a threat model is needed for this particular release and set a realistic deadline by which to produce it.

Forgetting Physical Access

It's not too surprising that most attention during threat modeling is given over to remotely accessible vulnerabilities. These are, after all, where the majority of threats will originate but sometimes the physical threats are never addressed or even considered.

But there are quite a few physical threats that may or may not be obvious. These include some of the issues I listed earlier as who has access to data but access also includes things like console or direct access to the systems or networks.

Forgetting the Registry

One of the places that information is stored and retrieved, and is still easily accessed is the Windows registry. There is a temptation to store some information in the registry that really should not be stored there, including security settings and sometimes user data in plain text.

Like some other risky storage schemes, this is sometimes used as "temporary" storage (often during installation and upgrade), and the registry key or value is supposed to be deleted after the process is completed. But the deletion isn't guaranteed to happen, and that can leave the plain text information sitting in the registry for easy access.

Sometimes the registry is used to save application settings because it's easy to access. But if settings are stored in the registry, there needs to be a review of just what is being stored. Settings relating to the security of the system or an application can be modified or deleted by anyone who obtains access to the registry. Any data saved in the registry is an asset that has to be assessed.

Threat Trees

Threat trees are a way to systematically examine each threat and determine whether it's a vulnerability or has been mitigated to a threat.

A threat tree begins with a root node or root threat. This root node then has one or more child conditions that must be true for an attacker to exploit the threat. Any of these child conditions can have one or more children of their own. An AND relationship is created by having two or more conditions at the same level and sharing the same parent node. Otherwise, an implicit OR condition exists.

Once the tree is created, each leaf node (a child node with no child nodes of its own) in each tree must be followed back to the root node. If a path can be found where there is no mitigating node or a path exists that involves a broken AND statement — that threat has now become a vulnerability.

In threat trees, the conditions in the trees can have mitigations associated with them. This is because the conditions represent specific actions or situations that must occur, while the threat is less concrete. The conditions also have a risk associated with them (usually rated via the DREAD system or a similar system).

Threat trees can be represented graphically as in Figure 6.2. Threat trees can also be represented textually as in Figure 6.3.

Neither of these two options is distinctly better than the other, so use any method that allows easy representation of the information, along with being the most usable when integrating with other processes in use.

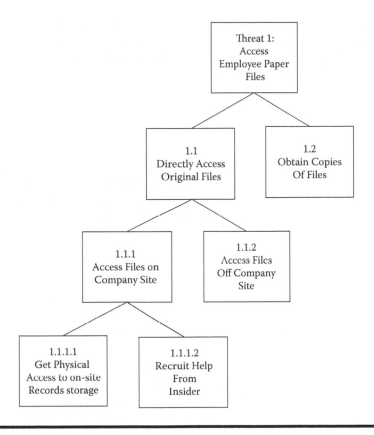

Figure 6.2 Sample graphic threat tree.

1. Access Employee Paper Files
    1.1. Directly Access Original Files
        1.1.1. Access Files on Company Site
            1.1.1.1. Get Physical Access to On-Site Records Storage
            1.1.1.2. Recruit Help from Insider
        1.1.2. Access Files Off Company Site
    1.2. Obtain Copies of Files

Figure 6.3 Sample text threat tree.

In addition to their usefulness in threat modeling, threat trees are also useful to penetration testers. They allow the creation of simulated attacks against a system by following the logical paths documented in the threat trees.

An individual threat tree can also be collapsed to act as a condition in another threat tree. A case where one or more threat trees are encased within another threat tree is called *attack chaining* and exists where a condition of one threat tree involves the successful exploit of another vulnerability.

Attack Path

An attack path is the route from a leaf condition (child node that has no children of its own) back to the root threat and including any AND conditions. These attack paths are mapped out on threat trees, and any attack path without at least one mitigating node is an exploitable vulnerability.

DREAD

DREAD™ (Microsoft Corporation, Redmond, Washington) is a method of evaluating security risks developed at Microsoft Corporation and documented in *Writing Secure Code, Second Edition* (Microsoft Press, 2003), by Michael Howard and David LeBlanc.

One thing that may be a little confusing about DREAD is that it is often called a "threat modeling" system, but I generally use it as a vulnerability evaluation system. Mitigated threats are generally not included. This is why I use "vulnerability" instead of "threat" in the descriptions of the process.

To compare the relative severity of vulnerabilities, a numerical score or rank is assigned to each one. This rank is the average of the scores in each of the categories that comprise the DREAD system. The typical implementation uses a scale of 1 to 10 for the score, with 1 being the lowest (least severe) and 10 the highest rank (most severe).

The problem I've discovered with using this 1 to 10 scale is that it's just too broad. A lot of time can be wasted while debating whether a particular score is a 7 or an 8. Some DREAD users cut the scale down to 1 to 3, but I prefer 1 to 5. That allows sufficient granularity while still remaining usable.

I also never use the Discoverability category because my own experience is that it's almost counterproductive. All vulnerabilities will be eventually found by external attackers or those people who will disclose the vulnerability publicly. Attempts to guess how hard or easy something is to find or to downgrade the overall rating of the vulnerability because "it's secret" is completely false security. There are quite a few vulnerabilities that were known to the software teams for months or years but remained unpatched because it was felt that they didn't need urgent attention, mostly because they would be so hard to find. But they were found and exploited, anyway.

All trust is misplaced: Never trust secrecy or obscurity to provide security.

Once the vulnerability has been given a score for each of the DREAD categories, the individual scores are totaled and then averaged to generate the vulnerability's overall rating. Then, the list is sorted by the overall rating (highest to lowest), resulting in a prioritized list of vulnerabilities that must be addressed and tested.

The DREAD categories are now examined:

Damage Potential

This is the amount of damage possible if the vulnerability is exploited. Note that this is not merely physical damage but can include intangible damage like reputation, customer confidence, etc. It can also include information disclosures like credit card information. It can even include items like violation of legal or regulatory mandates.

Reproducibility

This is a measure of how easy or difficult it would be to reproduce the successful exploit of the vulnerability. If the vulnerability could be successfully exploited on every attempt, that would rate a higher score than an exploit attempt that was only successful one time per year or one time per 10,000 attempts.

Exploitability

This is a measure of how easy or difficult it is to exploit a vulnerability. It includes factors like the preconditions required for the exploit, how many steps or separate actions are required, and how difficult it may be to find a system that meets all the preconditions. For example, if a system has to be running an application that has only sold several thousand copies, the rating would be lower than if the exploit didn't require that limited market package.

Affected Users

This measures how many users (or what percentage of total users) would be affected by an exploit of this vulnerability. This includes not just items like denial of service or server crashes but also the cases of information disclosure. Obviously, the greater the percentage of users affected, the higher the score; a total DoS or database access may be a 10, but something that only affects a few users may be a 1 or a 2.

Discoverability

This is a measure of how likely it is that a vulnerability will be found if it remains unpatched. As I mentioned earlier, I never actually use this category.

STRIDE

STRIDE is a system for categorizing the discovered vulnerabilities that have been identified so, in reality, it's actually more of a vulnerability classification system than a threat modeling system.

Classifying a vulnerability by its category or categories makes it easier to quickly understand what an attacker can do. It can also help in the assignment of priorities to vulnerabilities. The categories of vulnerabilities that are considered to have the highest level of risk are different, based on the program being tested. Elevation of Privilege is typically considered the most serious, but it's not mandated. If a particular business or industry has regulatory laws, this can have an impact on which categories are intrinsically more serious than others.

Because vulnerabilities can often be classified as belonging to multiple categories, it's very important to be certain that each vulnerability is classified according to its root cause. If a vulnerability enables tampering with data alone, it would be categorized as a Tampering threat. If it enabled tampering with data because of an elevation of privilege, it would instead be considered an Elevation of Privilege threat.

STRIDE is an acronym that stands for the services it renders, which are as follows:

Spoofing Identity

An attacker appears to be a user, component, or system that is afforded some level of trust by the system being modeled.

Tampering with Data

Data is added, modified, or deleted to further or achieve some malicious goal.

Repudiation

An intruder is able to deny performing some malicious activity because the system can't prove otherwise.

Information Disclosure

Attackers or users can see information they should not normally be able to have access to.

Denial of Service

An attacker causes legitimate users to be unable to use the normal functionality of a service, system, or resources.

Elevation of Privilege

An attacker uses illegitimate means to assume trust level with different (typically greater) privileges than the attacker should have.

MERIT

MERIT™ (Carnegie-Mellon University, Pittsburgh, Pennsylvania) (Management and Education of the Risk of Insider Threat) is a modeling system specifically focused on system sabotage by insiders. This is a pilot study or a proof of concept for a method developed by the Carnegie Mellon University's Software Engineering Institute and is in response to an analysis of insider crimes (the Insider Threat Study) conducted in conjunction with the U.S. Secret Service. There is a paper available on this new method on the CERT® Web site, and the link is listed in the Bibliography for this chapter. It definitely makes some interesting reading.

This is of the most use to you when determining mitigations and risk because insiders are a concern during this process as well as external attackers. This can also be useful when attempting to examine and develop attacker profiles or personas, or when developing test cases that include insider attack situations.

The MERIT information is really geared toward managers and employee policy makers as well as managers of employees, but it has some good points to make about the access granted and not recorded or tracked. It also really made me think about just what risks are posed by insiders because it's very easy to give fellow employees blanket trust.

The Insider Threat Study (also available from the CERT® Web site) examines 49 cases of insider sabotage that took place between 1996 and 2002 and met a rather stringent set of criteria. After verifying that these cases met the criteria, they were then analyzed for similarity and patterns with some interesting results.

The MERIT document has some excellent information and an interesting example situation for study.

Insider Threat Study Items of Note

Some of the interesting findings of the Insider Threat Study that I think are worth particular mention include:

- The majority of attackers were former employees at the time the attack was carried out.
- An overwhelming percentage of the time there was a specific incident that triggered the insider's actions. Most frequently the incident was the termination of their employment with the company.
- Most attackers began to act out in a noticeable and concerning way at work before their actual attacks took place.
- Most attackers planned their attack in advance, and other people had knowledge of the attacker's intentions, plans, or ongoing activities.
- Most attackers communicated negative sentiments to others, sometimes even including direct threats.

Analysis

Following are some of the aspects at play when it comes to Insider Attacks:

Attacker Behavioral Aspects

Some points to be noted are:

- A lot of the precursors to insider attacks are based on the degree or measurement of employee disgruntlement. An employee becomes disgruntled when the employee's expectations of what job and workplace freedom he should have are higher than the actual job and workplace freedom he enjoys. The further the employee's freedom falls below what he expects, the more disgruntled the employee becomes.

- Because of this disgruntlement factor, organizations can do more harm than good by allowing an employee too much freedom at first, and thus setting the employee's expectations too high too quickly.
- If the employee is sanctioned or disciplined, the level of disgruntlement can escalate. In many cases, especially if the problem is identified relatively early, the level of the employee's disgruntlement may be reduced with intervention or counseling.
- The symptoms leading up to the attacks follow a somewhat predictable path. This leads to the proposal that if management is attentive, these clues and behaviors can indicate the need for action. Attacks may be better prevented by taking earlier and more decisive action when there appears to be danger. For example, long periods of unmet employee expectations are periods of high risk for the organization, as are times when one or more employees have to be consistently reprimanded.
- Most attackers acted alone and did not actively collude with others. Despite the solo attacks, many times there are other employees that are aware of the actions or plans of the attackers. This can be because they observe the employee doing something out of the ordinary or suspicious. It can also be because such employees have told them that they will get even or have even revealed their actual attack plans.
- Most attackers carry out attacks that are in line with the skills and expertise that the employee demonstrated on the job. There weren't any cases in the study where the employee went outside their area of familiarity to carry out the attack.

Access Path Control Aspects

An access path is a set of one or more access points that lead to a critical system. These access points can include passwords, computer accounts, etc. There are three types of access paths:

- Paths that are legitimately granted by the organization. These can be known and quite logical at the time they are granted and then forgotten if records are not kept.
- Paths that are created by the insiders themselves. These include things like computer accounts created by the employee and network accounts or hacking tools installed by the employee. These can be either authorized or unauthorized at the time they are created and either known or unknown to the organization. They are also vulnerable to being forgotten over time.

- Paths that are discovered by the insider. These are existing paths that have either been revealed to or discovered by the employee. Although these can be used maliciously, they aren't necessarily created for the purpose of being malicious.

The employer should reduce the number of unknown paths as much as possible by auditing or otherwise identifying these paths, reviewing them, and then disabling all those that do not have a business need to exist. This requires periodic efforts that are focused on the task of finding these paths, because new, created, or existing ones are made redundant all the time.

Attackers who don't care if they are caught may use both known and unknown access paths. Those that are more concerned about being caught may use only unknown paths or paths they believe to be unknown. The employer needs to have monitoring systems in place that are adequate for the task of detecting the use of these unknown access paths.

As time goes on, more and more access paths become available to an employee, even without him actively attempting to obtain more access. This pattern is pretty standard across the study. Over time, some of these legitimately granted access paths can be forgotten by those who granted them, and they tend to remain in place as unknown access paths.

Attacker Technical Aspects

Once employees have reached a sufficient disgruntlement level, which is different for each employee, they begin to exhibit technical precursors to the attack in addition to the behavioral precursors.

These technical precursors can include signs such as the employee's creating backdoor accounts and attack tools, or even creating or planting logic bombs. These technical precursors are strong signs of an impending attack and shouldn't be ignored or excused.

An increase in the disgruntlement of the employee leads to a corresponding increase in the rate of technical actions taken by the employee. Employees can also begin to take more actions that are intended to facilitate the attack they are planning or increase the effectiveness of it. This can include moves such as destroying backup tapes, turning off monitoring, etc.

Because most attacks are motivated by revenge, the attacks will typically commence when the employee's disgruntlement reaches a sufficiently high level or the precipitating event (like being fired) occurs. If multiple attack paths are available, multiple attacks may be executed. If the attack execution is autonomous, the attacker doesn't even need an attack path to still be available at the time of the attack. Instead, the attack can be planted while the employee has access, and set to take effect after some trigger is tripped — such as on a preset logic bomb, etc.

Behavioral precursors come before technical precursors, and the study indicates that when the level of the technical precursors rises above the level of the behavioral precursors, the attack is imminent. This seems to be because the employee's emotions and effort are channeled into laying the technical groundwork for the attack. Technical precursors will drop off after an attack because the employee's disgruntlement is eased by the attack having been carried out.

Defense Aspects

The two best defenses for these insider attacks aren't a surprise at all:

■ Proactively model the organization's systems to discover access paths available to insiders that are unknown to management and eliminate those that are not necessary.
■ Reduce the ability for an insider to create new access paths.

For individual employees who are suspected to have the potential to turn into insider attackers, there are a few more possibilities:

■ If the employees have known access paths that are not needed to perform their job functions, these should be disabled as soon as possible.
■ If the threat posed by the employee is sufficiently high, the organization may choose to disable even the known paths needed by the employees to perform their job functions.
■ If the risk then reaches the point that the organization chooses to terminate the employee, all known access paths must be immediately disabled, but the organization must be aware that unknown access paths may still be available. Thus, knowing as many paths as possible will greatly reduce the risks.

OCTAVE and OCTAVE-S

OCTAVE® (Operationally Critical Threat, Asset, and Vulnerability Evaluation^SM) (Carnegie-Mellon University, Pittsburgh, Pennsylvania) is another method of evaluating security risks. This was developed and is taught by the Carnegie Mellon Software Engineering Institute. The documents and training materials are freely available on the CERT® Web site, but I will warn you that there are a lot of materials.

OCTAVE is primarily designed for use in very large organizations, and it takes more of an organizational approach to the tasks of risk assessment as opposed to the technical view of most other methods. Because of this, OCTAVE tends to be more sensitive to the needs of the business practices but also requires that the evaluations are carried out by a team internal to the company because of the need to interview for and understand the business needs.

OCTAVE-S® is a somewhat newer version of the original OCTAVE that has been modified to make it more suitable for smaller organizations (the target is approximately 100 people or less). The process is more streamlined and requires a smaller team (3–5 people recommended), and the computer exploration is very limited. As such, it's not as useful as OCTAVE may be, and therefore I'll be looking only at the original OCTAVE in this book — and that only at a fairly high level. If you do want more information on OCTAVE-S, it is freely available at the OCTAVE Web site listed in the Bibliography section of this chapter.

This system of threat analysis is very complex in execution, with a huge amount of required process and procedure that involves a lot of meetings and worksheets. In my opinion, this method is best suited for companies that use software and technology, and may even develop their own in-house software. The organizational focus and interview model of this system are not terribly well-suited to project-based, software development companies or divisions.

The three phases of the OCTAVE process are:

Phase 1 — Build Asset-Based Threat Profiles

This is the process of identifying and listing all information assets of the organization and what is being done to protect them. This relies heavily on meetings to interview representatives of various sections of the company to come up with a list of assets that are ranked by their importance to the company and the ways they are being protected at the time the model is created. This information is then consolidated, and a set of requirements are generated. Then, threat profiles are created for each of the critical assets that have been identified (the highest ranked assets).

Phase 2 — Identify Infrastructure Vulnerabilities

This phase takes a look at the technology that is associated with the critical assets from the prior phase, and what the key parts of the technological infrastructure are that support those critical assets. This is basically a way to focus the technological efforts on the most critical assets and look for ways in which the infrastructure protecting the assets is vulnerable.

Phase 3 — Develop Security Strategy and Plans

This last phase is where the key technological assets and vulnerabilities from phase 2 are analyzed for the associated risks, mitigations are developed, and an overall organizational protection plan is developed for implementation.

Bibliography

Cappelli, D.M., Keeney, M., J.D., Ph.D., Kowalski, E., Moore, A., Shimeall, T., and Rogers, S. Insider Threat Study: Computer System Sabotage in Critical Infrastructure Sectors. U.S. Secret Service and CERT® Coordination Center, May 2005. Available from http://www.cert.org/archive/pdf/insidercross051105.pdf.

Cappelli, D.M., Desai, A.G., Moore, A.P., Shimeall, T.J., Weaver, E.A., and Willke, B.J. Management and Education of the Risk or Insider Threat (MERIT): System Dynamics Modeling of Computer System Sabotage. CERT Program, Software Engineering Institute and CyLab at Carnegie Mellon University. Available from http://www.cert.org/archive/pdf/merit.pdf.

Howard, M. and LeBlanc, D. *Writing Secure Code*, 2nd ed. Microsoft Press, Redmond, Washington, 2003.

Octave. Carnegie Mellon Software Engineering Institute. Available from http://www.cert.org/octave/.

Snider, W. and Swiderski, F. *Threat Modeling*. Microsoft Press, Redmond, Washington, 2004.

Chapter 7

Personas and Testing

Personas have been becoming more and more prevalent as a more standardized method of trying to focus software development efforts on the system's customers and to give them a sort of "face" that is common across everyone involved in design, development, testing, and operations. The concept of personas was first introduced by Alan Cooper in his book *The Inmates Are Running the Asylum* (Sams Publishing, 2002) as a way to define user archetypes.

Note that personas are not the same as the actors that are used in Extreme Programming (XP) or Agile development, although they do have a relationship with each other. An actor is really the role a person plays in the system, i.e., secretary or customer. In comparison, a persona is an individual and a specific instance of an actor.

Creating Personas

Personas are expressed as one or more fictional people whose aspects are based on your knowledge of your real customers. However, this does not mean that these personas are created out of thin air. Instead, the process of gathering requirements and features for the system being developed should include the development of user personas. Sometimes other methods are also used to obtain extra data or insight to insure the accuracy of personas. These can include focus groups, customer visits, user surveys or interviews, product support reports, etc.

Table 7.1 Sample Aspect Matrix

Aspect Name	Aspect Values
Age	Young child
	Grade school
	Preteen
	Teen
	College age
	Young adult
	Middle age
	Senior citizen
Marital status	Single
	Married
	Divorced
	Underage
Parental status	N/A
	No children
	One child
	Multiple children
Technological familiarity	Nontechnical
	Somewhat technical
	Very technical
	Technical professional

There is generally a large variety of customers, and the multiple aspects need to be distilled down to a collection of customer archetypes that represent different mixes of different customer aspects. The actual aspects considered will differ somewhat based on just what the system in question is. The smaller the customer base of the system, the more narrow the list of aspects will be.

The easiest way to create this is to start with a matrix of aspects to consider. Table 7.1 demonstrates a simple aspect matrix.

These aspects are then combined into an individual set of aspects that can become a persona as demonstrated in Table 7.2. As you can see, I've already dropped the combinations that are impossible, or at least so improbable that there is no way they would be considered as part of a user persona. Sometimes I will create a large matrix with all aspects, and as I decide that a particular combination is invalid or unusable, I will make a note next to it and gray it out so that I have an ongoing record of everything that was considered and what the decisions were and why.

Now, this list of aspects needs to be narrowed down to create a set of personas that will be used. Typically, each user class (actor) has at

Table 7.2   Sample Persona Aspects

Age	Marital Status	Parental Status	Technological Familiarity
Young child	Underage	N/A	Nontechnical
Young child	Underage	N/A	Somewhat technical
Grade school	Underage	N/A	Nontechnical
Grade school	Underage	N/A	Somewhat technical
Preteen	Underage	N/A	Nontechnical
Preteen	Underage	N/A	Somewhat technical
Preteen	Underage	N/A	Very technical
Teen	Single	No children	Nontechnical
Teen	Single	No children	Somewhat technical
Teen	Single	No children	Very technical
Teen	Single	No children	Technical professional
Teen	Single	One child	Nontechnical
Teen	Single	One child	Somewhat technical
Teen	Single	One child	Very technical
Teen	Single	One child	Technical professional
Teen	Single	Multiple children	Nontechnical
Teen	Single	Multiple children	Somewhat technical
Teen	Single	Multiple children	Very technical
Teen	Single	Multiple children	Technical professional

least one persona. Generally, a page or two of documentation is needed to describe each persona, and multiple personas are created for any particular system. The goal of the persona documentation is to bring the persona to life by creating a name, a personality, a history and, often, even creating or selecting a picture for the persona. Anything that makes the persona seem like a real person allows the software team members to think and consider the persona as a real person and focuses their efforts toward a more concrete customer.

It's especially important that the motivations of the persona are clear. Why is this customer using this system? What is he or she trying to accomplish?

A sample persona may look like the one shown in Figure 7.1, although the amount of background information is highly variable depending on the needs of the system under development.

If personas are not being used by the software team as a whole, it can be useful to develop some specifically for use in testing.

Name	Troy
Age	24
Marital Status	Single
Parental Status	No Children
Income Status	$27,000
Employment	Retail Full Time
Story	Troy is an up and coming young professional with a BA in Business Administration who has just been named assistant manager of the electronics store he has been working at for the last 3 years. Troy is very technology savvy and his primary hobby is MMORG games. As he has spent more time at work, he has had less time to spend shopping and running errands and is now starting to explore online shopping and services. His new raise has offered a disposable income that will make these well within reach.

Figure 7.1   Sample persona.

Using Personas

Once personas are created, they can be used as stand-ins for the real users everywhere, from design to development to testing. They constitute an excellent way of getting all the team members into the mindset of their customers. They can also spark useful conversations about what the motivations and needs of each persona may be.

Sometimes, especially if there are quite a few of them, the set of personas is divided into primary and secondary personas. A primary persona is someone whose needs must be satisfied, and the secondary persona is someone whose needs should be satisfied.

Personas are often combined with use cases to create very specific scenarios. The persona is referred to by name, and the various aspects of that persona influence how the scenario will play out. These personas can also be used to develop alternate scenarios that may not have been as obvious without the personas to base them on.

Personas can be used throughout the software development process and by all disciplines. In my experience, the use of personas results in quite a few animated conversations around just what "Michael" would think of a particular menu arrangement, or what "Sue" would do if she forgot her password.

These functional personas are often used in testing to help develop functional test cases and to provide the necessary point of view to perform ad hoc testing. They can also provide a way to communicate bugs and concerns to the rest of the team in a way they can easily relate to.

Pitfalls of Personas

The use of personas, although very useful, does have some drawbacks, which you should be aware of because some of them specifically impact security testing.

Persona Tunnel Vision

When using personas, there is a tendency to develop some tunnel vision. Sometimes functional issues or concerns that may not fit neatly into one of the official personas do not receive the attention they deserve.

Such tunnel vision is a particular problem when it comes to testing, and you have to be attentive not to fall into it. The easiest way I've discovered to ensure that I am less likely to neglect other test cases or scenarios in favor of only those driven by personas is to make multiple passes through my test cases. I make one pass through for each persona and write those cases that are driven by that persona. Then I make another pass through to look for cases outside those I had already listed that need to be run.

Personas Are Customers, Not Consumers or Attackers

When it comes to security testing, the biggest problem associated with the use of personas is that security or attacker scenarios are not represented. Mostly personas are used to represent customers, not consumers or attackers.

This means that not only is security neglected in the process of testing but also the persona focus of the rest of the product team means that the other disciplines may not have adequately considered it either.

It also means that if bugs are filed for security vulnerabilities, you can meet some resistance to having them fixed because they are not related to a particular persona. This can make it a little more difficult to convey the seriousness of the security issues because the team members will not be able to easily move into the mindset of a persona from which to consider the issue as they are more abstract.

Persona Flaws

Another issue occurs when a set of customers isn't adequately or correctly represented. There are a number of possible reasons for this:

■ Lack of adequate research when the personas were created

- Using old personas for new product versions without reviewing them for any needed updates or modifications
- Narrowing the persona list down to too few so that the true customer base is not adequately represented
- Making the personas too general or too specific

Security Personas

The biggest problem with security testing and personas can be solved, at least in part, by creating specific security personas. These will allow you to take advantage of the benefits of persona testing while performing security testing.

The creation of security personas is similar to that of functional personas, but instead of them being based on the customers, you can start with the information already collected for threat modeling and risk assessment and begin to build an aspect matrix for the attackers, as shown in Table 7.3.

Now you can take this matrix and translate it into attacker descriptions that apply to a potential persona. A very basic sample is shown in Table 7.4.

Table 7.3   Sample Attacker Aspect Matrix

Aspect Name	Aspect Values
Motivation	Hacktivism
	Cyber-extortion
	Defamation
	Cyber-tagging
	Headlines/press
	Data theft
	Data destruction
	Data modification
	System resource theft
	Network resource theft
Identity	Security researcher
	Script kiddie
	Independent hacker
	Organized crime
	Attacker for hire
	Disgruntled current or former employee
	Competitors

Table 7.4 Sample Attacker Descriptions

Identity	Motivation
Security researcher	Hacktivism
Security researcher	Cyber-extortion
Security researcher	Defamation
Security researcher	Cyber-tagging
Security researcher	Headlines/press
Security researcher	Data theft
Security researcher	Data destruction
Security researcher	Data modification
Security researcher	System resource theft
Security researcher	Network resource theft
Script kiddie	Hacktivism
Script kiddie	Cyber-extortion
Script kiddie	Defamation
Script kiddie	Cyber-tagging
Script kiddie	Headlines/press
Script kiddie	Data theft
Script kiddie	Data destruction
Script kiddie	Data modification
Script kiddie	System resource theft
Script kiddie	Network resource theft

Now that you have a list of potential security persona descriptions, you can narrow this list down to the security personas you will expand and use for security testing. Just as in functional personas, details need to be added to bring the security personas to life.

Security personas should be reviewed and publicized to the rest of the product team as well as among the testers. This will serve to familiarize the rest of the team with the idea of having personas other than those associated with pure functionality. It will also tend to inspire the other disciplines to include security personas in their design and development efforts and will give quite a few of your security bugs a common point of view with which to be evaluated.

Just like functional personas, security personas need to be revisited regularly to insure that they still accurately represent the threats for and attackers of your system. As I read about or experience new attacks or vulnerabilities, I make notes on my set of matrices and personas so that I have a centralized location for updated information whenever I need to revisit the personas to maintain them.

Bibliography

Cooper, A. *The Inmates Are Running the Asylum: Why High Tech Products Drive Us Crazy and How To Restore the Sanity.* Sams Publishing, Indianapolis, Indiana. 2002.

Chapter 8

Security Test Planning

After all the techniques and background information, this is the chapter that really focuses on the reason why this book was written — teaching you how to develop a plan with which to conduct security testing on your system.

Like all methodologies or processes, there will certainly be aspects of what I present here that you will always use, there will be aspects you will only use for the first time or two you conduct a security test pass, and there may be aspects or steps that never apply to you. I would advise you to read the entire process before you decide to discard or change an aspect or step. After that, make the process your own and really integrate what you can use into your ongoing test arsenal.

This process should be started as soon as possible during the system's life cycle, but there are some interrelations with other parts of security testing, threat modeling in particular. So this seems like it would be a linear process but it really isn't, and you will often temporarily put aside your actual security test plan in order to produce or participate in another security-related task. Flexibility will be required, especially until this process is more familiar to you.

Overview of the Process

The process of developing a security test plan is broken out into major steps that are repeated for each release of your system. The first time you create this plan will be the most difficult because you really do have to start from scratch, whereas in future releases you will be able to review the plans and results from prior releases to give you a jump start.

I use a test case system called a TCO (test case outline) to document and organize my test cases as they are being generated. I use the information in my security TCO to also drive the actual test plan. The details of the number of test cases and scope of testing will give me something to base my time estimates on.

This test case outlining system is documented in Chapter 28 of this book. I would encourage all new testers to try the TCO system, but you may also use a different system to track and document your test cases if necessary.

Start Drafting Your Test Documents

Test Plan

Your test plan is the document that will outline:

- The basics of the system under test
- The location of all related documents (specifications, test case outlines, threat models, etc.)
- Special concerns for this release
- Documentation of how testing will be done, including the use of test case priorities
- What is included (in scope) of the testing for this release
- What is not included (out of scope) of the testing for this release
- The test schedule
- How and when results will be reported
- Any dependencies you have to carry out during the testing

There is generally one security test plan per release, but there may be one or more functional test plans, mostly depending on the size of the system and its complexity. If test plans need to be split up, you have to be sure that the plans overlap instead of having a gap between them where testing is lax or missing.

Test Case Outline/Test Case Documentation

Your test case outline or test case document is one that will outline the test cases to be run with each test case, including:

- Priority
- Explicit test case steps including validation

- Test case pass and fail criteria
- Vulnerability if the test case is to verify a particular vulnerability

Because this document can grow to an unwieldy size, there are often multiple TCOs for each release, and each one of them deals with a different security risk or area of the product.

Dissect the System

The first thing to do when beginning to create a security test plan is exactly what you would expect to be doing if you were assigned to perform functional testing on a system that is new (or new to you), and that is to familiarize yourself with the product.

You should have a good idea of all the areas of the system and how they relate to each other, but, to best facilitate security test planning, you are going to want to separate the system into different areas that are based on how you will address them in the test plan. I have suggested a list of categories below, but you may find that this doesn't make sense to you or with the system you are testing and want to use a different list.

You should, however, use a set of areas that are different from those being used for the functional testing. This is because you want to avoid being caught up in viewing your system in only that way, and a different structure will often force you into a different mindset.

These areas are loosely based on the same considerations used in threat modeling. If you have a threat model already completed, most of these areas can be taken from it. If you do not have a threat model, these can serve as part of the information needed to create one.

Separate the System into Security Areas

Start by noting the major security areas that you are planning to use at the beginning of your test case documentation. The following list is a good basic list to start with, although you can develop your own.

Be sure the list is the same between the test plan and the TCO so that they can be directly correlated.

Incoming Information

This corresponds with the entry points on the threat model. Each piece of incoming information must be listed separately as it must be tested, usually in multiple ways, as part of the security testing.

If you are testing a system such as an application programming interface (API) or another system that has many pieces of incoming information, you need to organize your outline so that you have a logical outline to work with. Sometimes the best way to set this up is immediately obvious, but sometimes I've had to restructure my list once or twice until I am happy with it.

Don't forget to list items that move from one part of the system to another.

Some ideas for items that could be included in this list are:

■ Initialization files
■ Registry data
■ User login data
■ User-supplied data (per API or per stored procedure)
■ Files
■ Database queries
■ Database query results

Outgoing Information

This corresponds with the exit points of the threat modeling process. This list is for any place where data or control leaves the control of the system. This list also includes items that move from one part of the system to another and those items that deliberately overlap incoming information and will serve to help you overcome the tendency to trust that data.

This list would include items such as:

■ Files
■ Database queries
■ Database query results
■ Registry data
■ User registration data

Dependencies

This is a list of the dependencies your system has on both its own subsystems and on external systems. The purpose of this section is to explore those dependencies and the assumptions made about them while conducting security tests.

A dependency is something that your system depends upon in order to work. Without that dependency, your system would fail to function.

This list would include items such as:

- Operating system registry access
- Operating system file access
- Database remote procedures
- DLLs
- Subsystems of your system under test
- Internet connection

Interactions/Interoperability

This is a list of all the systems that the system you are testing interacts with. The reason you are listing these is so that you can look at these interactions, challenge the assumptions made about them, and then examine their vulnerabilities to see if your mitigations will compensate if those vulnerabilities are exploited.

Remember to not just look at the most current version of these items. It's not at all unusual to have software of varying ages installed on the same system, trusting the user to have the most current version of everything, including patches, is definitely misplaced trust.

This list can include items like:

- Scripting language add-ins
- Browsers
- Operating systems

Gather Information

The next step is probably what you would expect: that of gathering the information you will need in order to proceed. Although this process appears daunting and tedious, once you start into it, it really isn't too bad.

As you gather this information, the easiest way to keep track of it is to note it in the appropriate section of the TCO. These are temporary notes but will serve to keep information organized and available for the next phase, where you are going to use it as part of the process of creating test cases.

If the information affects multiple sections of your TCO, it should be noted in each area it affects.

Your test plan, on the other hand, should document where you looked for this information.

Look At Existing Product Bugs and Known Security Issues

First, gather all the information you can find on known bugs and security issues. You won't really analyze this information immediately, but you need to have some familiarity with it and have concrete data at hand to refer to later.

At the end of this, you will also have a much better idea of what security issues exist and a list of the ones you specifically want to consider.

Your Own System

Start with the bugs and known issues with your own product. If you are working on a first-generation system where you do not have a bug history to review, you may not know the bugs, but you may still have other resources like design documents, design meeting notes, code review comments, etc., where notes have been made about issues or security concerns as the system was being brainstormed.

If you are not working on a first-generation product, you should have a bug history of some sort that you can go through. I start by looking for any bugs that directly mention that they are a security bug or a security concern. Read through these bugs thoroughly and make notes of security defects that have been found before and what was done to mitigate them. Pay particular attention to any bugs that required a patch or hot fix be done — this is an automatic sign of severity.

After you have read the bugs that are obviously noted as security related, skim the rest of the bugs to see if you notice any that are security related but just not tagged as such. Depending on how familiar you are with the bug tracking system in use, you may be able to move through the rest of the bugs fairly quickly.

Once you have finished familiarizing yourself with the bugs that have been filed, review the design documents and specs for any notes that may relate to security concern or risks, and any decisions made because of them.

I also sit down for a few minutes with the developers and designers/program managers on the current team — especially those that worked on prior versions of the system — and get their feedback and insight not only on what has happened in the past releases but also what risks they think currently exist. You will be surprised at what you can learn. Also, speak to other senior testers or testers who have been on the team longer than you have.

After all that, it's time to expand your perspective to that of consumers and those outside your own product group. Take a little bit of time and check to see if your system shows up on any of the common security bug tracking lists. (There are Web sites listed in Chapter 29 under section Recommended Web Sites and Mailing Lists.) These are security bugs that have been made publicly known, and despite the logic that says that anything publicly known should have a corresponding bug in the internal bug tracking system, experience has told me that is not always the case.

After looking through these bug databases, I recommend using your favorite search engine or two and trying a few searches for Web sites and Usenet groups that mention your system and any of a few keywords that are commonly used with security issues like the following:

- Hack, hacker, hacked
- Security, secure, insecure
- Virus
- Worm
- Spyware
- Crash, crashed, BSOD ("**blue screen of death**")

This is just to give you a feel for what the customers of your system are complaining about that may have to do with security.

Competitive Systems

Once you have exhausted the issues that relate directly to your own system, you should repeat the searches on the security bug databases and the search engines, but, instead of being targeted at your own system, you should see what relates to your top competitors. Similar competitive products are often based on similar technology, and it's possible for a security bug that has been found in one product to have the potential to appear in another. Web browsers are a good example of this.

This search can also give you some ideas on what has been done or is possible to be done with these security vulnerabilities, and you can integrate those ideas into your own threat modeling or plans.

Systems You Interface or Interact With

After your own system and your competitive systems, you need to turn your attention to related systems. There are usually quite a few of these from the operating system down, so you may have to focus your efforts on those you are most closely tied to. For example, if you are using a Web server and a database backend, some of your first research should be done on the specific Web server and database software you are using.

If these systems are produced by your own company, you may have access to that system's bug records and can start looking for security issues there. If not, you can only repeat the security bug database and search engine process again.

Review System Specifications

The next step is to take a careful look at both the functional and design specifications for your system, both for the current release and the last few releases. You are looking specifically for security-related designs and areas where security seems to have been neglected or not given the attention it deserved. You want to end up with a list of areas that you think are of particular concern.

Begin as Early as Possible

Always try to start this process as early as possible. As soon as there are functional specifications in even a draft state, you should be reading through them.

Always Question Security Concerns

As you read the functional and design specifications, you should note any security questions that come to mind. These can be specific to any new functionality that's being implemented or to any existing functionality that you have questions about.

No matter what explanation you get, make sure you understand what you are being told. If you don't understand, ask for clarifications.

If you have questions about security in regard to a specification, ask that the answer be integrated into the document so that it's clear in the future. After a release or two of these requests, you may find (as I did) that security becomes a subject that the program managers and developers include in their specifications and documentation without needing any more encouragement.

Review Existing Test Plans and Cases

If you have any prior tests plans and test cases, either functional or security, you may review those, as well as any test case results that may be obtainable.

This review is partly to see what has been tested before and also what hasn't been tested. If only functional testing has been done before, you can probably see pretty easily where there are possibilities of security vulnerabilities.

If security testing has been done before, there will be more data to go on that will tell you what has been tested, what cases were run, and even what vulnerabilities were discovered.

If you are not also doing the functional testing for your system, you will want to collaborate with the tester who is and keep up-to-date copies of the current test plan and test cases to refer to.

Review Existing Test Automation

If there is any test automation that has been run or is running, you should become at least familiar with what is being done and how. This is partly for you to know what testing is being done or has been done, and also to know how it was done. Certain methods of testing may or may not actually test what it is supposed to.

Sometimes test "hooks," methods, or user authentications are put in place for the convenience of testing but are accidentally left in at the time the system is shipped and can then be used by an attacker. Knowing how the automation is done or has been done will let you know what to check for in the released system.

Develop Security Cases

Now you need to begin to drill down to develop the actual test cases that you will run to security-test your product. As you examine each area, you need to write test cases that will give you an unambiguous result as the answer to the question of whether a test passes or fails.

The TCO process requires drilling down through the behavior to arrive at an atomic statement of behavior that can be tested. Some other test case systems are not as stringent and leave more room for ambiguity, so be careful to be extremely clear on what exactly you are testing and what results you expect to see as a pass result.

At this point you shouldn't really focus on how you will carry out these test cases. You really want to develop the best test cases possible, and later you will determine how to run them. If you start to worry right now about how to run a case, you will subconsciously narrow your test cases to accommodate the "how" instead of finding out how to run a test case you already have.

Known Vulnerabilities

Your System

The notes you made in the last step will now become items you want to have a test case or test cases specifically address. Reviewing these known vulnerabilities will also spark some ideas on other items to test.

The goal of these test cases is to verify that the known vulnerability is no longer reproducible and has been removed or mitigated.

Other Known Vulnerabilities

Remember to develop test cases for those vulnerabilities that exist in your system's dependencies and those systems that the system being tested interacts and interfaces with. The goal of these test cases is to verify that if these known vulnerabilities in these other products still exist and are unmitigated, your system will mitigate them so they do not become a vulnerability for your system as well.

You can also look at the known vulnerabilities in competing products and write test cases for each applicable one to ensure that these vulnerabilities are not also present in your system.

Unknown Vulnerabilities

Once you have developed a test case for each known vulnerability, you need to branch out and create test cases to search for vulnerabilities that are currently unknown.

These tests constitute the majority of the tests run in any security test passes. Unlike the known vulnerability cases, where you know exactly what you are looking for, these cases are designed to look for something that may or may not exist. I've found that the easiest way to do this is to go through each of my initial lists in turn and try to think of what vulnerabilities may be possible in each item in that list.

There are some potential vulnerabilities, which are pretty much of universal concern for any system. These include items like buffer overruns, plaintext storage of sensitive data, etc.

Then, there are potential vulnerabilities that are more dependent how your particular system functions. If your system has a dependency on a database, potential vulnerabilities may include structured query language (SQL) injection. But if your system has no Web site interface, there may not be a need (or a way) to test for XSS (cross-site-scripting) vulnerabilities.

In order to give a jump start to your test cases, Chapter 9 includes some ideas of what should be examined according to the type of system you are testing, and Chapter 10 through Chapter 21 give explanations of many of the most common vulnerabilities and ideas on how to test for them.

Prioritize Tests

Now that you have written your test cases, you need to be able to prioritize them so that you have a clear idea of what cases are considered to be the most important.

You need to know this now to be able to communicate this information both in your test plan and on the schedule for the system. If you are told that you have a set amount of time to run security tests, you will be able to then look at your highest priority test cases and determine how many of them you can run in that amount of time.

You will also want to be able to report the time needed by test case priority, i.e., priority 1 test cases will take four weeks to run, priority 2 cases will take another three weeks to run, etc.

This is also the way you can keep your testing on track and ensure that you are running those cases first that most need to be run, instead of just those that are easiest to run.

Test case prioritization is one of the harder test skills to teach, because so many of the factors that contribute to it are not easily quantified. You really have to do the best job you can, and, after each release of your system, continue to revisit and adjust the criteria you use for your test case prioritization.

At the end of this stage, your TCO or test case documentation will have a priority listed for each test case. I used a scale of 1 to 3 where the ratings have the following meanings:

- 1 = Must be tested in this release
- 2 = Should be tested in this release
- 3 = Can be tested in this release if time permits

The test plan should include the fact that the test cases are prioritized to allow better scheduling.

Use Threat Modeling/Risk Assessment Charts

If you or your team have conducted threat modeling for your system, these threat models are probably the best source of test case priorities. The test cases can be set to have the same priority as the vulnerability in the threat model, as a starting point.

If you have to narrow down the pool of test cases, you can pick a subset of the test cases for each vulnerability that you think is most likely to reveal the vulnerability's presence. Those will stay as the original priority and the rest of the equivalent cases would be downgraded to a lower priority.

Sometimes you will find that you have written test cases for vulnerabilities that were not considered in the threat model. These should be added to the threat model and prioritized.

Use Personal Experience Data

There is always a place for personal experience and hunches. You should never let this become a case of "test everything as the highest priority," but you may decide that you want to make a few of the test cases in a certain area a higher priority than they would normally be to appease your hunch that there is an exploitable vulnerability.

There is also a place for using your own experience. You may have information on areas of your system or its dependencies that seem to be rife with security defects. You may have experience with the work done by one of the team members who wrote a particular subsystem in which the code always seemed to be really careful and safe.

These types of information may cause you to adjust test case priorities.

Talk to the Developers for Special Concerns

Another source of information that may affect the prioritization of test cases is obtained by talking to the other team members, particularly the developers. These people may have their own concerns or hunches on the best places to test first for security vulnerabilities.

Develop a Test Plan of Attack

After your have written the test cases and prioritized them, you need to put more work into the test plan. Right now you have a very thorough TCO, but a very generic test plan.

To flesh out this test plan, you need to determine how you are going to approach the test cases you have documented. This is when you determine the "how" of running your test cases.

Start with your TCO and, in priority order, begin to add information on the steps needed to run that test. Then decide how that test can be run. Any methods or tools you are planning to use need to be noted in the test case and a summary description of the method, tool, or automation noted in the test plan.

Using "Normal" or "By Design" Test Methods

Some tests can be run via the system's normal access methods like a UI (user interface) or console command. Remember if there is any other way to run these tests, that method (or methods) should be used as well, so that you can bypass the UI checks as a lot of attackers will.

Using Commercial Tools

There are quite a few commercial tools that can make some types of testing easier to accomplish. Use of these can help you test aspects of your system that you would otherwise be unable to have direct access to, or the wherewithal to create such an item (like a file) that may expose a security vulnerability.

Using Custom Tools

Sometimes you will need to create or use custom tools that are built specifically in order to interface or interact with your product. This is common when creating or maintaining test automation.

Because the creation of custom tools is often expensive, careful thought and planning should be done before making an investment in one. If a custom tool is required, the justifications should also be included in your test plan.

Don't Forget Validation Tools

A lot of the emphasis is being made on the tools or methods used to run the test cases, but there should be equal documentation and thought given to how test case results are validated.

It's always better to validate test results both within the system under test and with a separate tool that will show you what actually happened where you cannot directly see it. Some of my favorite monitoring and comparison tools are shareware, which I've discovered over time.

Remember the Downsides

If you are using a tool or automation, always remember that any layer you put between yourself and your system introduces its own set of possible problems or biases that are not always obvious.

Each tool you use should be examined for these downsides and a way to compensate determined if those downsides would compromise the test results and make them unreliable.

These downsides and risks should be documented in the test plan, as well.

Untestable Code Is Unshippable Code

Although sometimes difficult to enforce, another tenet of software security is that untestable code is unshippable code. If you cannot get to the code to test it, it shouldn't be shipped because its actual behavior is unknown.

This tenet is one of the reasons that the once-popular software Easter eggs are an endangered species lately.

Draft a Schedule

The next step is to develop a draft test schedule for the security testing of your system. Scheduling is probably one of the least scientific and most disliked aspect of test planning, so don't feel like you are missing something obvious if it's not easy for you to do.

The goal at this point is to look at the schedule that has been determined for your system and any hard dates that must be met. You will have to work within those dates as much as you can.

There is always a trade-off to be made between a schedule and what can be tested, but this is where the test case prioritization can really pay off by allowing you to give three different time frames, depending on which priority of cases you plan to run.

One rule of thumb you always want to follow is building in your padding before you release a schedule. As soon as the dates are out there, no matter how much you explain, if they are raw dates and have no padding; they will become set in stone, and when the inevitable problems occur, you will immediately be behind schedule.

I typically build in a 50 percent to 75 percent padding on top of the actual time needed to perform tasks. If my meeting schedule is unusually heavy, I'll adjust the padding percentage to compensate. The amount of actual padding you need will be something that you discover over time, but I would always recommend building in at least 50 percent.

This is before any additional time is built in for things like tools, etc., and is used for investigation, issues, etc., that are inevitable.

Time to Develop or Learn Tools

If part of your test plan includes developing a new tool or learning a tool that is new to you, be sure to build in time for that. If someone else is building a tool for you, you need the time to meet with them, draw up specifications, wait for it to be completed, and then learn to use it.

If you have to develop a tool or have it developed for you, you will also want to note the schedule for that as it will have impact on the overall test schedule if it slips.

You need to be sure that the amount of time required for tool development or learning a new tool is built only into the schedule for the priority test cases that need to use it.

You also may be able to tighten the test schedule a little by seeing if some testing can be done as you wait for tools.

Time to Perform Tests

The raw time needed to actually perform the tests varies so much that you really can only make a guess by taking several different test cases of the average complexity and run those (or walk through the process of running them) and then derive the time needed to validate the results.

Multiply this by the number of test cases in that priority. This should give you a reasonable base number for just the test cases.

Now you need to add in some buffer time to account for the time you will need to spend on resetting between tests, documenting test case results, etc. Unless the reset between tests is really painful, I use about 15 percent for this overhead. This then gets multiplied by the number of test passes (of find/fix cycles) you plan to carry out.

Time to Investigate Issues

This is a really hard number to come up with because you don't know how many issues need to be investigated or how long it will take to investigate each one. In this case, you do have to guess based on whether you think there will be a lot of issues that need investigation.

The first time I do a security test pass on a product that is new to me, I use 25 percent of the test case performance time for this overhead. Then I adjust that up or down as I discover how it matches reality.

Time to Rerun All Security Tests on Release Candidate

This is the last security test pass before the product is released, so the time is usually the same as that required for the test cases for this release and the buffer time you've already built in. If your test is four days and you add two days of buffer to that, you would budget six days for this rerun as well.

Review the Plan and Test Cases

Now that you have your test documents in order, you should give them a formal review so that other people can offer what can be valuable feedback. It should be very clear to everyone just what is included and not included in the plan, as well as what your schedule is.

Review with Other Disciplines

Be sure to include disciplines other than test as they can have valuable feedback or insight to offer, especially when it comes to any assumptions you may have made.

The other places these reviewers can really help is in finding any areas that you may have overlooked in the system being tested or in recommending tools they may know about that will be able to fill one or more of your needs

Review with Other Testers

Also review both documents with other testers to get their feedback on missing or invalid test cases. They may also be able to point out ways to increase efficiency or speed.

Share the Plan with Others

Lastly, I would put the test plan and TCO out on a share or send it out as e-mail to anyone who wants to read it. This will help to publicize security testing as a whole but also may give other testers some examples they can use to develop their own security test efforts.

Run Test Passes

Now the planning is done, and it's time to actually run the tests. In addition to the standard testing process of run the case, verify the result, and either file a bug or move to the next case, I also do the following:

- Note any failures and their root causes, then look for any similar cases that could fail with a similar root cause, and if those have not been included in the test pass already, I mark them to be run
- Correct any false information that appears in my test documents
- Note any additional cases that I can think of as I am in the process of testing
- Mark any cases that took a huge amount of time
- Track how long I estimated for the test pass and how long it actually took so that I can continue to perfect my estimates
- Note when I was blocked from being able to make progress by something outside my control and for how long

All of these are to make easier the postmortem and any future planning for this system's security testing.

Postmortem the Results

After the system is released, it always pays to sit down and look through what happened during this release with a goal of improving the process. This means looking for:

- Items that worked well so that they can be continued
- Items that worked but not so well that they can't be revisited for improvement
- Items that didn't work or were really painful so they can be avoided in the future.

You should always postmortem the results for your own improvement, but I recommend you also write up an e-mail or a report that can then be distributed to your team, so that more people can benefit from the insight and lessons learned.

Chapter 9

Sample Security Considerations

This chapter gives a few sample ideas of what kinds of vulnerabilities may exist in products that have something in common. These are not exhaustive lists, nor are they intended to serve as a checklist. You should still be considering your specific system and its unique set of dependencies and functionality.

Universal

There are some considerations that are pretty much universal, in that most systems need to ensure they are addressed. It's not a guarantee that your system will need to have these tested, but it's likely.

Default Installation

These are considerations that are based on the default installation of the system and the trusts and assumptions that are made during the installation.

Too Many Features Enabled on Install

Although it can be considered a nuisance to have to enable a feature before you can use it, the alternative is to have features default to "enabled" during install so that people would have to deliberately disable them.

The problem with this approach is that people are likely to find and enable a feature they need and know that it is enabled. But if the features default to being enabled on install, the customers are not likely to know everything that is enabled. They will then be running features that may have security vulnerabilities, without knowing it; and human nature being what it is, they won't disable features they don't actually need, unless forced to.

More Risky Abilities Enabled by Default

This is a close cousin to the too-many features, but it differs in the fact that a feature can have multiple abilities, some of which are riskier to have enabled than others. This is evidenced in features such as automatically running script content in browsers.

It's far safer to disable the riskier abilities by default and make the user either turn them on or give permission each time they want to run.

High Permissions Required to Install but Not to Run

One of the biggest problems with this is that it means your users are more likely to just always run your system as the administrator because that's what they had to do to install it.

This shoots in the foot the security practice of running the system with the least security.

Hard-Coded Install Locations

Although this would seem rather innocuous and more of a nuisance than a security problem at first glance, it not only means users with nonstandard drive configurations would have a hard time installing your system, but it also means that the system is in a predictable location for every installation.

Such a predictability can make it easier for an attacker who is attempting to exploit a vulnerability in your system.

Authentication

These are considerations that have to do with how a user is authenticated by the system and when.

User Authenticated Only at Certain Points

If a user is authenticated only at certain points, this may mean that if attackers can get to a place where authentication is not done, they can carry out malicious activities as if they were authenticated.

Access Control Rules Not Enforced Consistently

If your system is using an access control list (ACL) or a similar method to enforce who has access to what functionality, and if this is not enforced consistently, attackers may be able to perform functions that their access level should not permit.

Input

These are considerations that have to do with the input your system consumes. Remember that all input is evil!

Input Contents Assumed Trustworthy

If your system trusts the contents of input to be intended as correct and appropriate instead of carefully validating it before use, any of the input can have malicious intent.

Input Formats Assumed Trustworthy

If your system trusts the format of its input to be correct and appropriate instead of carefully validating it before use, the system will try to consume data as if it were the format it expects.

Input Sources Assumed Trustworthy

If your system trusts input that appears to be received from a particular user, system, port, etc., without carefully validating it before use, the system will try to consume anything coming from that source as if it were trustworthy.

Security Validations

These are considerations that have to do with the way security is enforced and validation is done by the system.

Validations Are Faulty

If your system's validations are incorrect, it can be as bad as not having validations at all.

Validations Are Processed in Wrong Order

If your validations are technically correct but are processed in the wrong order, malicious content can still make its way inside the system.

Cryptographic Considerations

These are considerations that have to do with the use of encryption technology in your system.

Cryptography Not Being Used

If no cryptography is being used, only information being transmitted or stored has to be obtained to be used.

Home-Grown Cryptography

If your system uses home-grown cryptography instead of one of the proven and tested algorithms, the strength of the encryption isn't really known; therefore, any encrypted data is at increased risk.

Operational Environment

These are the considerations that have to do with the operating system or machines that the system runs on.

Registry Entries

If your system stores data in the registry and accepts it as trusted, that data is subject to tampering by the user outside the system that uses the registry.

System Pathing

If your system relies on information in the system path, it is vulnerable to path modifications when looking for resources such as DLLs, etc.

Hidden Files and Locations

If your system uses hidden files and directories, and trusts the contents of those files and directories, it is vulnerable to tampering.

Information Disclosure

This set of considerations has to do with the system giving the user too much information that the user doesn't really need.

Verbose Errors Displayed

If verbose errors are displayed, the attackers can use those error messages to help refine the attack they are attempting to craft.

Access to Temporary Files

If the system allows access to temporary files and then trusts the contents of those files, it is vulnerable to tampering as well as data theft from the files.

Access to Crash Dump Files or Reports

If the system writes sensitive information to crash dump files or reports, that data may be vulnerable to attackers.

Extraneous Code

These considerations have to do with code that exists in the system and which isn't necessary for the system's correct functioning.

Debug Code Still Present

If debug code is still present in the system after it is released, that extraneous code can cause unpredictable behavior in the system.

Test Hooks Still Present

If test hooks are still present in the system after it is released, these test hooks could be used by an attacker to bypass the system's security measures or to make writing automation code easier.

Security Bypass Settings

If code to permit security bypasses is still present after it is released, these test hooks could be used by an attacker to bypass the system's security checks.

Stand-Alone Applications

These are the considerations that are common in stand-alone applications.

Application Process

These considerations apply to the system's processes while running.

Processes Run at High Privilege

If the system's processes run at a high privilege, and an attacker manages to exploit a vulnerability and obtain control of the processes, whatever application the attacker uses with that process will run at a high privilege, which increases the damage that can be done.

Output

These considerations apply to the way in which the system's output is handled.

Setup Information Saved to Hard-Coded Location

If your system always saves its setup data to a hard-coded location, attackers know where to look for it, as well as other valuable information that may be there.

State Information Saved to Hard-Coded Location

If your system saves state information to a hard-coded location, the attackers know where to look for the data they can use.

This hard-coded location also means that attackers may be able to tamper with that state information.

Repair/Restore Information Saved to Hard-Coded Location

If your system saves its repair/restore information to a hard-coded location, attackers may be able to use that information to spoof the install.

Output Interceptable before Final Destination

If your system has output that somehow can be intercepted before it reaches its final (and, hopefully, secure) destination, the attackers may be able to copy or even tamper with this temporarily stored data.

Backward Compatibility

These considerations have to do with your system's ability to be backward compatible.

Defaults to Less-Secure Versions

If your system defaults to less-secure versions of its functionality, when faced with errors, it may be possible for an attacker to force the system into a less secure state and then exploit it.

Operational Environment

These considerations are centered around the environment in which your system operates.

Cached Information Not Safeguarded

If your system caches information in an unencrypted or open location, this can enable an attacker to retrieve and possibly use that cached information.

Information Revealed Unnecessarily

If your system reveals more information than is necessary (e.g., errors), an attacker may be able to use this information to help plan or further an attack.

Registry Keys Easily Accessible

If your system saves information in registry keys, it's easy to get to that information, and an attacker may be able to use it.

APIs

These considerations are centered around systems that implement an application programming interface (API) as a whole or part of their functionality.

Application Process

These are considerations that relate to the application's process.

Processes Run at High Privilege

If your system's API process or processes run at high privilege and an attacker takes control of the process, the attacker's code can then be run in the same high privilege process.

Default Accounts Used to Run Processes

If your system uses default accounts to run processes, an attacker can obtain access to these default accounts and use them for an attack. These accounts are easy to guess and misuse.

Input

These considerations have to do with how the system accepts input.

Data Submission Formats are Trusted

If your system trusts data without validation because it matches a particular format, an attacker can submit invalid or malicious data in the correct format to be consumed by your system.

No Validation of Data/Request Source

If your system does not validate the data or request source, it is easy for an attacker to submit malicious data for your system to consume.

Language

These considerations have to do with the programming language that your system uses.

Specific Language Details Relied On

If your system trusts the implementation details of a particular programming language to act as implicit security, an attacker can simply use another language or method to implement an attack.

Operational Environment

These considerations have to do with the environment in which your system operates.

Session Cookies Are Weak or Easily Reused

If your session cookies are not strong or are predictable, this leaves your system vulnerable to session replay or cookie-tampering attacks.

Session Persistence

If your system persists its sessions, an attacker may be able to locate and steal such session information and use it to implement an attack.

Specialized Considerations

These are considerations that are specific to APIs.

Safeguards on Perimeters Solely Relied On (Proxies, Etc.)

If your system relies on perimeter security alone, then any failure or breach of that security device means that your system is completely exposed to attack.

Insufficient Safeguards on API Abilities

If your system provides an API but insufficiently protects it, an attacker may be able to use an API method to implement an attack.

Web Applications/Web Services/Distributed Applications

These considerations are centered around systems that are Web applications, provide Web services, or are distributed applications of some sort.

Application Process

These considerations have to do with the process under which the system is running.

Local Processes Run at High Privilege

This is the same situation as for some other types of systems. If your system runs its processes at a high privilege, then attackers who obtain control of the process can run their own code at the same high privilege.

Server Processes Run at High Privilege

This is a similar consideration to that stated earlier, but instead of the client processes being at risk, the risk is to the server processes.

Default Accounts Used to Execute (Admin, Dbo, Sa)

If your system uses a default account to execute, attackers can easily gain access to the default account user id and password and begin to execute their own code.

Input

These considerations are related to the system's acceptance of input.

Custom Packet Format Relied On

If your system trusts input based on conformation to a custom packet format, an attacker can submit malicious data in that format for the system to consume.

Data Not Encoded Before Action

If your system carries out actions on data before or without encoding it, such plain text or unencoded data may be interceptable by at attacker.

Hidden Form Fields Not Validated

If your system uses hidden form fields and takes action on their contents without validating them, an attacker can insert malicious code into those fields for consumption by the system.

Data Transfer

These considerations have to do with the system's data transfer functionality. Traffic is considered trustworthy if specifically directed to or from ports, sockets, and Point-to-Point Tunneling Protocol (PPTP).

Named Pipes

If your system trusts data based on its transmission source, an attacker only has to use that transmission method to provide malicious code for consumption by the system.

Traffic Not Encrypted

If your system is transmitting unencrypted data, that data can easily be sniffed by an attacker.

Client

These considerations are related to the system's clients.

Rogue Clients Not Detected

If the system does not have a way to validate real clients and detect invalid clients, an attacker may only have to set up a rogue client to have access.

Server Verifies Only Client, Not Data (Client Hijacking)

If the system only verifies a client but not the data, an attacker may be able to hijack or spoof a client.

No Antirepudiation Validation

If the system does not maintain sufficient validation and records, an attacker may be able to repudiate an attack.

Server

These considerations have to do with the system's server functionality.

Rogue Servers Not Detected

If the system's clients have no method to validate the server they are interacting with and no way of detecting a rogue server, an attacker may be able to set up a rogue server for legitimate clients to connect to.

Client Verifies Only Server Identity, Not Data (Server Hijacking)

If the system only validates server identity but not the data, an attacker may be able to hijack the session by impersonating the server.

No Antirepudiation Validation

If the system does not maintain sufficient validation and records, an attacker may be able to repudiate an attack.

Remote Administration Available

If the system offers remote administration capabilities, its possible for an attacker to take advantage of these if they are not secured.

Specialized Considerations

These considerations have to do with the specialized functionality of Web servers/Web services/distributed systems.

Safeguards on Perimeter Only

If your system relies solely on perimeter security (like proxies, firewalls, etc.) and such perimeter security goes down, the system is completely exposed to attackers.

Encryption Keys Stored in Source Code

If your system uses encryption keys or other secrets that are stored in source code, they are vulnerable to an attacker who disassembles the source code.

HTML Comments Remain in Shipped Forms

If your system leaves HTML comments in the shipped forms, an attacker may be able to obtain enough clues to better craft an attack.

Chapter 10

Vulnerability Case Study: Brute Force Browsing

Pseudonyms

- Forceful browsing

Description

Most Web browsers have a standard behavior of listening on port 80 for HTTP traffic and port 443 for HTTPS traffic. A Web server is only supposed to access files reachable from its own document root directory. But the common gateway interface (CGI) is intended to allow ordinary programs (those that are not Web servers) to interact using a Web browser interface. Ordinary programs are not bound by the same rules as a Web server, and they can access any part of the file system. CGI interfaces are present at the core of almost all Web applications.

To add to the problem, most Web servers are only able to run as a single user: IUSR on IIS and nobody on most Apache systems. The identity of the remote user has no bearing on this as this is the Web server's own user identity. So, all human users are grouped into a single system user for the purposes of local file permissions. The Web server can restrict access to a CGI to specific users but cannot limit the files that the CGI can access.

These facts lead to a set of vulnerabilities called "forceful browsing" or "brute-force browsing" vulnerabilities. In these vulnerabilities, an attacker can manipulate values in the data they submit to a CGI program by way of the browser and thus force the Web server to return Web pages or other files that the attacker would be unable to access otherwise.

URL Guessing

The simplest form of forceful browsing is for an attacker to just guess the names of Web pages and enter them in the browser to see if they find a real page and if they can access it. Because the only security on these pages is that they are not linked to anywhere on the site that can be seen by a regular user; if the attacker correctly guesses the address, they succeed in obtaining access to whatever is on that page.

Session Replay Attack

Another type of forceful browsing takes place when the attacker knows the URL already. This can be done via saved URLs where the attacker had one instance of legitimate access to the URL and now replays the URL to regain access or replay a prior transaction. If this succeeds, the attacker has carried out a session replay attack.

The root cause of this vulnerability is the lack of state. HTTP and CGIs were never intended to be accessed in a stateful fashion. So, the user has to supply the CGI with all the information necessary to respond to the user for every request because the CGI can't retain that user information itself. To do this, cookies and hidden fields are often used, but both of these are very susceptible to tampering. By tampering with these, an attacker can impersonate another user or tell the CGI that a transaction has taken place, which actually has not.

Sometimes, a session variable is used to associate an authenticated user with a particular session, but these session variables can't be immediately expired by the server because any lag in the communication will cut off the legitimate user from his session. There is always delay — the Internet is not real time. If an attacker can obtain the session variable of another user before the delayed expiration of that session variable, the attacker can impersonate that user without ever needing to know a username or password because the server thinks that the stolen user identity is already logged in.

Session variables are often stored in hidden fields in the HTML pages of the site, or they are transmitted as part of the URL. This makes it relatively easy for an attacker to obtain session variables. Secure sockets layer (SSL) can be used to hide the session variable, but hardly any site uses SSL on all pages, even when the session variable is used. Other vulnerabilities (like cross-site scripting) can also be used to obtain the session variables from the cookies or browser history of other users.

Non-URL Forceful Browsing

URLs are the most common places from which to perform forceful browsing, but it is not the only place where browsing can be accomplished. Any of the CGI parameters that are present in the fields of the HTML page (both hidden and unhidden) can be tampered with.

Anatomy of an Exploit

URL Guessing

An attacker visits a Web site — for example, http://www.myweb-site.html/default.html. When the attacker browses the site, the attacker notices that there is a pattern to the URLs being seen.

The link titled "New Member" leads to the URL http://www.myweb-site.html/newmember.html.

The link titled "Consultants" leads to the URL http://www.myweb-site.html/consultants.html.

The attacker notices that there is no URL listed that seems to have anything to do with site administration and decides to see if he can find it. He guesses at a couple of URLs until he happens to guess the correct URL to achieve some level of access: http://www.myweb-site.html/admin.html.

Now that the attacker has guessed the correct URL, he has access to the administrative functions of the Web site.

Session Replay

An attacker sits down at a coworker's desk after the coworker has stepped away, and the computer is left unlocked. The coworker had just shown the attacker the new item he bought at a major online retailer.

The attacker opens the coworker's browser history and opens the link to the online retailer. When this link is opened, the attacker notices that the online retailer shows the user as logged on.

The attacker navigates to the account management page and changes the coworker's email address and password to his own, then logs out of the online retailer's site and closes the browser before returning to his own desk.

Real-World Examples

Kerio Personal Firewall™ (Kerio Technologies, Inc., Santa Clara, California) is a firewall for workstations. In 2003, a session replay vulnerability was reported.

The vulnerability reported involved a flaw in the authentication when the firewall's remote administration was being used. The traffic during the session is encrypted, but if the entire administration session is captured using a network sniffer and then replayed as a whole, the server recognizes it as a valid session.

The impact of this vulnerability is that an attacker could record a session and replay it at will to cause the same administrative commands to be sent to the firewall. These can be disabling to the firewall, etc.

Test Techniques

URL Guessing

Start testing for brute-force browsing vulnerabilities by mapping your site. Begin by creating a list of all the URLs that are intended to be safe and accessible to everyone, including those people who aren't logged in. This should be done from the documentation or specifications because you want to know the intended behavior, not the actual behavior.

Now log on to your site as an administrator and manually walk through all the pages you can access or find links to, noting the URLs of each page as you go. This can also be done via a Web spider program, if you want to use one.

The next step is to log out of the site completely, and clear your browser cache and cookies. Go back to your site and try all of the URLs — both from the safe list and the administrator list. Mark each of the URLs that is reachable.

Now repeat this process while logged in as a normal user. Again, mark each of the accessible pages. If there is any page that is accessible by nonadministrators and it is not on the safe list, then you have a URL-guessing security vulnerability.

Session Replay

To test for session replay vulnerabilities, start by seeing if you can detect how your system is storing session information.

Log into the system as a regular user, and navigate to a URL that requires you to be logged into the system to access. Look at the URL that is displayed in your browser's address bar. Does it contain any parameters with names like "session" or any long strings of seemingly random letters and numbers? If either of these are true, the URL probably contains the session variable.

Now save the current page to a local file, and log out of your site. Delete your browser's cache and clear your cookies, then try opening the saved file in your browser, and click on one of the links. If you can still navigate around the site, your system may be vulnerable to a session replay attack.

Try copying the URL to a file, and close your browser. Clear your cache and cookies again. Reopen your browser and paste the URL into the address bar and see if you can access the site without logging in. If you can, you may have a session replay attack.

To verify your findings, try the same process from a different machine with the locally saved file and the URL. If you can still access the site without logging in, you have a confirmed vulnerability.

Chapter 11

Vulnerability Case Study: Buffer Overruns

Pseudonyms

- Buffer overflows
- Stack buffer overruns
- Heap buffer overruns
- Stack smashing
- Heap smashing

Description

A buffer overrun is caused when data is stored in a buffer that is too small to contain the data being stored. This causes the data to "overflow" or "overrun" into adjacent memory.

If the software being tested is written in C or C++, even only in part, this is definitely something that should be carefully tested. Errors in, or failure to, bounds-check data before it is stored or used is an easy mistake for a developer to make.

This is becoming a less commonly reported flaw in released software because of the increased education of developers who program in C and C++ and the increased migration to managed code. But, it requires continued vigilance on the part of everyone who produces software.

A	A	B	B	B	B	B	B	B	B	C	C	D	D	D	D
0	1	0	0	0	0	0	0	0	0	0	3	'u'	's'	'r'	0

Figure 11.1 Sample buffer contents before overrun.

A	A	B	B	B	B	B	B	B	B	C	C	D	D	D	D
0	1	'e'	'x'	't'	'r'	'a'	'b'	'i'	't'	's'	0	'u'	's'	'r'	0

Figure 11.2 Sample buffer contents during overrun.

In Figure 11.1, adjacent memory has been allocated as follows: a 2-byte integer with contents of 1 (A), an 8-byte-long string buffer that is empty, application (B), a 2-byte integer buffer containing the number 3 (C), and a 2-byte-long string buffer with the string "usr" and the string terminating zero byte (D).

Now the program attempts to store the character string "extrabits" and the string terminating zero byte in buffer B. No bounds checking in advance means it fills buffer B and overflows to buffer C. The buffer contents now look like those in Figure 11.2.

If an attacker is aware of this buffer overrun vulnerability and knows that buffer D contains an access level variable, the string being stored in buffer B can be crafted to overwrite the buffer D data with the string that grants administrator privileges. It now might look like Figure 11.3.

There are two main types of buffer overruns that are the most problematic: Stack buffer overruns and Heap buffer overruns.

Stack Buffer Overruns

There is a special stack that holds information about the active subroutines of a program. It is sometimes referred to as the call stack, the function stack, the control stack, or the execution stack but is typically referred to as "the stack." One of the main functions of the stack is to keep track of

A	A	B	B	B	B	B	B	B	B	C	C	D	D	D	D
0	1	'e'	'x'	't'	'r'	'a'	'b'	'i'	't'	's'	0	'a'	'd'	'm'	0

Figure 11.3 Sample buffer contents after overrun.

where to return control when the current subroutine finishes executing. This is often done by putting the return address into the call stack.

There is one and only one stack that is associated with a running process, though if several processes are running on the system, there will be a stack for each one of these. For simplicity, it is just called *the stack*. It is called a stack because it grows from a higher memory address down to a lower memory address and is accessed in a LIFO (last in, first out) manner. The easiest way to think of it is as one of the little spikes people keep on their desks to jab notes onto. The item on top of the pile is the last item added and must be taken off before anything under it can be accessed. If too many things are pushed onto the stack, a stack overflow error can occur.

Depending on the environment, programming language, and other variables, the stack can also be responsible for:

■ Local data storage
■ Parameter passing
■ Pointer to the current instance
■ Evaluation stack
■ Context of the enclosing subroutine
■ Other return state information

The stack is comprised of stack frames, each one of which corresponds to a call to a subroutine that has not yet terminated with a return. The stack frame at the top of the stack (the last one pushed on) belongs to the routine that is currently executing. Stack frames may be different sizes depending on the needs of the subroutines involved. The stack frames are, however, generally comprised of the parameters passed into the routine when it was called, then the return address, and then the space for the local variables of the routine (in the order they are pushed onto the stack). Figure 11.4 is a sample view of a stack.

Stack buffer overruns depend on the fact that most C compilers store both return addresses and local variables on the same stack. When this is the case, an unbounded local variable can be used to overwrite the stack and create problems like substituting an address to an attacker's code or a command window in place of the subroutine's legitimate return address.

Heap Buffer Overruns

The heap is an area of memory, where dynamic memory allocation and deallocation is made at runtime by the C *malloc()* and *calloc()* functions, and the C++ *new* operator. The heap has mixed blocks of allocated and

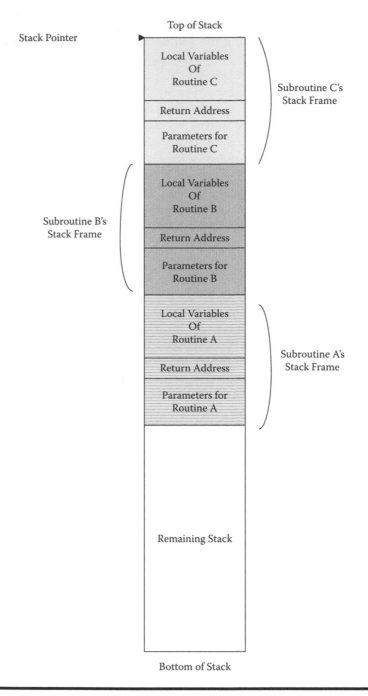

Figure 11.4   Sample stack frames.

Heap Buffer

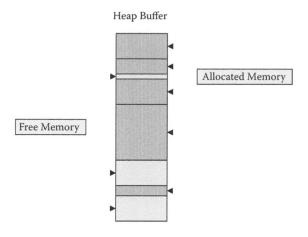

Free Memory

Allocated Memory

Figure 11.5 Sample heap buffer.

free memory, and is usually tracked with the use of a linked list where each block of memory has headers that point to the next allocated block of memory in the heap. These are updated as memory in the heap is allocated or freed. When the heap is corrupted by a heap-based buffer overrun, the results can be unpredictable, as some of the linked list structure is typically overwritten in the process of the overrun. A sample view of the heap is shown in Figure 11.5.

The number of vulnerabilities involving heap buffer overruns is expected to grow, as more and more steps are taken to protect the stack, and attackers turn to heap overruns instead. There is still a belief that not much can be done with heap buffer overruns because of the inherently dynamic nature of its storage structure, and this leads to heap buffer overruns not being subjected to scrutiny as they should be.

Anatomy of an Exploit

Most exploits of buffer overruns start with first knowing that buffer overrun vulnerability exists. This can be discovered in multiple ways, including personal experimentation and seeing it posted on one of the many boards frequented by hackers.

Once the vulnerability is known, the attacker needs to carefully craft a string to exploit the buffer overrun. Merely overflowing the buffer may be enough to crash the system or the application using the buffer that is being overrun. To achieve something else, the right information has to be inserted in the right place in the buffer.

In some cases, the attacker will be able to find out where in the buffer the application's variables are stored, but sometimes the attacker will start to systematically explore by overflowing the buffer via the exploit with a pattern of larger and larger data until a recognizable effect is achieved.

Once the attacker finds out how long a string is required to achieve the desired effect, they have an exploit of the vulnerability. Now, they can combine this exploit with other codes to create malicious software to distribute or install.

Real-World Examples

Buffer Overrun

Arguably the most famous example of a buffer overrun happened on November 3, 1988, now often known as "Black Thursday." A 99-line bootstrap program plus a large object file, both in C, infected Sun Microsystems' Sun 3 systems and VAX™ computers running variants of 4 BSD (Berkeley Software Distribution) Unix®.

One of the exploits used was a buffer overrun of the *fingerd* program's input buffer. *Fingerd* (a background process or daemon) was using the C gets call that takes input to a buffer without any bounds check. In this case, a string of 536 bytes was passed to *fingerd*, which overflowed its input buffer and overwrote parts of the stack. This string was specifically designed so the return stack frame for *main* was then a pointer into the buffer on the stack.

There were instructions written into the passed string at that location, which were then executed when *main* attempted to return. On VAXen, this meant the worm was connected to a remote shell via the transmission control protocol (TCP) connection, and the worm proceeded to infect the system. On Sun, this resulted in a core file error because the code wasn't in place to corrupt a Sun version of *fingerd*.

Stack Buffer Overrun/Stack Smashing

The first variant of Win32/Blaster (also called the Win32/Msblast worm) appeared on August 11, 2003, with many other variants that exploited the same vulnerability showing up over the next few months. Microsoft had released a security bulletin about the vulnerability exploited by this worm on July 16, 2003. This worm is notable because it was the first occurrence of a Windows command shell attack by a worm and because of the sheer volume of vulnerable machines despite the preexisting security bulletin. It also attempted to cause a huge DDoS (distributed denial-of-service) attack on the Windows update servers to prevent users from downloading the security patch.

This worm attacked vulnerable systems running Windows NT, Windows XP, Windows 2000, and Windows Server 2003. Although the vulnerability existed in all these versions of Windows, the worm could only infect the systems running Windows 2000 and Windows XP.

This worm scanned IP addresses and tried to connect to port 135 with a TCP connection, then used a security vulnerability in the Windows Distributed Component Object Model (DCOM) Remote Procedure Call's (RPC's) CoGetInstanceFromFile function. This function has as unbounded input string called szName, which was designed to hold a 32-byte NetBIOS machine name. The worm would then pass in an overly long crafted file name, cause a stack overflow, and then bind a cmd.exe command shell to port 4444/tcp.

This newly created shell is given a command to cause it to download the worm file from the attacking host over port 69/udp using the Trivial File Transfer Protocol (tftp), which is supported by a default tftp client on most Windows systems. Once the worm file (msblast.exe) is downloaded, the worm requests the remote system to execute the downloaded file. When the worm calls ExitProcess(), Windows XP systems will reboot and in Windows 2000 system there are a variety of side effects.

The worm added a key to the registry, (HKLM\SOFTWARE\Microsoft\ Windows\CurrentVersion\Run\windows auto update) to ensure that the worm is activated whenever Windows is started. Now the worm waits for an active network connection to start searching for more systems to attack.

The worm also conducts a DDoS SYN-flooding attack against the Web site windowsupdate.com, which is an alias of the main Microsoft Windows update site, on a predetermined schedule. For more information see the Denial of Service Case Study.

Heap Buffer Overrun/Heap Smashing

The Apache/mod_ssl (also called Smasher) worm appeared in September 2002 and affected Linux systems running Apache with the OpenSSL module (mod_ssl) on Intel Architectures. This particular worm is notable, because it is the first widespread worm that utilized a heap buffer overrun or heap smashing attack.

When this worm would find a system running Apache, it would check to see if the server had the cipher the worm was interested again. If that checked out as well, the worm would begin the first of the two buffer overruns to carry out its attack.

The worm would hand the server a key argument longer than the 8-byte maximum size allowed. When the incoming data was parsed on receipt, the information was not bounds checked and was copied into an 8-byte fixed length buffer in a heap allocated SSL_SESSION. Because the structure of the heap-allocated SSL_SESSION is known, the buffer was carefully overflowed with miscellaneous data until it reached the session_id_length field in the SSL_SESSION buffer, and then overwrote the data in that field with a value of 0×70 (112).

Then the worm terminated the connection with a "client finished" message in order to have the server respond with its standard "server finished" message, which contains the session_id data. But, because the worm overrode the session_id_length with a much larger value, the server tells the worm the entire 112 bytes of the SSL_SESSION structure, starting at the session_id.

Now that the worm has this information, it reuses the same attack vector again but this time it sets up shell code to run when the "client finished" message is received by the server.

Test Techniques

Testing for buffer overruns means testing every variable to see if it is bounded or not. The basic stages of buffer overrun testing are the same for both black-box and white-box testing.

Find and Document All Entry Points into the Product You Are Testing

Be sure that all entries are examined, not just the UI (user interface) or application programming interfaces (APIs). It is common for software that was once written as a standalone program to have been improved to include a public API, Web methods, or other ways of exposing the program's functionality to other uses. Too often, when this is done, there are places where assumptions are made instead of explicit checks.

As the entry points are documented, make special note of any input that may later be used to calculate a buffer allocation size.

Create an Attack That Targets Each Variable at Each Entry Point

If a passed variable is used to calculate the size of a buffer, some common values that should be attempted are as follows:

■   0
■   1

- Maximum size of datatype 1
- Maximum size of datatype
- Minimum size of datatype
- Minimum size of datatype + 1

For the strings, if the datatype is unknown, start with a string of 16,000 characters. If the input is supposed to conform to a particular format, each segment of the string should be tried with the test string separately and then in combination. For example, if you were submitting an e-mail address, you might try:

> \<test string\>@email.com
> \<test string\>.me@email.com
> Me.\<test string\>@email.com
> Me.me@\<test string\>.com
> Me.me@email.\<test string\>

In addition, a known and repetitive string should be used to recognize the test string.

Pass the Attack Data to Each Entry Point

Manual testing is usually possible but often time consuming and rather monotonous. This type of testing is a great place for test case automation.

Look for Any Crashes or Unexpected Behavior

Carefully examine any error messages for clues that will indicate what might be happening behind the scenes. Creating separate tests for each variable at each entry point will be helpful in tracking down the particular variable that is unbounded or improperly bounded.

The last point in this list is especially key. All too often there is a tendency to dismiss peculiar but not overtly dangerous behavior as a passing oddity, instead of possible evidence of a security vulnerability being exploited. All behavior needs further investigation, and the tester needs to be diligent about following up on any observed issues.

Black Box

Because there is no visibility into the code in black-box testing, the process of testing for buffer overruns is a little trickier than it would be during white-box testing. Use a trial-and-error approach to discover the data details like format and length. If there is a specification, then that can be used to determine the expected data details, but the actual boundaries must be tested for. Just because the specification says something does not mean it exists that way.

White Box

In white-box testing, all variables need to be traced back to where they enter the system, and then followed through the system from there. Any time the variable is manipulated or has memory allocated for it, the code must be carefully examined for any problems.

Run the tests under a debugger. This makes it easy to examine items such as what is on the heap or stack, or what is in the registers. If a portion of the test string appears on the stack, you may have found a stack overrun. If a portion appears on the heap, you may have a heap overrun. If a portion of the test string appears in the process register, you have a buffer overrun that is most likely exploitable. If a section of the test string appears in the instruction pointer (called the EIP register), you have definitely found a buffer overrun, and it is exploitable.

Bibliography

Baker, B. and Pincus, J. Beyond Stack Smashing: Recent Advances in Exploiting Buffer Overruns. *IEEE Security and Privacy*, 2004, pp. 20–27. Available online at http://www.lib.duke.edu/libguide/cite/printed_mag.htm.

Braverman, M. Win32/Blaster: A Case Study From Microsoft's Perspective. Virus Bulletin Conference. October 2005. Virus Bulletin Ltd. Available from http://download.microsoft.com/download/b/3/b/b3ba58e0-2b3b-4aa5-a7b0-c53c42b270c6/Blaster_Case_Study_White_Paper.pdf.

CERT Advisory CA-2002-27 Apache/mod_ssl Worm, CERT Coordination Center, 2002, Available from http://www.cert.org/advisories/CA-2002-27.html.

CERT Vulnerability Note VU#102795. CERT Coordination Center, 2002, Available from http://www.kb.cert.org/vuls/id/102795.

Donaldson, M.E. Inside the Buffer Overflow Attack: Mechanism, Method and Prevention. April 2002. Available from http://www.sans.org/reading_room/whitepapers/securecode/386.php.

Ferrie, P., Perriot, F., and Szor, P. Virus Analysis 3 Blast Off! Virus Bulletin. September 2003. Available online at http://pferrie.tripod.com/vb/blaster.pdf#search=%22win32%20blaster%20analysis%22.

Howard, M. Fix Those Buffer Overruns! May 2002. Available from http://msdn.microsoft.com/library.

Johnston, M. Revenge Is Sweet: Using the oc192-dcom.c exploit to accomplish revenge. SANS Institute. 2004. Available from http://www.giac.org/certified_professionals/practicals/gcih/0609.php.

Perriot, F. and Szor, P. An Analysis of the Slapper Worm Exploit. Symantec Security Response, 2003. Available from http://www.symantec.com/avcenter/reference/analysis.slapper.worm.pdf#search=%22slapper%20worm%22.

Seeley, D. A Tour of the Worm. Available from http://world.std.com/~franl/worm.html. (as posted by Francis Litterio)

Spafford, E. The Internet Worm Program: An Analysis. Purdue Technical Report CSD-TR-823. Available from http://homes.cerias.purdue.edu/~spaf/tech-reps/823.pdf.

Chapter 12

Vulnerability Case Study: Cookie Tampering

Pseudonyms

- Cookie poisoning
- Cross-site cooking
- Cookie theft

Description

Background

Cookies are technically small pieces of text that are sent to the Web client browser by a server and intended to be sent back to the server, unchanged, each time it accesses the same server or another server in the same domain. Cookies are used for authentication, tracking, maintaining state over stateless HTTP, as well as maintaining specific information about the user such as their site preferences, etc. The minimum size of a cookie is a name–value pair.

Cookies were originally developed for use in Web applications that used online or virtual shopping baskets. Cookies allowed for the contents of the basket to be changed, based on the user's actions and tracked items in the basket between browser sessions.

Cookies are also used when users log in to a Web site. Users enter their username and password into a login page and, if they are authenticated, a cookie is saved that allows the Web site to know the users are already logged in as they navigate around the site. This permits them access to any functionality that may be available only to logged-in users, probably the primary use of cookies at this time.

Cookies are also used to save user preferences for a site so that the site presentation and functionality can be personalized, based on the preferences of the user.

Cookies can also be used to track user actions across the site or domain. There are also some third-party cookies that allow for tracking across multiple sites. Most tracking done within a site or domain is done to gather usage data for that site. Tracking over multiple sites is done by advertising companies to build usage profiles to allow for more targeted marketing.

Cookies are destroyed at the point the user closes the browser unless a deletion date has been set. If a deletion date has been set, the cookie will be destroyed on that date instead. The cookies that have deletion dates are called *persistent cookies.*

Cookies are supposed to be sent only to the server that set them or another server in the same Internet domain. However, a Web page in one domain may contain images or components that are referenced on a page in the original domain but which are stored on a server in another domain. When these components are retrieved, cookies can be set for the second domain. These are called *third-party cookies.*

There are some privacy and security concerns around the use (and misuse) of cookies and that has caused some legislation to be enacted in the United States and the European Union. It is also important to know that the only real restriction on cookies is a maximum of 300 at a time, which is respected by most browser manufacturers. The site can create one cookie or a lot of cookies — the number is truly up to the site in question and its needs.

Cookie Risks

Cookie Theft

Cookies are supposed to be sent only between the Web browser and the server or servers in the same domain that set the cookie. But, if the cookie is being sent over an ordinary HTTP connection, it is visible to anyone across the network using a packet sniffer. This means cookies really cannot contain sensitive information. This is sometimes overcome by using HTTPS to encrypt the connection, but that's not the solution because it only solves one of the problems associated with having sensitive data stored in cookies.

For example, cross-site scripting can be used to send cookies to servers that should not be receiving that data. Encryption does not help stop this cookie theft, which is often done with a simple snippet of HTML posted to a site that users can be tricked into clicking on, and which will send their cookie for that site to a location that the attacker specifies. Because the request is coming from the same domain intended for the cookie, there are no problems. These cookies can then be exploited by connecting to the same site using the stolen cookies, thus spoofing the original owner of the cookie.

Cookie Poisoning

Cookies are supposed to be sent back to the server unchanged, but attackers can modify the value of a cookie before sending them back to the server. This is typically done to carry out some sort of attack against the server that relates to some sort of data contained in the cookie. For example, if a cookie contains the price per item for something in the shopping basket, a change to this value in the cookie may cause the server to charge the user a lower price for that item. This process of modifying a cookie before it is sent back to the server is called *cookie poisoning*. Sometimes, cookie poisoning is used after cookie theft.

Most Web sites only store a randomly generated unique session identifier in the cookie, and everything else is stored on the server. This pretty much eliminates the threat of cookie poisoning.

Cookie Inaccuracies

Even outside of deliberate cookie tampering, there are aspects to how cookies are used in some situations that cause cookies to carry inaccurate data on which to base sensitive transactions.

One issue is that separate people using the same computer, browser, and user account will unavoidably share cookies. Another is that if a single user uses multiple browsers, multiple computers, or multiple user accounts, it means that the user will have multiple sets of cookies.

Cross-Site Cooking

Despite the fact that each site is supposed to have its own set of cookies and to not be able to alter or set cookies for any other site, there are some browser flaws that cause cross-site cooking vulnerabilities and allow malicious sites to break this rule.

This is similar to cookie poisoning, but instead of the attacker attacking the site itself, the attacker is now attacking nonmalicious users with vulnerable browsers.

Many browsers have a flaw in how they deal with overly relaxed cookie domains. They are supposed to require a two-dot specification for all domains under the following top-level domains:

- .COM
- .EDU
- .NET
- .ORG
- .GOV
- .MIL
- .INT

This is supposed to prevent the setting of a cookie for a subdomain like .COM. So, the actual intent is that if you wish to set a cookie on a .COM site, you need to specify ".mysite.com" as the two-dot name. This breaks when you get to the international naming system for some domains like .COM.AU or .COM.DE. In some browsers, it's possible for a cookie to be set for the entire .COM.AU (for example) domain.

Another problem is how some browsers deal with periods. There is typically no check to see whether there is anything between the periods or if there is trailing period being used to override the local domain search path. This means that a cookie can be set for ".COM.," which then sends the user to http://www.mywebsite.com./

This address is not the "real" one, but how many users will care about the trailing period? Probably not very many. Even some seasoned users may not be adequately suspicious.

The third issue is that attackers can force cookies on random visitors, which are then relayed to a third-party site by setting IN A record and then redirecting users to the third-party site.

Anatomy of an Exploit

Cookie Theft

The attacker posts an auction that includes a link to what is advertised to be additional pictures or information about the object in the auction.

Instead, when users click on the link, their cookie for the auction Web site is sent to the attacker's server, where a CGI script logs the information.

Now the attacker can look through the list of cookies and pick some of the most recent cookies to use to try to log in to the auction site and spoof the user.

Cookie Poisoning

The attacker visits an E-commerce site and adds an expensive item to his shopping cart. Then, the user examines the cookie stored on his system from that site to see whether the cookie includes the total cost of the items in the attacker's cart.

The attacker then modifies the cookie on his system to change the total to be $5.00 and resaves the cookie. Then, the user returns to the E-commerce site and checks his cart to see that the total is now $5.00 and proceeds to order the items for the false price.

Cross-Site Cooking

The attacker crafts a cookie for the domain ".COM.UK" and sets up a Web site to distribute the cookie. Then, the attacker posts a link to his Web site on various bulletin boards or via e-mail, and when the users click on the link, they are given the attacker's crafted cookie that can then overwrite or disrupt the real business they do with Web sites in that international domain.

Real-World Examples

Cookie Theft

A cookie theft vulnerability was reported in January 2005 in the Froogle™ (Google, Inc., Mountain View, California) comparison shopping service. Although the details reported are sketchy, it appears that malicious Java-Script in a URL points to Froogle. Once a user clicks that link, the JavaScript executes a redirect to a malicious Web site, which then steals the user's Google™ (Google, Inc., Mountain View, California) cookie.

This stolen cookie apparently contained the username and password for the "Google Accounts" centralized log in service, information that is used by multiple Google services.

Cross-Site Cooking

At the moment, cross-site cooking is a proof of concept that demonstrates the vulnerability and hasn't emerged in the wild.

Test Techniques

Black-Box Testing

The first thing you need to do is know just what cookies are being created by the application and when. But all cookies are not kept as created. Some are modified by the application as it runs, and you need to know when and how the cookies are modified.

As a black-box tester, you really need to explore the application, track what cookies are being set where, and exactly what they contain. Then, delete or modify the cookie, and see where the system is looking for the data from the cookies. You need to see where the application modifies the cookies.

I generally start with a spreadsheet and have the page name on the left, a column for the date and time obtained, and then the contents of the cookies on the right, so I can compare them and the track changes. You should make multiple passes through the product with different user identities to give you a good amount of data to examine, and always include as many user states as you can (logged in, not logged in, a variety of user permission levels, etc.).

Analyze the Gathered Cookies

Once you have some data gathered, you need to examine the cookies you have gathered to try to get an idea of what they are supposed to tell the server or store. I typically start making notes on my spreadsheet if I think I see patterns or can make educated guesses at the cookie's contents or intent. In essence, you are trying to reverse-engineer the cookies. The major items to look for are:

- Predictability — By looking at several samples of the cookies, can you detect a pattern in the format or makeup of the cookies? There can be obviously predictable formats that are made clear by the use of delimiters or labels. There can also be hints in the name of the cookie itself. What changes in the cookies were issued from different sessions? For different users? What causes the cookie to be modified?

- Sensitive data storage — See if you can determine or guess what data is being stored in this cookie. Sometimes the labels help, but sometimes you can make educated guesses from hints of format, content, etc.
- Secure flag — Is the secure flag set? This would indicate the cookie is only supposed to be sent over a secure connection and may indicate the cookie contains sensitive data.
- Expiration data — If a cookie holds session information, it should either have a very short expiration date or no expiration, so that it will be deleted when the browser session is closed. If the cookie is meant to contain nonsensitive information, it may have a longer expiration date.

Compare to Documentation

Just because you are doing black-box testing does not mean that you cannot seek out any documentation on what the individual cookies are supposed to do and contain.

If there is any documentation available, compare that to your spreadsheet of notes and guesses and see if any issues are immediately obvious. Disparities can emerge between documentation and reality, and there may be cases where security measures (secure flag and expiration date) are not in place where they should be. These tested cookies become the first to manipulate and explore for vulnerabilities, as described in the next step.

Modify Cookies

Now you need to start experimenting with the cookies to see if you can find vulnerabilities. If you have documentation to use, you can start with the ones you marked as most interesting. Otherwise, you can start wherever you think the most risk is.

Start by modifying one field of one cookie at a time. If you have found a pattern to the cookie, test both inside and outside the pattern.

Naturally, cookies with one or more pieces of data in clear text are the easiest to modify, but to experiment with other cookies and cookie fields, too.

Don't stay within the field size the real cookie is using. It may be possible to create an overflow, and that should be explored as well.

Don't stay within the apparent data type of the cookie's field. The server should be checking all incoming data and validating type before use.

Write down the results of each attempt and listen to your intuition when it comes to potential vulnerabilities.

Cookie Misuse

Don't forget to try other cookie uses that go beyond cookie tampering. Try testing as if you had stolen someone else's valid cookie.

White-Box Testing

White-box testing of cookie vulnerabilities uses the same basic theories, but because you have direct insight into the code that saves and reuses the cookies, you don't have carry out the somewhat tedious task of reverse-engineering the cookie itself.

Chapter 13

Vulnerability Case Study: Cross-Site Scripting (XSS)

Pseudonyms

- Code insertion
- Malicious scripting
- XSS

Description

Cross-site scripting (abbreviated to XSS so as not to be confused with the abbreviation for cascading style sheets) is a vulnerability rooted in the way HTML content is generated and interpreted by client browsers. These vulnerabilities are usually found in Web applications and allow attackers to inject HTML or client-side scripting into the input of a Web-based application in the hope (or with the knowledge) that the input the attacker provided will be returned unparsed. If a dynamic Web page is output with the malicious code in it, the victim's browser attempts to render it as though it were HTML, complete with an attempt to execute the scripting.

This same scripting can post information it discovers to a third-party Web site as a parameter, which allows the attacker a way to collect it for subsequent use.

This basic vulnerability, depending on how it's exploited, can be used for a multitude of purposes. The number of these seems to grow all the time, but some of these are:

■ Cookie theft
■ Session ID theft
■ Defacing a Web site
■ Limited execution of arbitrary code on the victim's machine, particularly, if it's a trusted Web site or a Web-driven client application, or even if it is combined with an unsafe ActiveX control
■ Manipulating the DOM (Document Object Model)
■ Cookie poisoning
■ Changing user settings

Although this is called "cross-site scripting," the name is a bit deceptive because it's not particularly about scripting, and there doesn't have to be anything "cross site" about it. This was a name given before its application was well understood, and it stuck. It's really another case of trusting user input, and reusing it without validating or filtering it.

Malicious scripting can be created using a variety of languages or technologies, such as:

■ JavaScript
■ VBScript
■ ActiveX
■ HTML
■ Flash

There are three types of cross-site scripting generally recognized.

Nonpersistent or Reflected

This is the most common type of cross-site scripting vulnerability by far — a vulnerability where data from a Web client is immediately used by the server to generate a page to return to the user. If unvalidated user-supplied data is included in the resulting Web page without HTML encoding, this will allow client-side code to be injected into the dynamic page.

A classic example of this is encountered in search engines; if you search for a string that includes some HTML special characters, often the search string will be redisplayed on the results page to indicate what was searched for, or the search terms will at least appear in a new search text box for easier editing. If all occurrences of the search term are not HTML-entity-encoded, an XSS vulnerability will exist because that redisplayed search string would then contain the client-side script that your browser would execute.

This doesn't seem to be a serious problem and is often discounted because it appears at first glance that users can only inject code into pages that are returned to them, so they would only be attacking themselves. But that doesn't take the power of social engineering into account. Attackers can manipulate a potential victim into following a malicious URL, which injects code into the results page and gives the attacker full access to the content of the page.

Persistent or Stored

This is not the most common type of attack, but it is the most powerful. This vulnerability occurs when data provided to a Web application by an attacker is first stored persistently on the server, and then later it's displayed to users in a Web page without being HTML-encoded. This is a classic problem with message boards, where users can post HTML-formatted messages for other users to read.

One of the reasons this is a more serious or significant vulnerability is that an attacker can post an attack once and can potentially affect a large number of users without having to resort to social engineering. The attacker also doesn't need to use the Web application itself to exploit this vulnerability. Any data received by the Web application by other means, including e-mail, system logs, etc., is capable of exploiting these vulnerabilities.

DOM-Based or "Local"

This cross-site scripting vulnerability is one that is focused on the DOM (Document Object Model). When JavaScript is executed, the browser sends several objects that represent the DOM back to JavaScript.

One of these is the **document** object, which contains most of the properties of the page that executed the JavaScript. The **document** object contains multiple other objects, all populated from the browser's point of view — which is important to remember.

Basically, this type of XSS modifies the DOM itself to take advantage of any Web pages that then use the DOM information. Some DOM objects are not under the control of the server-provided page or are only partially under its control, yet the contents of those objects are used dynamically.

An example of this would be the **document.URL** that contains the URL the browser navigated to, not the URL extracted from the HTML body. This means that if a hyperlink is sent that contains scripting as part of the URL, and the page referenced uses that **document.URL** value in a dynamic page, the script embedded in the URL is executed.

Some DOM objects that are at risk:

- Document.URL
- Document.URLEncoded
- Document.location (and many of its properties)
- Document.referrer
- Window.location (and many of its properties)

Anatomy of an Exploit

Nonpersistent or Reflected Exploit

Here, the attacker discovers a Web site that has an XSS vulnerability by entering a string such as "<test>" to see if the string is reflected back with the greater-than and less-than symbols unencoded.

Once XSS vulnerability is found, the attacker crafts a URL that will exploit the vulnerability, and he sends the crafted URL to another user of the site, generally as a spoofed e-mail.

When the potential victim visits the site using the link contained in the e-mail, the malicious script contained in the crafted URL is executed by the potential victim's browser as if it came from the Web site with the XSS vulnerability. The script steals whatever sensitive information it can and sends the data to the attacker.

Persistent or Stored Exploit

This attack also requires that the attacker discover a Web site allowing users to post information for retrieval by other users in something other than plaintext (i.e., HTML-encoded, etc.). For HTML encoding of messages to be available, the browser reading the post or data has to be able to process the HTML.

The attacker can also test this by posting data to this Web site, using a test string to see if the user input is filtered or otherwise encoded.

Once the attacker finds that the site has an exploitable XSS vulnerability, the attacker posts a message designed to attract the maximum traffic possible (so it's generally controversial or even obnoxious), and in that message is embedded the code to exploit XSS vulnerability.

Now, whenever the posted message is viewed, the session cookies or other credentials are sent to the attacker's Web server.

The attacker can use the credentials of the other users to log in with their privileges.

DOM-Based or Local

Here, the attacker must know of a Web site with a page that uses part of the DOM not wholly under the control of the server-side page.

Once the attacker finds a page that parses the URL, or similarly uses information in the DOM to provide data for client-side logic, the attacker can craft a URL to take advantage of that vulnerability and e-mail or otherwise distribute the URL to potential victims.

When the potential victim receives the link and clicks on it, the malicious code is exploited; the vulnerable Web page is returned from the server and may now run a variety of commands with whatever privileges the user has on the computer it is running on.

Real-World Examples

There are multiple real-world examples of cross-site scripting vulnerabilities:

Bugzilla DOM-Based XSS

In December 2004, a vulnerability was reported in Bugzilla™ (The Mozilla Foundation, California) where, if an internal error was encountered, an error page used JavaScript to write the URL (using document.location) to the Web page without filtering or encoding it. This would allow someone to force an error and inject JavaScript code. The fix for this was to encode the special characters in the document.location string before it is written to the page. More details and some sample codes are available at https://bugzilla.mozilla.org/show_bug.cgi?id=272620.

PayPal XSS

In June 2006, PayPal® (EBay, Inc., San Jose, California) was hit by a complex attack that used a combination of an e-mail phishing that asked the users to click on a link leading to a URL on the real PayPal Web site. The link to this URL utilized cross-site scripting to present the users with some text (crafted to look official) informing them that their account is disabled because of suspicions that it had been compromised and that they would be redirected to a resolution center. Then the users were indeed redirected but to a trap site in South Korea.

This trap site was basically a phishing site. The users were asked for their PayPal login details, and even more sensitive information such as Social Security number, bank account numbers, etc.

One of the most interesting facts about this attack is that on the initial PayPal page the user is directed to is an SSL page; the valid 256-bit SSL certificate to confirm it belongs to PayPal. By the time users are actually redirected to the fake PayPal phishing site, they may be off guard because they've already done what they have been taught: They think they have verified that the original page is HTTPS, complete with its little lock icon and a security certificate.

Microsoft Passport

In October 2001, a security researcher, Marc Slemko, conducted some investigations into the integrated Passport™ (Microsoft Corporation, Redmond, Washington) system and its component services and brought one vulnerability to light: using Hotmail's HTML filtering and cross-site scripting can expose the user's Passport data.

In this case, an e-mail was sent to a Hotmail user that included a tag starting with "<_img." Hotmail thinks this is the start of an HTML tag and treats the information inside as attributes but Internet Explorer (IE) doesn't recognize any tag starting with an invalid character, so it just continues as if the tag isn't there.

Part of the problem is that IE is performing what is called a "white list" check for the tag. If the tag is not specifically considered to be valid, then it is invalid by default. Hotmail, however, is performing what is called a "black list" check. If the tag is not specifically considered to be invalid, then it is valid by default.

This Hotmail issue is merely an easy way to get around the necessity of sending some social engineering e-mails to get the user to click on the link — it's not actually a required part of the vulnerability demonstration. We recall that since the user is doing this through a Hotmail account, Passport has already been logged into and a Passport cookie has been issued.

Once the HTML exploit page is loaded, it opens two frames. One of these connects to a page in the Passport's secure path to enable the attacker to steal the Passport cookie. The second frame exploits an XSS vulnerability in Passport: if you are already logged in, a page is returned including the unencoded passed in information — in this case, executed by JavaScript on the attacker's server. This JavaScript then proceeds to capture the user's Passport cookie and sends the cookie off to a CGI script that captures them.

MySpace XSS Worm

The first incident of an XSS worm occurred in late 2005 when a MySpace™ (MySpace, Inc.) user figured out a way to increase his friend's list by first creating a script in his user profile that overcame the MySpace restriction against JavaScript. It achieved this by splitting it between two lines and then placing this script code within a cascading style sheet, exposing a leniency in IE.

Then, the attacker used a JavaScript object to load a MySpace URL that would automatically invite the attacker as a friend, and later as a "hero," into the visitor's own profile.

Next, he turned around and embedded this script into each of his visitor's profiles, so that the code continued to propagate to anyone who viewed their profiles. By 9:30 that night, there were over 1 million requests, and less than an hour later the entire MySpace site had to be taken offline while the worm was removed from all user profiles.

Test Techniques

One of the difficulties in testing cross-site scripting is that the more advanced efforts often involve encoding some of the telltale signs of cross-site scripting exploits in any one of a number of formats. Table 13.1 gives examples of texts that can represent the <script> tag in HTML.

If your application accepts UTF-8 characters, this becomes even more complex because you have multiple ways to encode each character. If this is the case for your application, it's a strong argument for deleting characters that are not explicitly safe and allowable.

Table 13.1   HTML <script> Tag Equivalents

Text	Scheme
<script>	HTML
%3cscript%3e	URL Encoded
%u003cscript%u003e	Unicode %U Encoded
%%3cscript%%3e	Double URL Encoded
\074cscript\076	C/Perl Octal Escape Characters
\x3cscript\x3e	C/Perl Hex Escape Characters

Question All Filtering and Encoding

A valuable exercise you can do before actually starting the test is to ask several questions about every field in your product:

- Does this field have a limited set of expected input?
- Is there filtering or error checking in place to enforce that only input that meets the requirements of the field is passed through?
- If your product accepts UTF-8 characters, is there filtering in place to delete all characters not explicitly safe?

There may be reasons that input cannot be as severely filtered as you might wish, but the fields should all be filtered as closely as possible without impairing necessary functionality.

In addition, there is a set of minimum characters that should always be encoded into their literal, printable equivalents. If this is done, any script code that makes it into the system can't be output again unless it's converted to safe formatting. This list is shown in Table 13.2.

The HTML characters should be entered into each field, and the resulting output examined to verify that each of the HTML characters is translated to its printable literal equivalent when it is passed back to the client browser.

Black-Box Testing

Basic Script Test

The best way to start testing for cross-site vulnerabilities is to test every input field you can find with a simple test script:

Table 13.2   HTML Literal Equivalents

HTML	Literal
&	&
<	<
>	>
"	"
(	(
)	)
#	#

- <script>alert('XSS Vulnerability Found')</script>
- <img xsstest=javascript:alert('XSS Vulnerability Found')>
- &(alert('XSS Vulnerability Found'));

If the message box displays "XSS Vulnerability Found," the input field you are testing has an XSS vulnerability. If it doesn't display the phrase but the HTML page returned displays incorrectly, the component may still be vulnerable and should be further tested.

Encoding Test

Now for each visible variable, submit the following string:

```
11;!-"<XSS_Check>=&{()}
```

On the page that is returned, search for the string "<XSS_Check>."

- If you can find that test string in the returned page, it's likely that the component has an XSS vulnerability.

If it's displayed literally (including the greater than or less than characters at any point), there is a definite XSS vulnerability.

- If only the phrase "XSS_Check" is displayed but the greater-than and less-than symbols have been stripped away completely, the component is not vulnerable.
- If there was some encoding done and you see something such as "<XSS_Check>" then a vulnerability may still exist.

Returned Code Examination

Now examine the other characters that were input around the test string to see what characters are filtered or encoded. This will indicate if the component may still be vulnerable.

Carefully examine the returned HTML page to see if you can identify what string an attacker could use to break out of the HTML code or sequence surrounding the test string. If these codes exist in an unfiltered form in the previous step it is very likely that the component is vulnerable.

White-Box Testing

The steps for black-box testing are still needed, but if you are doing white-box testing, you can follow the input string through the code to see wherever it may be used or returned to the client browser. Some of these places may not be obvious or may be difficult to find with black-box testing, especially pages that are not part of the well-known normal code path. This includes error pages, and the like.

There are two other tests that should be done if you are conducting white-box testing:

Hidden Fields

Repeat the set of black-box tests on every hidden field, the ones that are not normally editable. This may require the use of automation, a custom tool, or one of the proxy servers available commercially. You need to be able to edit HTTP requests between client and server.

GET Versus POST

If particular components are submitting data via an HTTP GET request, try turning the submission into an HTTP POST request for any components if the results of the prior testing indicate the possibility of an XSS vulnerability.

Bibliography

Klein, A. DOM Based Cross Site Scripting or XSS of the Third Kind. Web Application Security Consortium July 2005. Available from http://www.webappsec.org/projects/articles/071105.shtml.

Chapter 14

Vulnerability Case Study: Denial of Service/Distributed Denial of Service

---

Pseudonyms

- DoS
- DDoS

Description

A denial-of-service (DoS) attack is one in which an attacker uses multiple techniques to deny legitimate users access to a system or resource. This is generally done in one of two ways:

- Crashing the resource or a particular requirement for access to the resource
- Flooding the access so legitimate traffic is unable to reach it

DoS attacks are extremely common because they are so simple to carry out, and there is a wealth of ready-to-use tools available for script kiddies to download.

Ping of Death

The stereotypical "ping of death" is based on the fact that Internet Control Messaging Protocol (ICMP) echo messages are designed to be no larger than 65,535 bytes. Because most of the information of interest in ICMP echo packets is contained in the header, sometimes the data portion is unchecked. If an ICMP echo packet is sent that is too large, some operating systems (OSs) will crash.

Whereas a packet larger than 65,535 bytes is illegal, this limitation can be worked around by using fragmentation packets that, when reassembled on the receiving end, overflows the buffer on some systems. So it's basically a buffer overflow exploit. Because of the ease and prevalence of this attack, most systems are no longer vulnerable.

Teardrop

This attack is also dependent on fragmentation. Fragmented packets are sent but Instead of neatly lined-up fragmentation offsets, the offsets overlap. If the operating system does not have a plan in place for this eventuality, the system can crash, reboot, or lose stability. This is also an easy attack to learn; few systems are vulnerable anymore. It is named for the tool that exploits this vulnerability.

Ping Flooding

Ping flooding is an attack specifically aimed at denial of network resources. Ping flooding uses up the bandwidth of the network so traffic from legitimate users can't get through. It's the electronic version of the rush-hour traffic jam. The general rule is that if the attacker has a greater bandwidth than the victim, the attacker will succeed in the DoS.

This attack works as follows: The attacker sends many large ping packets as quickly as possible to the victim. This exhausts the victim's inbound bandwidth; if the person replies to the pings, the outbound bandwidth may be consumed as well.

Smurf Attacks

A smurf attack is a specific variation on a ping flood attack. Instead of a ping to a single system, a smurf attack uses repeated spoofed broadcast ping messages to flood the system. All of these ping messages use the spoofed IP address of the intended victim as their source address. If the ping is actually broadcast to the network, most hosts on that IP network will accept the ICMP echo request and reply to it with an echo reply per recipient, which will have the effect of multiplying the traffic by the number of hosts responding. On a multi-access broadcast network, potentially hundreds of machines may respond to each packet.

This attack is also named after the attack program created to exploit this vulnerability.

Amplification Attacks

This type of DoS attack uses both spoofing and broadcast addressing to amplify a single stream of packets several hundredfold to flood the victim's bandwidth.

To carry out this attack, the attacker needs to find a network that both allows communications to the network's broadcast address and has a good number of hosts active on the network. Because the amplification rate is directly dependent on the number of active hosts, the more hosts the better.

The attacker sends large ICMP echo request packets to the broadcast address of the amplifier network with a spoofed source address of the victim. The amplifier network then broadcasts these ICMP echo packets to all the hosts on that network, and each of these systems will then send corresponding ICMP echo replies to the spoofed source address of the victim, flooding their network bandwidth.

This is also called a *reflected attack*. If the attack relies on ICMP packets, it's also called a *smurf attack*. If the attack relies on User Datagram Protocol (UDP) packets, it's called a *fraggle attack*.

SYN Flooding

In SYN flooding, the attacker attempts to exhaust the space in the Transmission Control Protocol/Internet Protocol (TCP/IP) stack with spoofed and only partially complete connections, so legitimate users are unable to connect. TCP maintains the connections so it has to be able to track them and their state somewhere; that place is the TCP/IP stack. But only a finite number of connections can be tracked in the TCP/IP stack, and SYN flooding uses spoofing to exploit this.

The attacker floods the system with many SYN packets that have spoofed nonexistent source addresses. These packets behave as if a system that has the spoofed IP address wishes to open a connection with the victim computer.

Now the victim sends out a SYN/ACK package and waits for the connection handshake be returned in order to finalize or to complete the handshake process. In the meantime, the waiting connection goes into a backlog queue and will only be removed from the queue if either the SYN/ACK packet is received or the connection times out. The timeout can take quite a while, and the SYN packets continue to come in.

Distributed Denial of Service (DDoS)

This is basically a DoS attack coming from more than a single location. To carry out a DDoS, the attacker will generally compromise other systems and install daemons on them for later use. The daemons are waiting for the attacker to determine which victim to attack. When a victim is chosen, the attacker uses a controlling program to tell the daemons to simultaneously attack the target.

The fact that the DDoS attack is not coming from a single location has several impacts on its success:

■ More volume can be generated.
■ It's harder to filter or block multiple attacking systems.

Anatomy of an Exploit

Ping of Death

An attacker uses one of the ICMP ping tools available to construct an IP packet with a size larger than 65,535 bytes and sends it to the target of choice. The header source IP is usually spoofed to help hide the source.

Teardrop

An attacker targets a network that seems vulnerable and uses the Teardrop tool to set up the attack by sending several IP fragmentation packets that are structured so that when the receiving system attempts to reassemble them, they will overlap.

Ping Flooding

When an attacker thinks he has a vulnerable target, he tells his army of bots to begin sending ICMP echo requests to the target IP address as quickly as possible. The headers of the requests can be forged with random bogus IP source addresses to resist any attempts to filter the requests by source addresses.

Smurf

In a smurf attack, the attacker targets a vulnerable network and uses the Smurf tool to craft ICMP echo requests where it has forged the source IP address to match that of the target.

SYN Flooding

An attacker sends a continual series of TCP SYN packets to the target, each one with a different forged source IP address to exhaust the target's resources during this continual flooding.

Real-World Examples

Because of the overwhelming prevalence of DDoS compared to purely DoS attacks, both the following examples are DDoS.

WorldPay DDoS Attack

At about 6 p.m. on Saturday, October 2, 2003, the payment processing division of the Royal Bank of Scotland, WorldPay® (WorldPay Ltd.), was hit with a sustained DDoS attack. This attack, employing hundreds or possibly thousands of "zombie" computers to issue repeated automated requests, was designed to clog and slow the bank's systems. This attack lasted for three days, in spite of the attempts to block out traffic and restore functionality to the bank's customers. In April 2004, WorldPay was again hit with a DDoS attack.

There have been some conjectures that this was a case of attempted cyber-extortion by organized crime, but there never was a full disclosure of the exact events surrounding either DDoS. These attacks, however, did not reveal any of the data that WorldPay had stored.

Gibson Research Corporation DDoS Attack

On the evening of May 1, 2001, GRC.COM appeared to drop off the Internet. The network activity was analyzed quickly, and it was discovered that both of their T1 connections were maxed out with incoming traffic at their 1.54 megabit rate, and there was almost no outbound traffic. Capturing and analyzing the arriving packets themselves showed that the attack was a brute force UDP DDoS attack that was designed to use up all available network bandwidth and thus deny access to legitimate users.

GRC's firewalls and local routers easily recognized and discarded the bogus traffic but that meant the bandwidth to that point was still clogged. After 17 hr, filters were applied to the router that sat between the Internet and GRC's two T1 trunks to block out all UDP and ICMP traffic. From the type of packets generated, as well as other facts, it was determined that the attack was being carried out by 474 security-compromised Windows PCs. Because the attacks related to UDP, the TCP-based services could continue even while the attack was still under way and the router was blocking all UDP and ICMP traffic.

More attacks followed on the following schedule:

- May 4 — First attack took place; 17 hr to filter traffic and return to service.
- May 13 — Second attack. Identical to the first, including the same attacking Windows machines; 8 hr to reestablish the same filters used on May 4.
- May 14 — Attacked twice this day. The first attack of the day was targeted at the IP of GRC's firewall, and GRC disappeared from the Internet again. This time the router filtering was changed to add the firewall's IP to the filtering and then GRC was back.
- May 14 — Only 2 hr later, the attack resumed, aimed at one of the T1 interfaces of GRC's Cisco router. This again flooded the T1s, and GRC was off the Net again. The decision was then made to shut down that T1, which left one T1 to service GRC, but they were back on the Net again.
- May 15 — This attack took GRC off the Internet for 6.5 hr before stopping on its own. A decision was made to simply shut down for the night because of some bugs in the routing software that made it possible to effectively filter this attack.
- May 16 — Comprehensive filtering was put in place after the previous day's attack so traffic would be kept away from the entire GRC site. Another attack occurred, but the new filtering was completely effective. An estimate of how many packets were blocked by the filtering during this attack was 538,916,268.

- May 17 to May 20 — During this time the GRC was completely protected, but the number of packets filtered was estimated at 2,399,237,016.

Chat DoS Attack

A chat DoS attack that I experienced was somewhat low-tech, but I've included it as an illustration of how sometimes these low-tech approaches can be very disrupting to legitimate users of a system.

I was attending an online chat with a celebrity guest, and there were about 200 people in the online chat room. During the busy chat, two people who were logged in as anonymous guests began to repeat offensive messages as fast as they could paste the text and hit "send." The speed at which these messages were being posted made the chat room completely unusable by legitimate customers.

After a few minutes, an administrator booted the first of the attackers out, but before the second one could be booted as well, the first person (my own assumption) was back spamming again. This trade went on for about the next ten min before I gave up and left the room.

Test Techniques

Testing for DoS attacks really has two major branches, and whether you use one or the other (or both) will depend on the product you are testing and what dependencies it has or services it offers to others.

Network DoS

Most network DoS attacks boil down to one of two situations.

Protocol Vulnerability

In many cases, the DoS is caused by the fact that a network device or system is not able to deal with an exploit of a network protocol vulnerability. In these cases, fuzz testing is a good way to try to exercise the protocols to determine the reaction of the system under test to protocol fuzzing.

These are mostly network protocols and unless you are testing a system that deals directly with that low a level in the Open Systems Interconnection (OSI) model, you are a little bit helpless and dependent on your OS and network to handle these issues.

Lack of Limits

The other major factor is that limits on various types of transactions are either nonexistent or too high for the system to handle. In the latter case, it would pay if you can cause a DoS and then backtrack from it to question the limits that are in place to prevent DoS.

There are several aspects of input that you can experiment with in trying to trigger a DoS:

- Quantity from a single source
- Quantity from multiple sources
- Size of individual items

Think Outside the Typical DoS Box

In addition to the more standard DoS attack vectors, it pays to take a look at the more unusual attacks that might be able to be turned into DoS attacks.

Circular References

Is there any way you can cause a circular reference to occur in your system? If you can, you might be able to cause a DoS.

I had a recent experience with an e-mail system that treated notification messages not in the same way it treated regular e-mail messages; there were questions about whether or not a circular reference could be instigated with a combination of two different types of system notification messages. It turned out that it did not work, but it was an interesting experiment.

Any service- or system-crashing issues may become a DoS. If you run across a mysterious crash of your test system or a service on the system, sometimes the tendency is to dismiss it as a fluke. Perhaps it is, but never just shrug it off. Always keep looking for what might have caused it, because some of these crashing issues are very real vulnerabilities that may be exploitable as a DoS at some later date.

Bibliography

Gibson, S. The Strange Tale of the Denial of Service Attacks Against GRC.Com. Gibson Research Corporation. September 17, 2005. Available from http://www.grc.com/dos/grcdos.htm.

Kenney, M. Ping of Death. Insecure.org. October 21, 1996. Available from http://insecure.org/sploits/ping-o-death.html.

Chapter 15

Vulnerability Case Study: Format String Vulnerabilities

Pseudonyms

- Format string attacks

Description

The goal of a format string exploit is to take control of the execution of a program by overwriting data. It is dependent on programming mistakes or shortcuts made when using format functions such as printf().

If the software being tested is written in C, C++, or Perl, even in part, there is a possibility that it may use one or more format functions. The root cause of this vulnerability is that these languages allow functions to accept any number of arguments by "popping" as many arguments as they wish off the stack and trusting the early arguments to show how many additional arguments are to be popped and what datatypes they are. If this is combined with unfiltered user input as the format string, the vulnerability is created.

The following are the basic ANSI C functions that may be vulnerable to format string attacks:

- fprintf — prints to a file stream
- printf — prints to the stdout stream
- sprintf — prints into a string
- snprintf — prints into a string with link checking
- vfprintf — print to a file stream from a va_arg structure
- vprintf — prints to a stdout stream from a va_arg structure
- vsprintf — prints to a string from a va_arg structure
- vsnprintf — prints to a string with length checking from a va_arg structure

The format string itself contains the format parameters, similar to how inline formatting is done in HTML. The format parameters for printf() are:

- %c — Unicode represented by an integer – passed as a value
- %d — decimal (int) – passed as a value
- %e — scientific representation of a floating pount number – passed as a value
- %f — signed decimal string of the form xx.yyy
- %i — signed decimal string – passed as a value
- %u — unsigned decimal (unsigned int) – passed as a value
- %n — number of bytes written so far (int) – passed as a reference
- %o — unsigned octal string – passed as a value
- %p — formats a pointer to an address – passed as a reference
- %s — string ((const) (unsigned) char) – passed as a reference
- %x — hexadecimal (unsigned int) – passed as a value
- %% — used to print the escape character "%"

When a string is passed to a format function, the function evaluates the format string one character at a time and if the character is not the percentage sign (%), it is copied to the output. If the percentage sign is encountered, the next character specifies the type of parameter that requires evaluation. Figure 15.1 illustrates the stack when a format string has been pushed onto it.

For every parameter found in the string, the function expects an additional variable to be passed in. So if four format parameters exist in a format string, there should be a total of five arguments passed to the function — the format string itself and one additional argument for each of the format parameters. The problems occur when developers use a format string function without explicitly stating that the input must be treated as a string. For example:

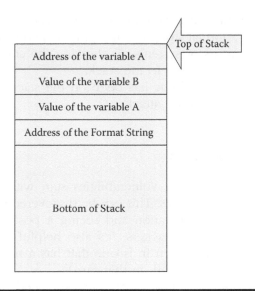

Figure 15.1 Sample format string stack.

`Correct: printf("%s", inputString);`

As opposed to:

`Incorrect: printf(inputString);`

If the prior two uses of printf() are used where inputString = "Testing%s":

`Correct: Testing%s`

Incorrect: Testing?? (where the ?? is whatever string is being pointed to by whatever memory address was at the top of the stack).

For a simple string that contains no format parameters, this will result in the same output. But if a string is provided to the function that includes one or more of these format parameters embedded in it, the function will treat the string (that the user wanted to treat as merely a string) as a format string. The danger in this is that some of the format string functions take a pointer to memory — specifically %s (string) and %n (number of bytes written so far), for example:

- %s expects a memory address and then will print the data at that address until a null byte terminator is encountered to signal the end of the string.
- %n expects a memory address and will write the number of bytes written so far into memory at that address.

So if an attacker can create an input string that is passed to a vulnerable implementation of a format string function, the individual can do anything from crashing processes or systems, to showing the contents of parts of the stack, to writing your data to the stack.

Note that although the focus has been on the stack, the heap is not immune to these format string attacks.

Anatomy of an Exploit

Most exploits of format string vulnerabilities start with knowing that a format string vulnerability exists. This can be discovered in multiple ways, including personal experimentation and seeing it posted on one of the many boards frequented by hackers. It's also helpful to know that the language the software is written in is one that has a risk for this vulnerability to exist (C, C++, and Perl, in this case).

Once the vulnerability is known, the attacker needs to carefully craft a string to exploit the format string vulnerability. The exact string or strings will depend on what the attacker wishes to accomplish.

In some cases, the attackers will be able to find the stack information from others, but in some cases, they will start to systematically explore by having the format string function output the contents of memory for examination.

Once the attackers determine what they want to accomplish, they can craft one or more strings to exploit the vulnerability. Now they can combine this exploit with other code to create malicious software to distribute or install.

Real-World Examples

Although considerable numbers of format string vulnerabilities have been reported, few actual exploits are listed among the reports of real incidents. But a very interesting toolkit that did use string format vulnerabilities in some of its functionality was reported "in the wild" in January 2001.

Ramen Worm Toolkit

This intruder toolkit was recovered from several compromised systems and analyzed to discover that it contained several tools for attempting to exploit vulnerabilities in common software.

Ramen is self-propagating and restarting, and once it has completed modifications of the compromised host system, Ramen starts to scan and attempts exploits against external systems. Similar to all root compromises, Ramen is painful and time consuming (and therefore expensive) to recover from.

The vulnerabilities Ramen attempts to exploit will cause a root compromise if even one of them is successful. These vulnerabilities are described in the following subsections.

wu-ftpd (port 21/tcp)

The initial advisory for this vulnerability was reported in July 2000 — five months prior to the Ramen worm. There are actually two separate vulnerabilities under this advisory:

The "site exec" functionality allows a user logged into the ftp server to execute a limited number of commands on the server itself. However, this functionality uses the printf() function and, if the user passes carefully crafted strings when calling that functionality, the daemon can be tricked into executing an arbitrary code as the root. So, in other words, the developers didn't use a format specifier when they used printf().

The "setproctitle()" call sets a string used to display process identifier information. This functionality eventually calls vsnprintf() and passes the buffer created from the setproctitle() as the format string. The developers didn't use a format specifier when they used vsnprintf().

rpc.statd (port 111/udp)

The initial advisory for this vulnerability was reported in August 2000 — four months prior to the Ramen worm.

The rpc.statd program passes user input data to the syslog() function as a format string. This means a user can create a string that put executable code into the process stack and overwrite the return address, forcing the code to be executed. The developers didn't use a format specifier when they called syslod().

This was made worse by the fact that rpc.statd maintains root access privileges even though those privileges are only needed for it to initially open its network socket. This means that whatever code the attacker injects is run with root (administrator) privileges.

lprng (port 515/tcp)

The initial advisory for this vulnerability was released on December 12, 2000 — only one month prior to the Ramen worm.

The lprng software accepts user input that is later passed to syslog() as the format string for a function call to snprintf(). This particular instance of the format string vulnerability can allow users who have remote access to the printer port to overwrite addresses in the printing service's address space. This can cause segmentation that will lead to denial of printing services or can be used to execute an arbitrary code injected by other methods into the memory stack of the printer service.

All the incidents were caused by the lack of a format specifier when syslog() was called.

Test Techniques

Out of the list of formatting functions, sprintf and vsprintf are the functions that deserve some special care and attention as they are the ones that "print" formatted data to a buffer. The fix for this vulnerability is to always use a format specifier to format data.

Black Box

In Black-Box testing, it becomes important to include some of the formatting parameters in all input fields. These should include the following, but more can be used:

- %x
- %s
- %n

Then watch all output and the program itself for unusual output or behavior. You can also try testing with several %s parameters embedded in the input string. If a format string vulnerability exists, the resulting behavior would be likely to be an access violation error or another error that would cause the application to crash.

White Box

White-Box testers have a relatively easy time finding these vulnerabilities. The code base needs to be searched for any use of the C format string functions, and each time they are used, there must be a format string in place to insure that the data is correctly interpreted.

There are some additional functions that use formatted output, which must also be scrutinized, and are fairly OS specific. These include functions such as syslog().

Tools

There are a number of potentially useful free tools that can provide additional checks of the C code. Although automated tools can add significant value to test efforts, they do not take the place of security reviews and dedicated security testing. They also have a tendency to generate a large number of false positives and thus a great deal of noise.

Flawfinder

This is an open source tool that does security scans of C code. It can be obtained from http://www.dwheeler.com/flawfinder/.

ITS4 Security Scanner

This is a freeware tool from Cigital, Inc., that scans for potentially dangerous function calls in C code (including format string calls). It can be obtained from http://www.cigital.com/its4/.

Pscan

This is an open source tool that scans C code for potentially dangerous function calls. It can be obtained from http://www.striker.ottawa.on.ca/%7Ealand/pscan/.

Rough Auditing Tool for Security (RATS)

This is an open source code analysis tool designed to check C source code for potentially dangerous function calls (including format string calls). It can be obtained from http://www.securesw.com/rats/.

Smatch

This is an open source tool that scans C and C++ code for known bugs and potential security defects but is mostly focused on checking the Linux kernel code. It can be obtained from http://smatch.sourceforge.net/.

Splint

This is an open source code tool that scans C code for potential vulnerabilities and dangerous programming practices and can be obtained from http://splint.org/.

Bibliography

CERT® Advisory CA-2000-13: Two Input Validation Problems In FTPD. Released July 7, 2000. Last updated November 21, 2000. Carnegie Mellon Software Engineering Institute CERT® Coordination Center. Available from http://www.cert.org/advisories/CA-2000-13.html.

CERT® Advisory CA-2000-17: Input Validation Problem in rpc.statd. Released August 18, 2000. Last updated September 6, 2000. Carnegie Mellon Software Engineering Institute CERT® Coordination Center. Available from http://www.cert.org/advisories/CA-2000-17.html.

CERT® Advisory CA-2000-22 Input Validation Problems in LPRing. Released December 12, 2000. Last updated January 27, 2003. Carnegie Mellon Software Engineering Institute CERT® Coordination Center. Available from http://www.cert.org/advisories/CA-2000-22.html.

CERT® Incident Note IN-2001-01: Widespread Compromises via "ramen" Toolkit. January 18, 2001. Carnegie Mellon Software Engineering Institute CERT® Coordination Center. Available from http://www.cert.org/incident_notes/IN-2001-01.html.

Multiple Linux Vendor rpc.statd Remote Format String Vulnerability. July 16, 2000. Security Focus. Available from http://www.securityfocus.com/bid/1480.

Multiple Vendor ftpd setproctitle() Format String Vulnerability. July 5, 2001. Security Focus. Available from http://www.securityfocus.com/bid/1425.

scut/team teso. Exploiting Format String Vulnerabilities. March 24, 2001. Available from http://julianor.tripod.com/teso-fs1-1.pdf.

Chapter 16

Vulnerability Case Study: Integer Overflows and Underflows

Pseudonyms

- Integer manipulation bugs

Description

Integer overflows and underflows are made possible by the way numbers are handled in computer memory. Each bit in computer memory has only two possible values, 1 or 0, and different numbers of bytes (units of 8 bits) are used to store integers based on the size of the number to be stored. If no negative numbers are needed, a signed datatype will often be used. In a signed datatype, the value is always positive, and a larger positive number can be stored in the same number of bytes than can be stored using an unsigned datatype because the first bit is not reserved to indicate whether the integer is positive or negative.

The ranges of some common C datatypes are shown in Table 16.1.

Integer math is handled with a method called *two's complement* arithmetic. This, along with the fact that computers are very literal, can cause a security vulnerability. When told to add or subtract, they do so based

Table 16.1   C Datatype Ranges

Integer Type	Bytes	Minimum Value	Maximum Value
Signed character	1	–127	127
Unsigned character	1	0	255
Short integer	2	–32,767	32,767
Unsigned short integer	2	0	65,535
Integer	2	–32,767	32,767
Unsigned integer	2	0	65,535
Long integer	4	–2,147,483,647	2,147,483,647
Unsigned long integer	4	0	4,294,967,295

on this specialized type of arithmetic with no regard to whether the results make logical sense. This method of doing arithmetic is used on almost all systems because the overhead of doing floating point math is so high.

In two's complement, if you are dealing with a signed integer datatype, the binary value can be translated directly to decimal, and nothing special needs to be done. If you are using an unsigned datatype, and the leftmost bit (the one that indicates the sign of the number) is a 0, then your number is a positive number and can be translated directly to decimal. If, however, it is a negative number, then the following must be done to obtain an accurate decimal translation.

First the two's complement needs to be translated back to normal binary. Starting with the rightmost (least significant) bit, copy the bit pattern of the two's complement number until you copy the first bit that is a one. Then, write down the complements of the remaining digits. If the original bit was a one, write down zero and *vice versa*. Once the two's complement has been translated back to a standard binary number, you can translate it to decimal using normal rules and then add a negative sign.

When integer math is performed, the appropriate bits are flipped, but the result of incrementing a large positive number can be a large negative number or zero. The result of decrementing a large negative number can be a large positive number. If the results require that another bit than is available in the datatype be allocated, the leftmost digit is simply truncated. Two samples of incrementing and decrementing are shown in Figure 16.1 and Figure 16.2, respectively.

Integer errors, by themselves, are not directly usable but the consequences of them can be.

Table 16.2 Two's Complement Translations

Bit Pattern	Decimal Value
0111	7
0110	6
0101	5
0100	4
0011	3
0010	2
0001	1
0000	0
1111	−1
1110	−2
1101	−3
1100	−4
1011	−5
1010	−6
1001	−7
1000	−8

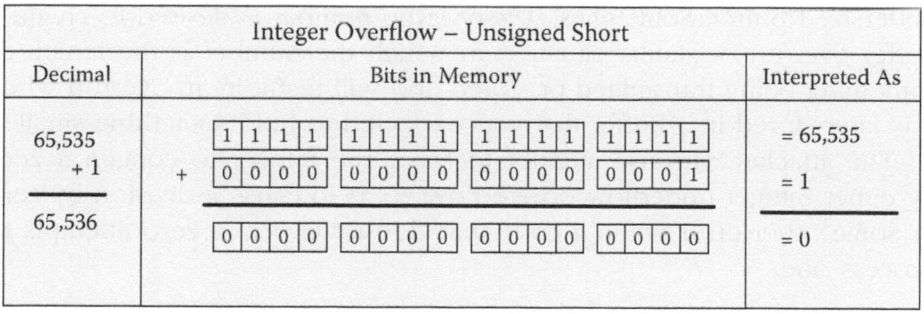

Integer Overflow – Unsigned Short		
Decimal	Bits in Memory	Interpreted As
65,535	1 1 1 1 1 1 1 1 1 1 1 1 1 1 1 1	= 65,535
+ 1	+ 0 0 0 0 0 0 0 0 0 0 0 0 0 0 0 1	= 1
65,536	0 0 0 0 0 0 0 0 0 0 0 0 0 0 0 0	= 0

Figure 16.1 Unsigned short integer overflow.

Anatomy of an Exploit

Integer overflows are most useful as a way to set up for a stack overflow if the attacker is able to create an integer overflow in a variable that is later used in the dynamic allocation of memory. Because no widespread exploits are in the wild, an attack is pretty much based on logic and conjecture.

Integer Overflow – Signed Short		
Decimal	Bits in Memory	Interpreted As
-32,767	`1 0 0 0` `0 0 0 0` `0 0 0 0` `0 0 0 0`	= -32,767
- 1	- `0 0 0 0` `0 0 0 0` `0 0 0 0` `0 0 0 1`	= 1
-32,768	`0 1 1 1` `1 1 1 1` `1 1 1 1` `1 1 1 1`	= 32,767

Figure 16.2   Signed short integer overflow.

To carry out an attack based on an integer overflow, the attackers would need to know that an integer overflow or underflow vulnerability exists and what that integer affects in the program under attack. Based on the desired effect (a very large or very small number) after the vulnerability is exploited, the attackers will craft their exploit to achieve that end.

Sometimes, a very small number is desired, for example, the quantity of items being purchased, so that the amount owed is very small, zero, or even negative (which would result in a credit to the buyer). A small number can also be desired if that number is used to determine how large a buffer to allocate, and later a large number is stored in that undersized buffer. Sometimes, a very large number is desired to create a buffer overrun or similar situation in which the number is the length of something being transmitted or stored and will result in an overrun when it is later stored in a buffer that was expected to hold something smaller.

The attacker can also attempt to force the integer to contain a zero by either integer underflow or overflow so as to cause a division by zero or some other error when a code that doesn't expect a zero attempts to process one.

Real-World Examples

No widespread exploits have been reported as being based on an integer overflow, but quite a few vulnerabilities have been reported and patched, especially in the last few years. This is only smart because there will certainly be attention paid to how to successfully exploit the known vulnerability.

An example of one of these patched vulnerabilities is one reported in early 2004 in Microsoft's Internet Explorer 5.5 SP2. In this case, there is vulnerability in the bitmap file processing functionality, which uses an unsigned integer during bounds checking. If an attacker submitted a carefully crafted bitmap file, the affected integer could be forced to wrap to a negative value. This integer is later used to read data into a 1024-byte buffer and may cause an overly large amount of data to be read into the buffer, thus creating a stack buffer overflow. The resulting stack buffer overflow could then be exploited.

Another example is a vulnerability reported in August 2002 in the SunRPC-derived XDR libraries. In this case, there was an integer overflow vulnerability in the xdr_array() function (External Data Representation). Exploiting this integer overflow could result in improperly sized dynamic arrays, and then those arrays could later be used to cause exploitable buffer overruns.

Test Techniques

Black Box

Black-box testing of integer overflows and underflows is very difficult. All variables still need to be examined, and the tester should know or discover what calculations are carried out with those variables and then attempt to influence those results. Sometimes you will seemingly get no response; sometimes you will get an error message that gives more clues to the actual datatype being used. The ranges typically returned in some of these error messages can often be translated directly into datatype range values, thus revealing a potentially useful bit of data to the attackers but also to the tester. It's particularly useful, whenever one of these is encountered, to try to set the variable to a maximum or minimum value and then try to increment the maximum or decrement the minimum.

Always try long strings in input fields and remember that "long" tends to be a rather fluid description. I generally try a string slightly longer than I would expect, then a string that is about 5 times as long, and then a string perhaps 50 times as long. This is useful if a calculation is being done based on the input length. If this succeeds, the program may crash.

Always try the largest and smallest allowable values in numeric fields to see if there is a case in which the individual integers are correctly checked but perhaps operations performed with them are not.

Always verify the data coming from other sources for the same flaws as data being input directly into the program itself. *All trust is misplaced.*

Don't forget applications programming interface (API) calls and methods of passing data other than the user interface (UI). Never trust what is calling your functionality to do so correctly and with the correct data. All trust is misplaced. Your program needs to be able to protect itself.

White Box

There are several places in a code where an integer underflow or overflow can occur. These include:

- Arithmetic operations
- Conversions and casts
- Copying and reading

If the expected value of a variable is easily defined, the variable should be checked for that value or range/size before it is used or stored. This allows the system to protect itself, at least in part.

All integer values need to be followed through the system to examine the bounds of each variable and then the bounds possible (not just expected) when an arithmetic operation or cast is carried out. Then, take combinations of the maximum values of each variable and carry out the operation to determine if the resulting value is larger or smaller than the resulting integer type. Next, carry out the same process using combinations of the smallest possible values and check the result of that against the resulting integer type as well.

Static analysis tools are often very useful for detecting these types of vulnerabilities at or prior to compile time.

Bibliography

CERT® Advisory CA-2002-25: Integer Overflow In XDR Library. Original Release Date August 5, 2002. Last updated October 3, 2002. Available from http://www.cert.org/advisories/CA-2002-25.html.

Howard, M. *Reviewing Code for Integer Manipulation Vulnerabilities.* April 28, 2003, Microsoft Corporation. Available from http://msdn.microsoft.com/library/default.asp?url=/library/en-us/dncode/html/secure04102003.asp.

Symantic Security Response Newsletter. January–February 2004. Available from http://www.ldeo.columbia.edu/ldeo/it/Symantec/News-Jan2004.

Chapter 17

Vulnerability Case Study: Man-in-the-Middle Attacks

Pseudonyms

- MITM attacks
- Eavesdropping attacks

Description

Man-in-the-middle (MITM) attacks are named for the attacker's position as quite literally the man in the middle. The attacker sits between two other parties, and both of them believe they are talking to each other but, instead, they are really talking to the man in the middle, the attacker. To accomplish the classic version of this attack, the attacker must either be located between the two communicating systems or must share a network path with one of them.

When encrypted connections are set up, a secret key is generated between the two parties and transmitted. This key is used to encrypt any communications between the two parties from then on. Traffic between these two parties is not readable by would-be attackers who may be sniffing the network, because the key is sent securely and used to encrypt the subsequent traffic.

In an MITM attack, the two parties trying to communicate securely are tricked. Although the server thinks it is talking to the user, and the user thinks it is talking to the server, they are both wrong; they are really talking to the attacker. The original request to open a secure connection was intercepted by the attacker, and the attacker is maintaining the originally requested secure connection with the server and a separate secure connection with the user.

Packets from the server are encrypted with the first key and sent to the attacker, which the server actually thinks is the user. The attacker then decrypts these packets with the first key and reencrypts them with the second key. Then the attacker sends the newly encrypted packets to the user, who believes these packets are actually being sent by the server. By sitting in the middle and maintaining these two separate keys, the attacker is able to sniff and even modify traffic between the server and the user without either side being the wiser.

This process is illustrated in Figure 17.1.

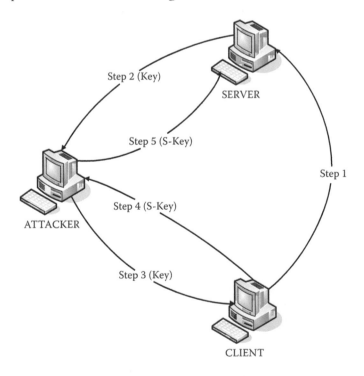

Figure 17.1   Man-in-the-middle complete handshake.

Anatomy of an Exploit

The attacker is sitting on the same network as the server and the victim but wants to intercept the traffic between the two. In preparing for the attack, the attacker has routed the network traffic through itself so that the attacker can see the traffic.

The user now tries to open a Secure Sockets Layer (SSL) conversation with the server, but the attacker intercepts the traffic and responds as if he were the server, issuing a key with which to encrypt the traffic between itself and the user. The user responds with its key and a two-way SSL conversation is now in place between the user and the attacker, but because the attacker responded to a request made to the server, the user thinks he is talking directly to the server.

At the same time, the attacker opens an SSL conversation with the server itself as if it were actually the user. The server responds to the request with a key with which to encrypt the data between the attacker and the server. The attacker responds with its own key, and there is now a two-way SSL conversation in place between the attacker and the server.

At this point, the server and the user think they are talking to each other, but the attacker is actually sitting between them, holding a secure connection to both of them. When data is sent, the attacker takes the data, decodes it with the appropriate key and then reencodes it with the other key and sends it on to the intended recipient. The attacker now has the transmitted data as unencoded to use as it wishes.

Real-World Examples

An interesting variation of the MITM attack was reported in July 2006. This attack targeted the users of CitiBank's CitiBusiness functionality.

This attack was carried out by sending to Citibank customers an e-mail that claimed to be from Citibank. The e-mail informed the victims that someone attempted to log onto their account, and they need to confirm their account information. The e-mail included a link to do so. This is a fairly standard phishing email.

Now CitiBusiness customers are required to use one of the seldom-supplied security tokens to access their account online. This is one of the little fobs generating a password that changes frequently (every minute perhaps). This is a much-touted way to improve security.

Once the victim clicks on the link in the e-mail, they are taken to a very well-done spoof of the Citibusiness login page. Even its address appears believable as it ends with Citibank.com. However, it is really a Web site in Russia.

This spoofed Web site is set up to act as the MITM between the victim and the real Citibusiness login site. When victims enter their username, password, and token-generated key, the Russian server forwards that information to the real Web site to validate it. If an error is generated by the real Citibank Web site, the spoofed Web site also generates an error.

Now the Russian site is logged into the Citibusiness site with the victim's credentials and can do whatever it wants.

Test Techniques

Most testing of MITM attack vulnerabilities is begun by looking carefully at all protocols in use in your system to determine what information they exchange and how. In the clear? How is the remote server identified?

If your method of identification is to put out a call and trust whatever system answers to be the correct one, you are most likely vulnerable to an MITM attack.

Once you find a likely candidate to test, you can use one of the session-hijacking and MITM tools available to see if you can demonstrate the vulnerability. A good tool to try is Ettercap (http://ettercap.source-forge.net/).

Bibliography

Lam, K., LeBlanc, D., and Smith, B. Theft on the Web: Prevent Session Hijacking. *Technet Magazine*, Winter 2005. Available from http://www.microsoft.com/technet/technetmag/issues/2005/01/SessionHijacking/default.aspx.

Chapter 18

Vulnerability Case Study: Password Cracking

Pseudonyms

- Password cracking
- Password guessing

Description

There are actually multiple password issues that are not uncommon across many applications. For simplicity, I have combined most of them into this single section on passwords rather than spread them out.

Probably the single most common root cause of password issues is the human issue. Passwords are annoying, and it seems like there are far too many of them to remember. There are frequent admonishments to have strong passwords that are changed regularly and aren't reused for several months. There should be a different strong password for every site that is used, as well, but how are we supposed to remember all these passwords?

Despite knowing better, most people come up with a short list of passwords that they find easy to remember and stick with those, reusing them for multiple sites and not changing them often, if at all. This is even despite the knowledge that these passwords may be the only defense against the loss of personal data that is of great value.

These very facts of human behavior mean that the potential victims make it easier for attackers, and this is one of the reasons why password attacks are very common and surprisingly effective. The victims, in essence, shoot themselves in the foot all too often with their password behavior. This is not isolated to just personal passwords but sometimes server or software administrator passwords.

Default Passwords

Many pieces of software are installed with either blank or default passwords with the assumption that the users will change these passwords as soon as the software is installed. Except, even if the user's guide, administrator's guide, or online reminder tells the user to change the password for security, a surprising number of users never bother to do so.

This can leave all the system's security wide open, as has been shown many times on many products. There are extensive lists available online of the default account names and passwords for just about every piece of major software that ships with defaults.

Weak Passwords/Password Guessing

Password guessing is the most common password cracking techniques but it is one that requires some personal knowledge of the victim if it's going to be more than moderately effective.

To start, the attacker takes some effort to discover various personal information about the victim. This can include items ranging from a girlfriend's name, pet's name, parents' names, birth dates, etc.

After gathering the above information, the attacker simply tries to guess the victim's password by trying various combinations of different names and numbers. People are relatively predictable, and there are some common password patterns like:

- Loved one's name + birth date/phone number
- Victim's name + birth date/phone number

Insecure Password Storage

Another password vulnerability is centered around how passwords are stored. Unfortunately, despite the improvements in the encrypted and protected password storage by operating systems, a lot of systems are very trusting in how they store passwords.

One common mistake is to store passwords in plaintext in any one of several places:

- Windows registry
- Configuration file
- Authentication file
- Custom file

Storing passwords in plaintext is really the equivalent of writing them on the playground wall.

If passwords must be stored, at the very least they should be encrypted. A better option is to store a hash that is calculated from the user's password instead of the password itself.

Insecure Password Transmission

Similar to the problems associated with plaintext password storage, this vulnerability centers around transmitting passwords in plaintext.

If passwords are transmitted in plaintext, they are easily obtained by network sniffing, and reliance on a Secure Socket Layer (SSL) connection still leaves the vulnerability of a spoofed or man-in-the-middle attack.

All transmission of sensitive information should require that the data be encrypted.

Dictionary-Based Attacks

This is a version of a password attack that relies on an automated tool that simply starts trying every word in whatever dictionary it uses as a resource to find the victim's password.

When it meets with success, the tool displays the password for the attacker.

This type of password attack is very slow and uses a lot of system resources to function. It's also useless if the user's password isn't in the dictionary.

Brute Force Attacks

The fall back password attack is a simple brute force attack. This type of attack uses a tool to try all the possible combinations of the available keys on the keyboard. This takes a long time as there are a huge number of combinations to be tried out, but it isn't reliant on the user's choice of password. Because of this, it has a good success rate if the attacker wants to invest that sort of effort.

Anatomy of an Exploit

Default Passwords

An attacker sends a packet to a target machine, which is directed to a port used by the software they are targeting, to see if their potential victim is running the target software. If they get the response they are expecting, they know they might be able to attack this victim.

Once the attacker knows the target software is installed, he attempts to connect to that software using the well-known default administrator password.

If the default password works, the attacker now has administrative rights to that software.

Password Guessing

An attacker is attempting to log in to the network of the company he was fired from with the username of his ex-boss. Because the attacker had worked with the victim for awhile, he begins trying to guess at possible passwords until he succeeds with the ex-boss's wife's name and the day of their anniversary.

The attacker is now logged onto the network with the credentials of his ex-boss.

Insecure Password Storage

An attacker merely has to obtain access to the place the password is stored to change or steal the password.

Insecure Password Transmission

Network sniffing of the various network traffic can expose plaintext password transmission.

Dictionary-Based Password Attacks

This is the simple use of a tool to keep submitting the username and dictionary password guess until success is reached or the dictionary is exhausted.

Brute Force Attacks

This attack also uses a tool and keeps submitting the username and password guess until either success is reached or the tool exhausts its options.

Real-World Examples

Default Passwords

In 1995, it was reported that the IRIX system of Silicon Graphics, Inc. (SGI) was being shipped with multiple accounts preconfigured with no passwords to provide easy plug and play install and operations.

Insecure Password Storage

In 1993, it was reported that a flaw in the LOGIN.EXE program in some versions of Novell's Netware software would temporarily write a user's password and username to the disk in clear text.

Insecure Password Transmission

In 2002, a vulnerability was reported in the driver for the SunPCi II VNC, which would allow an attacker that is sniffing unencrypted network traffic during the authentication process to see the plaintext password.

Test Techniques

Insecure Password Storage

The easiest way to detect plaintext password storage is to exercise your system while you run monitoring software in the background to monitor what is being created and stored on the local system. It's important to include install and uninstall on your system while running this same monitoring software.

It's also important to see what storage is being done on the server, if applicable, to eliminate the possibility of insecure password storage on the server itself.

Insecure Password Transmission

Setting up a network sniffer and then performing functions that would require the user to log onto the system will disclose plaintext password transmission.

Remember that wireless networks can also have this vulnerability, so they should be verified as well.

Password Cracking

Attempting to brute-force crack the password of a user account by simply entering a variety of different incorrect passwords will not test the security of the password itself, but it will demonstrate whether there are any mitigations in place like those that lockout the user after a certain number of incorrect password entries.

Password cracking and guessing can also be made more difficult by setting and enforcing password length and complexity rules.

Bibliography

CERT® Advisory CA-1993-12: Novell LOGIN.EXE Vulnerability. Original Release Date September 16, 1993. Last updated September 19, 1997. Available from http://www.cert.org/advisories/CA-1993-12.html.

CERT® Advisory CA-1995-15: SGI Ip Vulnerability. Original Release Date November 8, 1995. Last updated September 23, 1997. Available from http://www. cert.org/advisories/CA-1995-15.html.

Chapter 19

Vulnerability Case Study: Session Hijacking

Pseudonyms

- Session theft
- Connection hijacking

Description

Session hijacking is when an attacker takes over a TCP session between two machines, quite often in midstream, and usually for the purposes of either stealing information or disrupting or inhibiting the flow of information. Because authentication only occurs at the start of a TCP session, an attacker can use captured, brute-force, or a reverse-engineered session ID to seize control of a legitimate user's Web application session while the session is still in progress.

A session is designed as a way to track the state between multiple connections from the same server and is a series of interactions between the two communication end points that occurs during the span of a single connection. When a user logs in to an application, a session is created on the server to maintain the state for other requests originating from the same user.

Sessions are used to store parameters that are relevant to the user. The session is kept alive on the server as long as the user is logged on to the system. The session is destroyed when the user logs out from the system or after a predefined period of inactivity. When the session is destroyed, the user's data should also be deleted from the allocated memory space.

A session ID is an identification string (usually a long, random, alphanumeric string) that is transmitted between the client and the server. Session IDs are commonly stored in cookies, URLs, and hidden fields of Web pages.

Sometimes cookies are set to expire (be deleted) upon closing of the browser. These are termed *session cookies* or *nonpersistent* cookies. Cookies that last beyond a user's session (i.e., "Remember Me" option) are termed *persistent* cookies. Persistent cookies are usually stored on the user's hard drive. Their location is determined according to the particular operating system and browser.

There are several problems with session IDs. Many popular Web sites use algorithms based on easily predictable variables, such as time or IP address to generate the session IDs, causing them to be predictable. If encryption is not used (typically, SSL), session IDs are transmitted in the clear and are susceptible to eavesdropping.

Session hijacking involves an attacker using brute force captured or reverse-engineered session IDs to seize control of a legitimate user's session while that session is still in progress. In most applications, after successfully hijacking a session, the attacker gains complete access to all of the user's data and is permitted to perform operations instead of the user whose session was hijacked.

- Brute force — attacker tries multiple IDs until successful.
- Calculate — in many cases, IDs are generated in a nonrandom manner and can be calculated.
- Steal — using different types of techniques, the attacker can acquire the session ID (sniffing network traffic, using Trojans on client PCs, using the HTTP referrer header where the ID is stored in the query string parameters, and using cross-site scripting attacks).

In a "referrer" attack, the attacker entices a user to click on a link to another site (a hostile link — say, www.hostile.com). The browser sends the referrer URL containing the session ID to the attacker's site. The attacker now has the session ID of the user.

Session IDs can also be stolen using script injections, such as cross-site scripting. The user executes a malicious script that redirects the private user's information to the attacker.

Anatomy of an Exploit

In blind hijacking, the attacker injects such data as malicious commands into intercepted communications between two hosts commands such as "net.exe localgroup administrators /add EvilAttacker." Called *blind hijacking* because the attacker can only inject data into the communications stream, he or she cannot see the response to that data (such as the command completed successfully). Essentially, the blind hijacker is shooting data in the dark, but as you will see shortly, this method of hijacking is still very effective.

In a session theft attack, the attacker neither intercepts nor injects data into existing communication between two hosts. Instead, the attacker creates new sessions or uses old ones. This type of session hijacking is most common at the application level, especially Web applications.

Session hijacking at the network level is especially attractive to attackers. They don't need host access, as they do with host-level session hijacking. Nor do they need to customize attacks on a per-application basis, as they do at the application level. Network-level session-hijacking attacks allow attackers to remotely take over sessions, usually undetected. But successfully hijacking a session at the network level requires an attacker to overcome various obstacles.

Real-World Examples

In 2001, a vulnerability was reported in Sun's NetDynamics application server platform, where a user who authenticates with NetDynamics receives a session id and a random unique identifier.

This session id and identifier remain active for up to 15 s after the user logs in, and a subsequent user can make use of those credentials to hijack the logged-in account.

Test Techniques

Most testing of session-hijacking vulnerabilities is begun by looking carefully at all protocols in use in your system and determine what information they exchange and how. In the clear? How is the remote server identified? Is authentication done only at the start of a session?

If your system authenticates your user only at the start of a session, and after which the system on the other side of the connection is trusted, your system is most likely vulnerable to a session-hijacking attack.

Once you have a good idea of what your system does, you can use one of the session-hijacking and man-in-the-middle (MITM) tools available to see if you can demonstrate the vulnerability. A good tool to try is Ettercap (http://ettercap.sourceforge.net/).

Bibliography

Lam, K., LeBlanc, D., and Smith, B. Theft on the Web: Prevent Session Hijacking. *Technet Magazine*, Winter 2005. Available from http://www.microsoft.com/technet/technetmag/issues/2005/01/SessionHijacking/default.aspx.

Session Hijacking, Imperva Application Defense Center. Available from http://www.imperva.com/application_defense_center/glossary/session_hijacking.html.

Chapter 20

Vulnerability Case Study: Spoofing Attacks

Pseudonyms

- IP address spoofing
- IP spoofing

Description

This is an attack based on the creation of Internet Protocol (IP) packets with a forged IP source address. This forging makes the packet appear as if it was sent from a different machine. This technique is very useful as part of certain other attacks, as a way of trying to disguise identity, and as a way to defeat portions of network security like IP address authentication.

Carrying out an IP spoofing attack can be difficult, because it often means the headers of thousands of packets must be modified, one packet at a time. This can't usually be done on a computer that's running Microsoft Windows.

To perform IP spoofing, the header of the packet must be modified. This header contains the following (among other data):

- Source IP

- Destination IP
- Checksum value
- Order value

When packets are transmitted to the Internet, they will most likely arrive at their destination out of order and must be reassembled using the order sent value.

When trust relationships exist between machines, these spoofing attacks can be especially effective. Some corporate networks make it a common practice to have trust relationships between various internal systems, so that a user can access other machines without a username or password as long as they are connecting from another machine on the internal network. Because of this connection from another system, they are assumed to have been authenticated by that system. By spoofing a connection from another machine in a trust relationship with the target, an attacker might be able to access the target machine without authenticating.

Nonblind Spoofing

To perform this type of spoofing attack, the attacker needs to be on the same subnet as the target. The attacker can then use a packet sniffer to view the sequence and acknowledgment numbers, which means that the attacker doesn't have to worry about calculating them accurately and correctly. The biggest threat of spoofing in this case is session hijacking.

Blind Spoofing

In this attack, the sequence and acknowledgment numbers are unreachable and unknown. To try to provide a basis for guessing or calculating the sequence and acknowledgment numbers, several sample packets are sent to the target machine to obtain sample sequence numbers. It was once a common practice to use simple methods to generate these sequence numbers, which also made them easy to guess and calculate. Now, sequence numbers are typically the result of random number generation, which makes it harder to predict the sequence.

Denial of Service Attack

IP spoofing is almost always a component of denial-of-service, or DoS, attacks. Because the goal of these attacks is to consume bandwidth or other resources, there is no need to worry about properly completing the handshake or transactions. To consume these resources, the attacker wants to flood the victim with as many packets as possible and as quickly as possible.

To prolong the attack, the attacker will forge source IP addresses on these packets to make tracing and stopping the DoS as difficult as possible. When multiple hosts are involved, and all of them are sending spoofed traffic, it can be very hard to block the traffic quickly. This tends to be a task where attackers use their army of bots.

Anatomy of an Exploit

Nonblind Attack

The attacker sets up a packet sniffer and collects the packet data from the system they are targeting to see what the pattern of sequence and acknowledgment numbers are. If a pattern can be detected, the attacker can construct a packet that uses that pattern and spoofs the IP address they want to attack.

Real-World Examples

The most famous use of an IP spoofing attack is probably that of Kevin Mitnick's attack against Tsutomu Shimomura in December 2004. It's important to note, first, that IP spoofing was a component of this attack but not the sole vulnerability used.

The initial sign of this attack was some probes against various machines, apparently to see if there might be an exploitable trust relationship between these machines.

Then SYN flooding was used to make the first victim computer unable to respond to requests, while the attacking machine first probed for specific TCP behavior and sequencing. Then the spoofed IP address of the first victim computer was used to issue a SYN request to the second victim computer, and Mitnick eventually gained root access on the second victim computer.

Test Techniques

IP spoofing really isn't a solvable problem, but the use of encryption and decryption should be tested as in some of the other attacks like man-in-the-middle or session-hijacking.

Chapter 21

Vulnerability Case Study: SQL Injection

Pseudonyms

- SQL insertion
- Script injection

Description

The very first thing to point out is that this section is entitled "SQL Injection," but injection attacks are not limited to applications running against a particular database server. MySQL, SQL Server, Oracle, etc., are all potentially susceptible.

SQL injection vulnerabilities are common in Web applications that access an SQL back end. The vulnerability has its roots in the use of client-supplied data in SQL queries.

Successful SQL injection attacks can result in the attacker possibly being able to:

- Run commands as the SQL Server user on the database server, using the xp_cmdshell extended stored procedure

- Read registry keys, potentially including the SAM (if SQL Server is running as the local system account) using the xp_regread extended stored procedure
- Run other extended stored procedures
- Run queries on linked servers
- Create new custom extended stored procedures to run explicit code with the SQL server process
- Use the "bulk insert" statement to read any file on the server
- Use bcp to create arbitrary text files on the server
- Create OLE Automation applications that can do everything that an ASP script can

The goal of an SQL injection attack is to attempt to manipulate queries or information sent to an SQL back end to gain control of the SQL server. This control can mean the ability to modify queries to get unauthorized information, but it can also go as far as modifying data on the server, invoking stored procedures, or even shutting down the SQL server, depending on the skill of the attacker and the level of control that can be gained.

This is usually done by bypassing or tricking whatever safeguards are in place to validate or scrub data before it's sent to the back-end SQL server.

An example would be that if the SQL query looks like this:

```
SELECT FieldList FROM Table WHERE field = 'user-
clause';
```

Now, if the clause supplied by the attacker is "myclause'" (notice the trailing single quote), the SQL query now looks like this:

```
SELECT FieldList FROM Table WHERE field = 'myclause'';
```

Typically, this will result in a syntax error because the trailing single quote will confuse the SQL server. Now, what if we try to change the nature of the WHERE clause by injecting a clause designed to always be true, such as "anything' or 'z'='z'". Our query then becomes:

```
SELECT FieldList FROM Table WHERE field = 'anything'
or 'z'='z';
```

This version, because the conditions will always be met, will return all rows in the table.

The attacker can continue on from there with some guesses at table names and even get to where, instead of just copying or stealing the information in the database, the attacker is writing data to the database, if that is not forbidden.

Anatomy of an Exploit

Look for a Possible Vulnerability

The start of an SQL injection attack generally begins with the attacker looking for vulnerability in a site. This could be just about anything that accepts input: a search string, a form, ASP, JSP, CGI, or PHP pages. Note that this can include hidden fields, not just those displayed through the UI. Anything the attacker can see in the source is as vulnerable as what is openly displayed; perhaps more so, because sometimes there is less security on those fields that are hidden.

Once a possible vulnerability is found, the attack can begin in earnest.

Test the Vulnerability

To test the vulnerability, the attacker often starts with what is the most common vulnerability: the single quote. In SQL, a single quote is the string literal delimiter. If user input is submitted directly to the SQL back end without sufficient validation or input "scrubbing," it's incredibly easy to gain control of the SQL server.

If the attacker is working with a hidden field in the source, it's only a bit more complicated in that the source needs to be downloaded from the site, saved, the URL and the hidden field modified, and then the source executed.

If the user input is not being sufficiently validated and scrubbed, the additional information after the apostrophe will be treated as a part of the query string submitted to the SQL server and will be executed.

Now the attacker takes a look at what is returned.

All Errors Are Not Created Equal

Unfortunately, error pages can reveal a lot of information about exactly what is happening behind the scenes. If you know what to look for, they're a great tool to use when trying to diagnose and refine attack attempts.

The first thing to do is see just what error page is returned. If it's an ODBC error page, the attacker knows right away that this is a true vulnerability because the error was generated from the SQL, which means the single quote inserted in the prior step was successful in passing from the front end to the SQL back end.

If the attacker gets a different error, he will then look carefully through the source of the error page for any references to "SQL Server," "ODBC," or "syntax." Sometimes the details of the error are hidden in the headers or in comments that aren't visible except in the source.

If an error page is returned that includes links, the attacker will search the links to see of they contain more details of the error.

If a 302 Page Redirect is called, the attacker will try to capture the page it is redirected from; this may have more error details in it that can't be easily read before the redirect occurs.

If a 500 Error Page is returned, the attacker knows that the injection may have been successful as this is the default error page for most Web servers. Though the attacker may not be able to determine much from this page, it will spur him on to greater attempts to exploit a possible weakness.

The Hunt Continues

The attacker will continue to try other options as to how to bypass the site's validation and scrubbing routines. In each case, the server's responses will be carefully examined. These other options include:

- Using the single quote in different places in the string to try to take advantage of any ordered validation routines (for example, an e-mail field may be validated to require an @ and a period, and if the attacker entered "joe'@mysite.com," it would fail that validation. However, it's never actually tested for a single quote, so "joe@mysite.com'" would succeed and expose the vulnerability).
- Using the single quote at the end of a maximum length string. If the site is escaping single quotes, the attempt to escape a single quote when it is already at maximum length for the string may lead to the string's being truncated right back to the single quote and the vulnerability exposed.
- Using two dashes. Two dashes in an SQL server indicate a single line comment and may be passed to the back-end server, causing the server to ignore the rest of the line.
- Using a semicolon. This is a character that indicates to the SQL server that a new command follows. If this is passed through to the back end, the attacker may be able to concatenate another command and essentially piggyback on the prior query.
- Using all of these techniques in not just string fields but in fields that appear to be set for other data types. For example, a back-end SQL server may implicitly translate an integer into a varchar. Or a format may only be enforced by the Web code and never checked after that UI check.
- Using a # character. This is sometimes used as a date/time delimiter.

- Using char equivalents to the suspicious characters (for example, char(0x63)).

Real-World Examples

Arguably, the most serious and widely publicized SQL injection attack is the one that was carried out on CardSystems in September 2004, where 263,000 credit card numbers were stolen and 40 million more numbers were exposed.

Although the exact details of the attack are not available (or at least not that I've been able to locate), the attack is acknowledged to be the product of the exploit of an SQL injection vulnerability on the Web application that allows the customers to access account information. The attackers injected a script that would run every four days to extract records, zip them, and then export them to an FTP site.

It is worth pointing out that the data that was exported had been kept in an unencrypted form and in violation of regulatory rules for supposed "research purposes."

Test Techniques

Every parameter of every call must be tested separately to have a good picture of the Web service's/site's SQL injection vulnerabilities. Table 21.1 shows the list of characters I recommend testing with.

Black-Box Testing

For black-box testing, you need to use a browser and perform parameter tampering in any query or parameter you can locate on the site.

The basic process is to replace the argument in every parameter on every script on the server with a test argument, one parameter at a time. Leave all the other parameters with valid data intact. Submit this parameter (or set of parameters) to the server, and then examine the returned page for the signs of possible vulnerabilities listed in the earlier section titled "Anatomy of the Exploit."

White-Box Testing

Determine if the Web site is performing any type of input validation. Strings tend to be more susceptible to parameter injection than other data

Table 21.1   SQL Injection Test Characters

Character Name	Unicode Value	Reason
Required		
Single quote/ Apostrophe (')	[U+0027]	SQL character used to escape strings. Remember to test all fields, not just string fields • Use alone • Use as the first character in otherwise valid input • Use in the middle of otherwise valid input • Use as the last character in a maximum length otherwise valid input • Use in places specific formatting is required after formatting requirements are met
Recommended		
Double quotes (")	[U+0022]	Used to encapsulate SQL query as a whole; also test as its URL escaped equivalent (%22)
Semicolon (;)	[U+003B]	SQL command terminator; also test as its URL escaped equivalent (%3B)
Dash/hyphen (-)	[U+002D]	Use two as a SQL server single line comment indicator
Left single quote	[U+2018]	Often downgraded to the single-byte single quote character
Right single quote	[U+2019]	Often downgraded to the single-byte single quote character
Prime (′)	[U+2032]	Often downgraded to the single-byte single quote character
Other Ideas		
Percent sign (%)	[U+0025]	SQL wildcard character; also test as its escaped equivalent (%25); this doesn't so much test for vulnerability as it does that the character is properly escaped and doesn't cause unexpected results
Double left quotes	[U+201C]	Often downgraded to the single-byte quote character
Double right quotes	[U+201D]	Often downgraded to the single-byte quote character
Double prime	[U+2033]	Often downgraded to the single-byte quote character
Soft hyphen	[U+00AD]	Often translated to the dash/hyphen

Table 21.1   SQL Injection Test Characters (Continued)

Character Name	Unicode Value	Reason
En dash	[U+2013]	Often downgraded to the single-byte hyphen character
Em dash	[U+2014]	Often downgraded to the single-byte hyphen character

types. One parameter at a time, replaces the argument of each parameter on each API, with each of the listed single-quote test scenario, and submits it. Then, examine the entire response from the server to see if you received an error and whether you can tell if it's an SQL error.

Bibliography

Friedl, S. SQL Injection Attacks by Example. January 2005. Available from http://www.unixwiz.net/techtips/sql-injection.html.

SQL Injection Walkthrough. SecuriTeam, May 2002. Available from http://www.securiteam.com/securityreviews/5DP0N1P76E.html.

Chapter 22

Fuzz Testing

Fuzz testing (also called *fuzzing*) is a test technique that attempts to find security vulnerabilities by passing unexpected and malformed data to a program's entry points. Because a very large percentage of security vulnerabilities are due to input validation issues, where a program is unable to deal with one or more pieces of unexpected input, fuzz testing can be used to find a good number of these vulnerabilities.

Fuzz testing is actually so effective that there is supposition that attackers are using fuzz-testing techniques to search for exploitable vulnerabilities. Blaster and Slammer are both said to have been based on vulnerabilities discovered by fuzzing.

Fuzz testing is also a way to challenge any assumptions made about how a program will behave. To create and carry out functional tests for a program, assumptions are invariably made and often never challenged to ensure that they are not masking vulnerabilities. Fuzz testing allows all sorts of random data to be used with no regard for any preconceptions or assumptions.

This can be a useful technique whenever you are dealing with input during security testing.

Assumptions

At its most basic level, fuzz testing is the process of testing the assumptions made about how a program should or will behave, and how dependent your program is on the trusts it has in these assumptions.

Some of the common assumptions focus on:

- Data length
- Data type
- Data order
- Data timing
- Data capacity
- Source
- Machine state
- Success
- Failure
- Authentication
- Authorization

Also, do not limit your list of assumptions to data input fields only. Do not forget about:

- RPC endpoints
- ActiveX controls
- Network ports
- Files

Assumptions are often made based on "standards" that anything interacting with the program is trusted to follow, even though the program itself does not enforce or validate them

All trust is misplaced. What stops someone from passing the link to a huge graphic file instead of one to a tiny text file? If all URLs are well under 1 KB, what stops someone from passing in a 10-MB one?

Process Steps

This is the set of basic steps that are needed for a fuzz testing effort.

Prioritize and Choose Targets

This should be done in conjunction with your threat model or risk assessment so that you are in line with the areas of greater risk. A well-written threat model should include all entry points, and if yours does not, they need to be added to be able to effectively determine trust and attack surface.

This can also be done with the data from your test plan and test case outline (TCO) by reviewing the input test cases and determining which entry points have the highest priority based on the priority of the test cases that test them.

Some of these entry points are as follows:

- Network clients
- Network servers
- Protocol handlers
- APIs
- ActiveX controls
- Remote procedure call (RPC) endpoints
- Stored procedures
- Windows messages

Set the Bug Fix Bar

This should be done in advance, because even security bugs are not all created equal. What bugs must be fixed right away? What bugs can wait for a while?

This can also be tied back to the threat model or risk assessment, as the risk of the discovered vulnerabilities being exploited should already be known.

Choose Tactics

Some thought must be given to just what kinds of malformed data to send to the targets determined in step 1. There are some categories that can be mixed and matched to provide the correct level of testing for your project:

"Smart" Fuzz Testing

This is not smart as in "more intelligent," but rather smart as in "guided by human decisions." This uses input changes you specify, tends to be more specific, and requires a level of technical knowledge about the program being tested and some of its inner workings. It's equivalent to knowing the required input format and using that format but inserting invalid data into the fields.

This is most useful when you are looking for very specific issues or you are trying to look at specific areas of code. It is also more susceptible to assumptions and trusts, and not as useful if you do not have the insight and experience with the project being tested.

"Dumb" Fuzz Testing

This uses random and unspecified changes to inputs, and disregards any data formatting conventions.

This is useful for broad testing of the code and is more immune to biasing by assumptions and trusts than smart fuzz testing. It's also useful for defect estimation and the creation of exclusion lists. It's not as useful for cases where data may be rejected for syntax issues.

Mutation

Mutation is the process of taking existing data and modifying it. This is useful if you happen to have the existing data and a way to modify it. Beware of attempting this if your data has validation like checksums or digital signatures.

Generation

Generation creates new data, typically using tools. This is useful when you have a tool to create the input that can be scripted. Beware of attempting generation, when you do not have well-defined formats and no tools in place to generate the data for you.

Mixed Fuzz Testing

There are also times when you have to use a mix of smart and dumb fuzz testing. Perhaps you know a part of a format, or you want to use smart fuzz testing on those areas that are parsed for acceptance and dumb fuzz testing on other parts.

You can also use mixes of generation and mutation, depending on the needs of your product and the test efforts.

Build Tools and Test Harnesses

Now, based on the information gathered and decisions made in the prior steps, tools need to be either chosen or designed, and built if no ready-made tools are available that meet your needs. There are some commercial and some shareware and open source fuzzing tools available, and rather than reinvent the wheel, it often pays to adapt or use tools already available instead.

Run Tests

This is the all important step of actually running your tests. No matter how well you have planned and designed, count on the fact that it will take longer than you initially think it should, especially the first time or two you attempt it. So it's important to be alert for ways that you can streamline the process or otherwise save time.

During testing, it's very important to keep accurate and complete records of all tests run, their actual input, and their results/output. Without this information, especially with the randomly generated fuzzing cases, vulnerabilities may be difficult to track down and reproduce.

Analyze Results

There are three basic types of real results in fuzz testing:

- True positive — crashes and access violations (AVs), best diagnosed with a good reproduction
- False positive — inappropriate failure
- False negative — inappropriate success, usually due to poorly designed fuzz tests

Then there's the one result that you cannot really determine through testing:

- True negative — not possible to have this determination through testing

Now the raw results need to be reviewed and analyzed to determine which of the three main result types they fit into. I generally start with the reported test failures and analyze those first, so that the type which has the greatest likeliness of being a security vulnerability is identified soonest, followed by sorting out the true positives from the false positives.

If any results are determined to be false negatives, the cases need to be redesigned and rerun to have a valid test.

Fix Vulnerabilities

Now the process of fuzz testing returns to a standard test process of filing the bug and getting it fixed. Note that you should never wait for an exploit to appear in the wild before filing the bug and getting it fixed.

Repeat

The fuzz testing needs to be repeated, results reevaluated, and any new vulnerability fixed until a clean set of tests is achieved.

Case Studies

1990: UNIX

In 1990 there was a study done by three people from the University of Wisconsin–Madison, which was the first testing done on the subject of fuzz testing. In this study, 88 utility programs on seven versions of UNIX were tested on several hardware configurations. The rather simple set of test cases that were run in this study was able to crash or hang between 25 and 33 percent of the utility programs on each system.

1995: UNIX

This study was repeated five years later with over 80 utility programs on nine UNIX platforms, including three of the same platforms that were tested in the 1990 study. The following additional areas of testing were added:

- Testing network services with random input streams
- Testing X-Window application and servers with random input streams
- Additional checks of the utility programs to see if they check the return value of system calls

This study found that although there was a noticeable improvement over the systems that had been tested in 1990, the failure range over all the systems was 9 to 29 percent. Unfortunately, approximately 40 percent of the bugs that were reported in 1990 as a result of that study were still present in their original form in 1995.

In the X-Window testing, more than 25 percent of the programs tested crashed or hung.

2000: Windows NT and Windows 2000

In this study, Windows NT 4.0 (build 1381 SP 5) and Windows 2000 (version 5.00.2195) were tested with over 30 application programs. This study revealed the following:

- Twenty-one percent of the applications tested on Windows NT 4 crashed when given random valid keyboard and mouse events.
- Twenty-four percent of the applications tested on Windows NT 4 hung when given random valid keyboard and mouse events.
- Up to 100 percent of the applications tested failed (crashed or hung) when given completely random Win32 messages.
- Any application running on the Windows platform was vulnerable to random input strings that generated other applications on the same system.

Bibliography

Forrester, J.E. and Miller, B.P. An Empirical Study of the Robustness of Windows NT Applications using Random Testing. 2000. University of Wisconsin-Madison. Available from http://www.cs.wisc.edu/~bart/fuzz/fuzz-nt.html.

Fredriksen, L., Miller, B.S., and So, B. An Empirical Study of the Reliability of UNIX Utilities. 1989. Miller, Fredriksen, and So. Available from ftp://ftp.cs.wisc.edu/paradyn/technical_papers/fuzz.pdf.

Koski, D., Lee, C.P., Maganty, V., Miller, B.P., Murthy, R., Natarajan, A., and Steidl, J. Fuzzing Revisited: A Re-examination of the Reliability of UNIX Utilities and Services. October 1995. University of Wisconsin-Madison. Available from ftp://ftp.cs.wisc.edu/paradyn/technical_papers/fuzz-revisited.pdf.

Chapter 23

Background: Cryptography

Crypto is a blanket term that has come to mean the combination of the techniques of encryption, decryption, and cryptology. None of these are new concepts; coded messages existed in the ancient world, and they played a big role in recent wars, with the cracking of Enigma machine encryption being one of the pivotal developments. These concepts have just moved to the realm of computers.

In 1993, the U.S. government tried to protect the security of cryptographic software that it uses by making it a crime to export any cryptographic software with over 40-bit keys outside the United States without a special munitions export license. After years of outcry and study, this law was changed in 1996, and crypto developed outside the military was no longer considered munitions, and thus no longer prohibited from export.

One really important concept to understand about crypto is that it is rarely, if ever, unbreakable — given an unlimited amount of time, computing power, and incentive to break it.

Encryption

Encryption is typically used for the following purposes:

Authentication

This can be through encrypted passwords but also through the use of digital signatures. A digital signature is a method of ensuring the source of a message or file by processing it in such a way that the actual message or file is tied to the person who signed it and is therefore much less likely to have been spoofed. Most digital signatures employ a trusted third party.

Integrity

This applies to the integrity of both the system and the data, thus allowing users to confirm that the system has not been breached and that the system retains its expected completeness, consistency, and integrity.

Confidentiality

The most basic data security is the enforcement of confidentiality, preventing the data from unauthorized viewing. By converting the message to ciphertext, encryption allows the senders of messages to obscure the original message so that the confidentiality of the message is assured. This also applies to processes like the encryption of an entire hard drive to ensure that if the network has been hacked, the data on the disk is still secure from unauthorized viewing by someone on the outside. It would also ensure its security even if an unauthorized person has physical access to the storage media, such as a laptop or hard drive.

Crypto can also be used to insure the confidentiality of e-mail messages being sent over the Internet and to keep those messages secure from sniffing or interception.

Nonrepudiation

This is the defined as the ability of both parties in a transaction to prove that the other party has, in fact, participated in that transaction. Thus, neither party can effectively deny that they have exchanged messages with the other party. This may apply to situations in which intellectual property is discussed or shared, or terms of a transaction are agreed upon. Nonrepudiation is generally considered to constitute undeniable proof of delivery through the multiple ways the users and the transaction are bound together. These can include the origin of data, the data sender, and time of receipt. The use of encryption keys to encrypt and decrypt messages can also be considered proof.

How Encryption Works

Any form of data can be encrypted, including single bits, small strings such as passwords, individual files, or huge databases of multiple files. Different encryption algorithms work in different ways, so what is being encrypted often determines the best algorithm to be used. Sometimes, a combination of several strong algorithms is used to ensure even tighter security.

Methodology

To perform encryption, data is passed through an algorithm or a series of mathematical operations that generate an alternate form of that data. A cryptographic algorithm is the mathematical formula or function that is used specifically for encryption and decryption. Because it's a set procedure and doesn't change, it can be reversed so that the encrypted data can be unencrypted and restored to its original readable form.

A very simple example of a basic cipher is the childhood decoder ring. This ring has 26 letters of the alphabet, and users agree on how far to rotate the ring to send each other secret messages. If the users agree to a setting of +2, each letter in their original (plaintext) message is replaced by the letter that occurs two characters later in the alphabet. Thus, a B in the plaintext message would appear as a D in the ciphertext.

An algorithm is considered computationally secure if it cannot be broken with available (current or future) resources. Strong cryptographic algorithms can be made even stronger by publishing the algorithm and allowing anyone and everyone to try to prove its insecurity. Sometimes these take the form of distributed computing challenges. This is why open source suits crypto development.

Key-Based Ciphers

A key is the means by which messages are encrypted or decrypted. Key-based encryption is generally considered to be very secure, because even if the attacker has the ciphertext (the encrypted form of the data) and the algorithm itself, neither the plaintext (data to be secured) nor the key can be determined from those two pieces of information.

One way to increase the security of an encryption is to increase the length of the key. In crypto, key length is equal to the number of possible options of keys available to decrypt a certain code. An example would be that a 1-digit numeric key has 10 options: 0 through 9. A 2-digit numeric key has 100 options: 0 through 99.

The length of the key has an exponential effect on the strength of the encryption. An 8-bit key has 2^8 (256) possible outcomes. A 40-bit encryption has 2^40 or 10^12 (1 trillion) possible keys for decrypting ciphertext. Each time we increase the number of individual keys that potential crackers have to try to brute-force crack the message that is encrypted with that key.

Key-Based Algorithms

Symmetric (Single-Key) Cipher

In symmetric encryption, the same key is used for both encryption and decryption and must be kept secret. To do this, both the sender and receiver have to agree on the key to be used before making any data transmissions. Symmetric algorithms tend to be very fast, so they are often used to encrypt and decrypt large amounts of data.

Digital Encryption Standard (DES) is the most common symmetric cipher. It was adopted in 1977 and has a 56-bit key. DES was proven insecure in 1997 and cracked in 56 hr by a machine built in 1998. This gave rise to Triple DES, a way of using DES on itself for greater security. Typically, this would consist of a three-step encryption operation, i.e., encrypt the file with one key, decrypt it with another, and encrypt it again with a third key.

Advanced Encryption Standard (AES) — originally called Rijndael — was adopted by the National Institute of Standards and Technology (NIST) in 2000 from entrants in a competition between numerous algorithms developed in the crypto community. The cipher has a variable block length and key length, usable with keys of 128, 192, or 256 bits to encrypt blocks with a length of 128, 192, or 256 bits. Both block length and key length can be extended very easily to multiples of 32 bits.

Asymmetric Encryption

Also known as public-key encryption, the key used to perform encryption differs from that used to perform decryption. The key used to encrypt is generally called the "public key" and the decryption key is the "private key" or "secret key." The cool thing about asymmetric ciphers is that they can authenticate transactions across a public channel, providing a receipt ("signing") when the private key is used at the receiving end.

If copies of any keys are stored anywhere outside the main user's traditional storage location, they are considered to be in escrow. Some tools, such as Pretty Good Privacy (PGP), put these in certificate authorities (CA) for trust in the public keys. Its key certificate contains the public key, user ID related to the key, date created, and, if desired, a list of digital signatures on the key ring, signed by people who "attest to that key's veracity." RSA (Rivest–Shamir–Adleman), released in 1977, is the most common asymmetric cipher. It is now in the public domain, open for anyone to use or improve.

Hash Cipher

In essence, a hash is a string of text that is generated by a message that serves as a unique identifier of that message. The text of the message, as well as date and time of submission, is put into the hash algorithm, which spits out a string of text. This hash string is used to verify the document integrity by placing the document through the hash function again to see if the two hashes match. If the hashes are the same, there is a very high probability that the message was transmitted intact.

MD5 is the most widely used hash algorithm, with a 128-bit fingerprint. MD5 is also in the public domain.

SHA1 has a 160-bit output and is often used for digital signatures.

Encryption Tools

Here are some of the most widely used (and, generally, more secure) encryption tools, though encryption tools are constantly evolving. With greater open source development and use, crypto will probably only continue to change and improve in the future. Open PGP and GPG lead the way, with OpenSSH and OpenSSL running on OpenBSD, etc. Bugs crop up occasionally, but developers in the open source community are usually able to resolve them quickly.

PGP

PGP is probably the most famous encryption tool. It is based on the RSA algorithm and is most commonly applied to e-mail transmissions. In fact, according to Phil Zimmermann, creator of the PGP tool, over 90 percent of e-mail encryption is done with PGP. PGP is available on a few sites now as a commercial product, further developed by Network Solutions (NAI) in the late 1990s, but they no longer support the product. PGP freeware is available all over the world. Phil Zimmerman has been attempting to regain rights to PGP so he can continue to evolve it for future needs.

GPG

Gnu Privacy Guard (GPG) replaced PGP to some extent. Because of its development outside the United States, it is a more widely available open solution internationally. GPG is gaining in popularity, particularly after NAI shut down the commercial support of PGP and with the rise of Linux.

S/KEY

The best way to secure a password, S/KEY is a true one-time pad-based password scheme. Passwords are long, so that key length is long. To use S/KEY the user must carry around a list of one-time passwords for each password entry. The keys should never be stored online.

SSH and SCP

Secure Shell (SSH) is a secure version of Telnet, whereas Secure Copy (SCP) is a secure version of copy, which also replaces the insecure FTP. They work by authenticating known hosts using RSA.

SSL

Developed by Netscape, the Secure Socket Layer (SSL) handshake protocol authenticates servers and clients by using the RSA algorithm. OpenSSL is a newer version available for open platforms.

Crypto Is Not Always Secure

Given enough time and computing power, all key-based algorithms are theoretically breakable. Although encryption sounds like it's always the best thing for security, there are a few things to consider:

Key Length

Keys can be cracked by brute force and the right hacker. Most current data considers symmetric algorithm keys shorter than 128-bit keys to be at risk for a brute force attack. So far, Triple DES and AES are yet to be broken. This is because of their extraordinary key lengths.

As for asymmetric or public-key lengths, there are multiple recommendations for 1280 through 2005 bits for individuals and 1536 for corporations and 2048 for governments.

Programmer Error

Even with strong encryption algorithms, some software programs contain other bugs that can make passwords, etc., easy to hack, which, in turn, means that no matter how good the encryption is, the supposedly secure information can be read.

User Error

Using encryption poorly may be worse than not using encryption at all. Although this might be an overstatement, the point is that poorly implemented encryption can give a false sense of security. If users know a file is encrypted, they may disregard fundamental security practices for a file. This is a security weakness because some information should never be sent — encrypted or not.

Obscurity

The term "security by obscurity" is one that is often heard these days. It usually refers to the practice of hiding important data, rather than securing it in a known location.

An example of security by obscurity would be a letter, not locked in a safe merely hidden in an undisclosed location within one physical area of the country. Stronger security in this case would be locking the letter in a safe, knowing the safe's location, and providing design specifications of that safe along with 100 safes of the same type to anyone who wants to try to break in, but guarding it actively all the while.

Security by obscurity may work for keeping physical items safe from the random burglar, but it will not work for data on a network.

Cryptanalysis

This is the study of breaking ciphers (uncovering codes and algorithms). Assuming that an algorithm or product is breakable, cryptanalysis on it can be conducted in a variety of ways, the most common being the brute force method. Brute force means trying all keys until the end result resembles the estimated plaintext. This can only realistically be done with special hardware, or multiple machines running in parallel. Sometimes, codes are deduced by using the ciphertext of several messages. The deductions definitely have better results if some plaintext is available as well. The 56-bit key in 1995 took one week and 120,000 processors to break.

The Future of Crypto

Crypto is becoming easier all the time — easier to install and understand and with more types available to the average user. As a result, NIST created the federal Public Key Infrastructure or PKI. Currently, the NIST PKI is mainly a center of information on various encryption tools and technologies.

Cryptography is increasingly becoming a central focus as companies try to protect their intellectual property. This is particularly true in the case of the TCPA (Trusted Computing Platform Alliance) or Microsoft's Palladium.

The attempt to apply cryptography to protect copyrighted material against unauthorized reproduction (called DRM or Digital Rights Management) is still creating tremendous debate, particularly regarding the CBDTPA (Consumer Broadband and Digital Television Promotion Act), not to mention the BPDG (Broadcast Protection Discussion Group).

The general idea behind all of these groups and concepts is to mandate strong security through crypto hardware, which greatly benefits the entertainment industry, while potentially threatening the open source community.

Chapter 24

Background: Firewalls

Firewalls are tools that can be used to improve the security of computers connected to a network, such as a LAN or the Internet. A firewall separates a computer from the Internet, inspecting your packets of data as they arrive at either side of the firewall, both inbound to or outbound from your computer, to determining whether each packet should be allowed to pass or be blocked.

Firewalls act as guards at the computer's entry points (which are called *ports*) where the computer exchanges data with other devices on the network. They ensure that packets attempting to enter the computer abide by certain rules that have been established by the user of the computer. Firewalls operate in two ways: by either denying or accepting all messages based on a list of designated acceptable (white listed) or unacceptable (blacklisted) sources, or by allowing or denying all messages based on a list of designated acceptable (white listed) or unacceptable (blacklisted) destination ports.

Although they sound complex, firewalls are relatively easy to install, set up, and operate.

TCP/IP

TCP/IP is spoken and understood by all computers on the Internet, even those using different operating systems. In fact, for a computer to communicate on the Internet, it has to use TCP/IP.

Packets

Firewalls read the IP addresses in the header of the packets that they receive to determine the source of the message. That information will be used as part of the determination of whether or not the message will be allowed access.

Ports

The destination port number is also included the packet's header information. This is important for firewalls, because by reading the packet, the firewall can tell what application the message is trying to run. Firewalls can be configured to deny certain applications, which they determine by reading the port number of the incoming header.

For example, FTP uses port #21, so computers running FTP will be open to accepting FTP packets and will accept packets that indicate that they are FTP packets by the inclusion of port #21 in their header. If the recipient is not running FTP, it would not be open to receiving any info addressed for port #21. The firewall should be configured to deny access to any packets that are destined for that port number.

Some common TCP/IP ports are:

- 21 — FTP (File Transfer Protocol)
- 25 — SMTP (Simple Mail Transfer Protocol)
- 49 — Login (Login Host Protocol)
- 80 — HTTP (Hypertext Transfer Protocol)
- 113 — Auth (Authentication Service)
- 114 — Audionews (Audio News Multistream)

Port Scanners

Port scanners are used to find the services running on systems, such as the ones mentioned earlier. Once the port scanner finds a service or an application that is running, the attacker can then determine whether or not that specific service is vulnerable or one they are targeting for attacks.

There are 65,535 virtual ports on a typical personal computer that can be used to gain entry. The firewall has to keep an eye on each one of these ports.

Types of Firewalls

Firewalls have a set of rules that determines if any one packet should be allowed access. But different types of firewalls have different methods of inspecting packets for acceptance or rejection.

Packet Filtering

Also known as a network layer firewall, this is the most common type of firewall. When a packet filtering firewall receives a packet from the Internet, it checks the information stored as the IP source address in the header of the packet and compares it to a table of access control rules to determine whether or not the packet is acceptable. These access control rules are determined by the firewall administrator to say whether a packet is acceptable or not. The rules can also state that certain actions must take place when a particular criterion is met, including source or destination IP address or port number.

Packet filtering firewalls are fast, but they are fairly easy to get around. One way to do so is via IP spoofing in which attackers use the IP address of a trusted source as the source IP address in their packet and which fools the firewall into thinking that the packets are actually from that trusted source.

The other issue is that they still allow a direct connection between the source and destination computers. Once an initial connection has been approved by the firewall, the source computer is directly connected to the destination computer, and all the computers that are connected are vulnerable to potential attack.

Stateful Packet Inspection

This is like a stepped-up form of the packet filtering that examines not just the headers of the packets but also the contents of the packet to determine more about the packet than just its source and destination information. It's called a *stateful packet inspection*, because it examines the contents of the packet to determine what the state of the communication is; it ensures that the stated destination computer has previously requested the current communication. This is a way of ensuring that all communications are initiated by the recipient computer and are taking place only with sources that are known and trusted from previous interactions.

In addition to being more rigorous in their inspection of packets, stateful inspection firewalls also close off ports until connection to the specific port is requested. This allows an added layer of protection from the threat of port scanning.

Application-Level Proxy

This is a type of firewall that determines if a connection to a requested application is permitted. Only connections for specified purposes, such as Internet access or e-mail will be allowed. This allows administrators to control what applications their systems' computers will be used for.

An application-level proxy can be set up to only allow Web and e-mail applications to gain access. It can also be programmed to stop all packets with the destination port of 23 (Telnet). Any attempt by attackers to telnet into the user's computer will fail, because the application-level firewall will recognize this telnet collection as a non-Web/e-mail application and reject the information trying to enter the user's computer.

This type of firewall is called an application-level proxy because, in addition to screening incoming packets for the type of application it wants to run on the user's computer, it also serves as a proxy server. A proxy can be thought of as a computer that sits between a computer and a Web server, and acts as a middleman between the computer and the Web server.

The application-level proxy receives all communications requests from the computers behind it (or inside the firewall). It then proxies the request; it makes the requests on behalf of its constituent computer. What this does is effectively hide the individual computers on the network behind it. The targeted computers are protected from view because outside sources never make direct contact with the computers; every communication is conducted through the proxy server.

Network Address Translation (NAT)

Also known as network masquerading or IP masquerading, this serves as a firewall by keeping individual IP addresses hidden from the outside world. Similar to a proxy server, a NAT acts as an intermediary between a group of computers and the Internet. A NAT allows multiple computers to appear on the Internet with a single address. This means that people scanning the Internet for addresses cannot identify the computers on the network or capture any details of their location, IP addresses, etc.

Drawbacks to Using Firewalls

Some attacks that firewalls can't prevent or protect against are things like eavesdropping or interception of e-mail. Although firewalls may provide a single point of security and audit, they are also a single point of failure.

Firewalls are really a last line of defense, not a first line of defense. If an attacker breaches the firewall, he will have gained access to the system or network and may have an opportunity to steal data that is stored in that system or to create other havoc within the system.

Firewalls may keep the bad guys out, but what if the bad guys are already inside? Firewalls do nothing against dishonest or disgruntled employees.

Chapter 25

Background: OSI Network Model

The Open Systems Interconnection network model (OSI network model, also called the OSI seven-layer model) is a layered diagram designed to abstractly describe communications and computer network protocol. Although developed as part of the OSI initiative, it is mostly followed in the software industry and is defined by the International Organization for Standardization in ISO standard 7498-1. By the time the ISO Standard was written, TCP/IP had already been used for years.

The OSI network model has seven layers, each layer only using the layers underneath it in the model and only providing functionality to the layer above it. This layered approach, when implemented in hardware or software (or a mix), is called a *protocol stack*. This means that each layer performs services for the next.

One of the main functions of this OSI model is that it defines how each layer interacts with another through an interface. It also offers interoperability across various platforms by allowing all network elements to operate together, regardless of who they were built by.

The seven layers of the OSI network model are (Figure 25.1):

OSI Model			
	Data Unit	**Layer**	**Function**
Host Layers	Data	Application	Network process to application.
		Presentation	Data representation and encryption.
		Session	Internet communications.
	Segments	Transport	End-to-end connections and reliability.
Media Layers	Packets	Network	Path determinaiton and logirigel addreessing (IP).
	Data Link	Data Link	Physical addressing (MAC & LLC).
	Bits	Physical	Media, signal and binary transmission.

Figure 25.1   OSI model.

Application Layer (Layer 7)

This layer provides the user with a way to interact with the application and thus the network. The protocols operating on this layer include Telnet, File Transfer Protocol (FTP), Simple Mail Transfer Protocol (SMTP), and Hypertext Transfer Protocol (HTTP). It performs common application services for the application processes. Virtual file, virtual terminal, and job transfer are examples of services performed in this layer.

Presentation Layer (Layer 6)

This layer is responsible for delivering and formatting information to the Application Layer for further processing or display. This deals with issues like how strings are displayed, etc. Encryption is typically done at this layer, but it's not limited to it. Representing structure is standardized at this level, often using XML. Much of the time, no differentiation is made between this layer and the Application Layer.

Session Layer (Layer 5)

This layer is optional in a lot of protocols used today, but it is useful as a way to outline protocols that manage the combination and synchronization of data from two higher layers. These protocols are responsible for ensuring the correctness and synchronization of the data before it is transmitted.

Transport Layer (Layer 4)

From this layer up, data is assumed to be at the correct destination node. This layer is responsible for dividing the data that it transmits by assigning port numbers to the packets for this layer, which are called "segments." When data reaches a protocol at this layer, the segment is examined to determine the destination port for its data. Once the port is discovered, the wrapper information is stripped off and the data is passed up to the Session Layer.

These ports allow a way for more than one protocol to exist for OSI model layers 5–7. A lot of higher-level protocols that service applications, such as e-mail, instant messaging, chat, etc., operate on their own unique port in this layer.

Transport Layer protocols can perform a checksum on their payload data to help determine both validity and can request a resend if there appears to be a problem.

Network Layer (Layer 3)

This is the first layer that is purely software and deals only with software. This layer directs network traffic to a destination node when its physical address isn't known. This is done by utilizing something called "logical addressing." *Logical addresses* are software addresses assigned to a node at this layer of the OSI Model.

These software-assigned addresses can be made hierarchical, and this allows very large networks to be possible by using a concept of *routing* to take care of the collisions that occur when data is addressed to all nodes on a large network. This is accomplished by having a network router that handles the network signals from each node directly, instead of having nodes just keep repeating packets at the Physical Layer until they happen to reach their destination. The network router sits at the center of the nodes, and all nodes are connected to it instead of to each other. Thus on a routed network, packets from the Network Layer are no longer broadcast to all nodes but rather only to the router, which then forwards the packet to the appropriate node. Routers can be linked to other routers, either chained or connected to a single central router.

When a node begins a transmission, the information is passed down from higher layers to the Network Layer and is wrapped with the logical address of the destination node in a *packet*. Once this packet has been transmitted through the Data Link and Physical Layers and out onto the network to the router, the router compares the logical address in the packet to a list of the physical nodes connected directly to that router. If the router finds the address in its list, it sends the packet directly to the destination node. If the router does not find the address in its list, it forwards the packet onto another router to repeat the process.

Data Link Layer (Layer 2)

This is the first pure software layer in the OSI model, but it's also the only layer that specifically addresses both hardware and software. It's sometimes called the Physical Address Layer. This layer takes information from the layers above it, wraps it in the physical addressing information, and passes it down to the Physical Layer. The wrapping is called a *frame*.

When the computer at the other end receives this data, it is passed from that computer's Physical Layer to its Data Link Layer, and the Data Link Layer on that system checks the addressing information in the frame to see if the physical address (Media Access Control or MAC address) in the frame matches its own MAC address. If it doesn't match, the data is not intended for that computer, and the frame and data are discarded. If the MAC addresses match, the frame is stripped from the data, and the data is passed up to the next higher layer in the OSI Model on the recipient computer.

Although MAC addresses are often treated as if they are guaranteed to be unique, that's not actually true. Although each manufacturer is assigned prefix codes by the Internet Assigned Numbers Authority (IANA), the manufacturers may then only make cards within that assigned range of prefix numbers; however, some manufacturers occasionally recycle MACs while others allow MACs to be changed via software. So they aren't actually guaranteed to be unique.

Physical Layer (Layer 1)

This layer is the physical infrastructure of the network. It includes the actual wires — the cabling or other transmission medium — and the network interface hardware that is placed in the computers, as well as any other hardware that makes it possible for the computers to connect to the transmission hardware.

The purpose of this layer is to take the binary information sent to it by the Data Link Layer, translate it into whatever transmission method is suitable for the physical network, and send the data across the transmission medium. It also receives incoming data from the network and translates it back to binary before it sends it back to the Data Link Layer.

The Physical Layer does not examine the binary information, nor does it do any validation. It does participate in flow control and contention resolution.

Some of the hardware devices that operate at this level are Ethernet hubs, repeaters, modems, and wireless cards.

Chapter 26

Background: Proxy Servers

A *proxy server* is a computer that offers a network service to allow clients to make an indirect network connection to other network services. Client systems connect to the proxy server and then request a connection, file, or other resource that is available on another server. The proxy then obtains the requested resource on the behalf of the client system.

Types of Proxy Servers

Web Proxy

The most common type of proxy server is a Web proxy or a caching Web proxy. This provides a cache of Web pages and files that are available on remote servers to allow LAN clients to access them more quickly and reliably than if they had to be fetched every time.

When the Web proxy receives a request for a Web resource (by URL), it first checks its local cache to see if it already has the document. If it exists in the local cache, it returns the document from the cache immediately. If it does not have the document in its cache, it obtains the page from the server that it resides on, returns it to the requestor, and saves a copy in its local cache. Items kept in the cache are regularly expired out, based on a number of factors that include access history, age, etc.

Specialized Web Proxies

- Censoring — Some proxies are implemented to enforce standards of content access, often to block offensive content.
- Reformatting — Some proxies are implemented to provide translation or reformatting functionality between the original page format and something similar to a mobile browser format.
- Protection — Some proxies are implemented to help protect the users from malicious content that would normally be received by them from remote Web pages.
- CGI Proxies — CGI proxies are really Web sites that allow users to access another site through them. They tend to use PHP or CGI and are often used to gain access to Web sites that are blocked by the policies of the local network. Because they also hide the user's IP address from the Web sites that they access, they are also used to perform anonymous browsing or actions.

SSL Proxy

These are also called HTTPS proxies and are designed to be able to decrypt, apply policy, cache, and reencrypt SSL traffic. These are necessary because HTTP proxies are not able to cache encrypted traffic, so there was no benefit to be had for SSL applications using an HTTP proxy.

HTTPS proxies can monitor, control, and accelerate SSL traffic. They can also screen for malware and apply content filtering to inhibit phishing, spyware, and viruses that are hiding inside encrypted tunnels.

There are definite privacy concerns with having SSL proxies and the sensitive data the HTTPS proxy may be capturing or revealing.

There is also a form of proxy that is also called an SSL proxy but which really refers to a CGI Web proxy that is accessible via encrypted SSL connections. SSL adds another level of security on top of the CGI proxy system, lessening the chance of data interception.

Intercepting Proxy

These are proxies implemented to enforce acceptable network use policies or to provide security, anti-malware, or caching services. A traditional Web proxy is not transparent to the client application, which has to be configured to use the proxy, but an intercepting proxy doesn't require that configuration.

When client applications require special configuration, users may reset the client configurations to bypass the proxies if there are alternative means of connection to the Internet available. Enforcing the browser policies can be time consuming for network administrators.

An intercepting proxy, sometimes called a transparent proxy (though incorrectly so), combines a proxy server with a NAT. Connections made to NAT are intercepted and redirected to the proxy without having to change the client-side configuration — or even having to have the client know about the redirect. These are often used in businesses to avoid abuse of policy and not require individual administration.

ISPs also use them to reduce upstream traffic by providing a local shared cache to the ISP's customers.

The downside is that you cannot use user authentication. This is because the browser doesn't know there is a proxy in the middle, so it can't send any authentication headers.

Open Proxy

An open proxy is one that will accept client connections from any IP address and make connections to any Internet resource. Abuse of open proxies is implicated in a significant portion of e-mail spam delivery.

Spammers will often install open proxies on systems they have compromised by means of viruses. Internet relay chat (IRC) abusers also frequently use open proxies to cloak their identities.

Reverse Proxy

This is a proxy that is installed in the neighborhood of one or more Web servers. All traffic that comes from the Internet to one of these Web servers has to go through the reverse proxy server. These are installed for the purposes of:

- Security: They can serve as an extra level of defense and protect the Web servers further up the chain.
- Encryption/SSL acceleration: When secure Web sites are created, the SSL encryption is often not done by the Web server itself but by a reverse proxy that is equipped with SSL acceleration hardware.
- Load balancing: The reverse-proxy server can redistribute the load to several Web servers. In such a case, the reverse proxy may need to rewrite the URLs in each Web page (to translate from the externally known URLs to their internal locations).
- Serve/cache static content: A reverse-proxy server can reduce load on the Web servers by caching static content like pictures or other static graphical content.

- Compression: The proxy server can optimize and compress the content to speed up the load time.
- Slow connection compensation: If a program is producing the Web page on the Web servers, the Web servers can produce it, serve it to the reverse proxy, which can then slowly send it to the clients, however slowly they need it. The Web servers can close the program after the Web page is served to the proxy server, rather than having to keep it open to accommodate the slow clients.

Split Proxy

A split proxy is a pair of proxies that are installed across two computers, usually not in close physical proximity. This split install lets the two proxies communicate with each other extremely efficiently, and this is ideal for compressing data over a slow link such as wireless or mobile data connections. It also helps reduce issues associated with high latency (such as with satellite Internet) where establishing a TCP connection is time consuming.

Take the example of Web browsing: The user's browser is pointed to a local proxy, which then communicates with its other half at some remote location. The remote server fetches the data, repackages it, and sends it back to the user's local proxy, which then unpacks the data and presents it to the browser in the standard fashion.

Circumventor

A circumventor is a Web-based page that takes a site that is blocked and circumvents the block through to an unblocked Web site so the user can view the blocked Web page. A famous example is "elgoog" that allowed users in China to use Google after it had been blocked there. Elgoog differs from most circumventors in that it circumvents only one block.

The most common use of these is in schools where many blocking programs block by site rather than by code. Students can access blocked sites (messenger, games, chat rooms, porn, etc.) through a circumventor. As fast as the filtering software blocks circumventors, others spring up. Circumventors are also used by people who have been blocked from a Web site.

The use of circumventors is usually fairly safe except that the circumventor sites run by an untrusted third party can have hidden intentions and risks, such as collecting personal information. As a result, users are typically advised against running personal data such as credit card numbers or passwords through a circumventor.

Anonymous

When a proxy server is used, all data sent to the service being used must pass through the proxy server before being sent to the service, mostly in unencrypted form. It is possible (and has been seen) that a malicious proxy server can record everything sent to it, including unencrypted logins and passwords.

By chaining proxies that do not reveal data about the original requestor, it is possible to obfuscate activities from the eyes of the user's destination. But more traces will be left on the intermediate hops, which could be used or offered up to trace the user's activities. If the policies and administrator of these other proxies are unknown, the user may fall victim to a false sense of security just because those details are out of sight and therefore out of mind.

Be careful when using proxy servers. Only use proxies of known integrity (the owner is known and trusted, has a clear privacy policy, etc.), and never use questionable proxies. If there is no choice but to use unknown proxy servers, do not pass any private information (unless it is properly encrypted) through the proxy.

More an inconvenience than a risk, proxy users may find themselves being blocked from certain Web sites as numerous forums and Web sites block IP addresses from proxies known to have spammed or trolled the site.

Chapter 27

Background: TCP/IP and Other Networking Protocols

Together TCP and IP are referred to as the *internet protocols*, but TCP stands for Transmission Control Protocol and IP stands for Internet Protocol.

At the very basic level, a TCP/IP packet is merely a package of data that has source and destination addresses, and data contained inside.

TCP

TCP is a Connection-Oriented Protocol that operates at the transport layer of the Open System Interconnection (OSI) Model. It attempts to guarantee delivery of packets by generating and comparing a sequence of numbers to see what data has been sent and received. In cases where data loss occurs, a resend can be requested. It can sense network delay patterns and can throttle data to dynamically prevent bottlenecks. TCP also uses a set of flags to manage the connection.

TCP delivers data as a series of packets that are individually numbered with a sequence number and passes them to IP for delivery, where the sequence numbers allow the packets to be reassembled at their destination. TCP also allows packets whose sequence numbers are not acknowledged to be retransmitted. It offers efficient flow control and is what is called *full duplex*, which means that sending and receiving can be done at the same time.

A sample TCP packet is shown in Figure 27.1.

TCP Packet Fields

- Source port and destination port.
- Sequence number — A unique number assigned to the first byte in the segment.
- Acknowledgement number — The sequence number of the next byte of data expected on the receiving end.
- Data offset — The number of 32-bit words in the TCP header.
- Reserved — For future use.
- Flags — These control markers such as SYN, ACK, and FIN bits that are used for beginning and ending connections.
- Window — The size of the receiving buffer (window) for incoming data.
- Checksum — Used to verify the integrity of incoming data.
- Urgent Pointer — This marks the start of urgent data.
- Options — Numerous options are available.
- Data — This is the data payload.

TCP Flags

These are the most common flags used in the TCP Packet's "Flags" field, and their basic meaning is as follows:

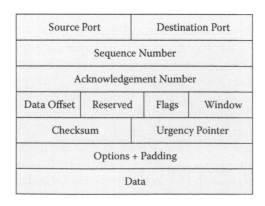

Figure 27.1 TCP Packet.

Table 27.1   Common TCP Application Port Numbers

Port Number	Application
20	FTP (File Transfer Protocol) nonpassive transfers
21	FTP (File Transfer Protocol) control stream
22	SSH (Secure Shell Protocol)
23	Telnet
25	SMTP (Simple Mail Transfer Protocol)
53	DNS (Domain Name Server Protocol)
80	HTTP (Hypertext Transfer Protocol)
110	POP3 (Post Office Protocol v.3)
137	NetBIOS (Windows Networking) Name Service
138	NetBIOS (Windows Networking) Datagram
139	NetBIOS (Windows Networking) Session Protocol
143	IMAP (Internet Message Access Protocol)
443	HTTPS/SSL (Secure HTTP over Secure Sockets Layer)

- ACK — Acknowledgment of last packet. All packets in a session other than the first have this.
- FIN — Closes a connection.
- PSH — Send immediately, even if the buffer isn't full.
- RST — Resets connection (error occurred).
- SYN — Starts a connection.
- URG — This packet has important data.

Common TCP Application Port Numbers

Table 27.1 shows a small sampling of the port numbers used by the most common TCP applications.

IP

IP is a protocol that takes place at the network layer of the OSI Model. It is a connectionless protocol and is used to carry data, but because it has no mechanism to assure data delivery, it is used along with a protocol that sits on the transport layer such as TCP.

IP headers contain a 32-bit address that identify the sending and receiving hosts, and routers use these addresses to select the appropriate path for the packet. Because of the possibility of IP spoofing, the validity of the source address should always be questioned, and another method of authentication should be used to at least corroborate the IP header information.

Version	IP Header Length	Type of Service		Total Length	
Identification				Flags	Fragmentation Offset
Time To Live			Protocol	Header Checksum	
Source Address					
Destination Address					
Options					
Data					

Figure 27.2   IPv4 Packet.

Version	Traffic Class		Flow Label	
Identification		Next Header		Hop Limit
Source Address				
Destination Address				
Data				

Figure 27.3   IPv6 Packet.

If a network can only handle smaller packets, IP packets can be split according to the MTU (maximum transmission unit), and the IP packets reassembled at the receiving end.

The IP version currently in use is IPv4, but IPv6 was introduced in 1996 and is the standard for new development as IPv4 is being phased out. The adoption of IPv6 has been slow. A sample of IPv4 packet is shown in Figure 27.2, while a sample IPv6 packet is shown in Figure 27.3.

IPv4

Packet Fields

- Version — The version of IP in use (4 bits).
- IP header length — The IP header length is 32-bit words. The maximum IPv4 header length is 60 bytes.

- Type of service — Level of importance and processing instructions intended for the upper OSI model layers of the recipient.
- Total length — The length of the IP datagram (IP header + payload) in bytes.
- Identification — A unique identification number that allows the data to be put in order at the destination (16 bits).
- Flags — The fragmentation flags specify whether a packet can be fragmented or not, and if so, whether this packet is the last fragment of a packet sequence. Only two bits of three 3-bit fields are defined, but if bit 1 is set, the PMTU (path maximum transmission size) is calculated to ensure all packets sent along the route are small enough to avoid fragmentation. The bits are:
  - Bit 1 = Do not fragment
  - Bit 2 = Last fragment of the datagram
- Fragmentation offset — Order of this particular fragment in the packet sequence.
- Time-to-live counter — This is designed to keep packets from looping endlessly. Once this is set, each time the packet is forwarded by a router along the route, the counter is decremented, and at the point it reaches one, the next router will drop the packet. This prevents the problem of infinite packet looping of undeliverable packets.
- Protocol — This field defines the protocol that will receive the packet from IP.
- Header checksum — This field checks for IP header integrity but it's not a cryptographic checksum and is easily forged.
- Source address — The sender's address (32 bits).
- Destination address — The recipient's address (32 bits).
- Options — Various options are available.
- Data — The data payload.

Addresses

Logical addresses appear as four sets of numbers that can be up to three digits long and are separated by periods. IP addresses have an order, i.e., from left to right. These numbers have a minimum value of 0 and a maximum value of 255, and leading zeros are not used.

The first section refers to a router, which is either the top level router in the network or the top level router in this section of the network. All addresses beginning with the same number are managed by the same router (i.e., addresses XXXX.0.0.1 through XXXX.255.255.255 are all managed by the same router). If you have a routed network, you must have a minimum of one router, but more routers may exist on a larger network.

Fragmentation Variables

These are the fragmentation variables used in IP packets to give information about the fragmentation.

- Fragment ID — Same as the unique IP identification of the parent packet.
- Fragment offset — The sequence of each fragment in the original packet. This is used to reassemble the fragments on the receiving end.
- Fragment length — The total length of this fragment.
- More fragmentation flag — Value of 1 means there are more fragments of this packet to follow; 0 means this is the final fragment in the packet.

IPv6

Packet Fields

- Version — A 4-bit field describing the version of IP in use
- Traffic class — Similar to the IPv4 type of service field
- Flow label — A 20-bit experimental field to signal special processing in routers
- Payload length — A 16-bit field indicating the length of the data payload
- Next header — Similar to the IPv4 Protocol field but also includes the IPv4 options field, as well
- Hop limit — An 8-bit field similar to the IPv4 time-to-live field
- Source and destination address — A 128-bit fields that represent the source and destination addresses in IPv6 format
- Data — Includes the payload

Addresses

Iv6 addressing is designed to allow many more addresses than the addressing scheme of IPv4 by using hexadecimal numbers separated by colons. An IPv6 address may look like this:

1844:3FFE:300:1:4389:EEDF:45AB:1029

IPv6 is still being developed and has some remaining privacy concerns focused around certain items such as the address space in some cases using a unique ID that is derived from hardware information and can be traced back to a single machine.

UDP

UDP stands for User Datagram Protocol and is faster than TCP, but less reliable. It is often used when zero percent packet loss is not an important factor. Because there is no handshake or sequence tracking, it's a lot easier to spoof UDP packets than TCP. This is often used in online games.

ICMP

ICMP stands for Internet Control Message Protocol. It's basically a protocol designed for testing and debugging and which runs on top of a Network Protocol. It serves as a way to get information from a router or network dynamically. Ping uses ICMP. Routers use ICMP to determine if a remote host is reachable. If there is no path to a remote host, an ICMP packet is generated to say so. It's also used to determine the PMTU, and if a router needs a smaller packet but the "no fragmentation" flag is set, it can use ICMP to request smaller size packets from the host.

To prevent some of the vulnerabilities of ICMP from being exploited, sometimes a decision is made to simply turn off all ICMP, but this has an unfortunate side effect of allowing packets to be dropped without notice. Most firewalls allow for selective dropping of ICMP messages as a better way to limit abuse of items like Ping.

There is the possibility of ICMP Source Quench messages being generated when a router is bottlenecked and has to buffer too many packets. This message tells the host to slow down the rate of transmission. This isn't often used though.

Traceroute is another tool that uses ICMP to map networks by sending out packets with small TTL values and then watching for the ICMP timeout messages.

ARP

ARP stands for Address Resolution Protocol, and it enables hosts to convert a 32-bit IP address to a 48-bit Ethernet address (the MAC address). ARP broadcasts an ARP packet to all hosts attached to an Ethernet network that contains the desired destination IP address. Ideally all hosts without the matching IP address ignore the packet, and only the one with the correct matching IP address returns an answer. If the packet is destined for a machine outside the local LAN, an ARP request, which has to be specified in advance, would be sent to the local gateway.

ARP is vulnerable to a spoofing attack (ARP spoofing) that occurs when compromised nodes have access to the LAN. The compromised machines can send phony ARP replies in order to mimic a trusted machine.

This protocol takes place at level 3 of the OSI Network Model.

RARP

This is Reverse ARP, and it allows a host to discover its IP address by broadcasting its physical address, and the RARP server responds with an IP address.

BOOTP

This is the Bootstrap Protocol, and it allows diskless network clients to learn their IP addresses and the location of their boot files. BOOTP is done at the application layer of the OSI model via UDP.

DHCP

DHCP stands for Dynamic Host Configuration Protocol. It's an extension of BOOTP, and provides a method to dynamically assign IP addresses and configurations parameters to other IP hosts or clients in an IP network. It allows a host to automatically allocate reusable IP addresses and additional configuration parameters for client operations. DHCP allows clients to obtain an IP address from the pool of reusable IP addresses for a fixed length of time called a *lease period*. When the lease expires, the DHCP server can either assign that same IP address to a different computer in the network, or the host that had that IP prior to the lease expiration can renew the lease for another period.

Chapter 28

Background: Test Case Outlining (TCO)

Early in my career as a software tester, I was introduced to a method of creating and distilling a product into something called a test case outline (TCO). Although this book is not focused on test case or test plan design, I am including the basics of this technique as it has been very useful to me in making sure I question my assumptions and trusts while performing security testing.

Test Case Outlining is an extremely effective and yet deceptively simple technique for the design of test cases. Once the basics are learned, the process becomes a great addition to any tester's arsenal and can simplify not just the writing and maintenance of test cases, but also the review of those test cases with others, especially nontesters.

Over the years I have been using this technique in my daily work. I have made my own modifications to the purer form I was originally taught so that it better served my needs and the needs of my projects.

Goals

Test planning itself is an often arduous task that seeks to achieve the following goals:

- Improve overall test coverage

- Avoid unnecessary duplication and repetition
- Provide a structure to test passes
- Improve the efficiency of test
- Provide an ability to report test suites
- Provide scheduling information for resource and project planning

Accompanying these goals is a somewhat daunting set of challenges to be met, including:

- Effective test plan organization
- Test plan maintenance and updating
- Running tests from the test plan
- Broad reviewing of the test plan
- Spotting redundancies and omissions
- Ascertaining the current state of testing
- Extraction of scheduling information

TCOs, if used consistently and routinely, are an effective way of meeting both the goals and challenges of test planning.

What Is (and Is Not) a TCO

A TCO, in its purest form, consists of an organized and comprehensive set of atomic statements of behavior (also called predictive statements of behavior) for testing. It can also be said to be an organized and comprehensive set of test cases.

A TCO is not any specific tool or software application and is not a mandated set of rules on how to structure test cases. In many cases, the structure of your TCO depends greatly on just what is being tested and how — a TCO for testing an API will differ from the one for stress testing. Even a TCO for functional testing of an API will differ from the one for security testing of the same API. The needs of the testing dictate the structure of the TCO. Forcing a particular structure on disparate test needs tends to result in a loss of most of the benefits of creating a TCO in the first place.

Benefits of a TCO

Using the TCO process has multiple compelling benefits to an entire product team, not merely to the testers. A few of these benefits are:

- If the TCO process begins as soon as there are draft specifications and requirements to work from, the process of writing the TCO itself will often bring to light issues in both design and development that otherwise may be discovered much later in the process or may not be discovered until the product is released and the defect is reported by a user.
- The TCO process encourages and facilitates the review of the test cases by more than just the test team. Development and program management are often able to correct errors, assumptions, or add valuable feedback on missed areas or duplicate code paths that would otherwise not be known.
- Having a well-written TCO makes turning over test responsibilities to another tester or even another group much less painful. The cases are clear, they are well organized, and they are very binary in nature, which leaves little room for misinterpretation or assumptions that the new person may not have. In fact, one group I was in had a set of people responsible for writing the TCOs and a different set of people responsible for executing the tests from the TCOs.
- TCOs also make the popular option of outsourcing basic testing much easier because of the very binary nature and very clear statements of behavior.
- A good TCO makes the maintenance tasks much easier. The very atomic and binary nature means the case stands on its own, and if a change is made in the product, finding the test cases that need modification is easy.
- TCOs often serve as great additions to specifications when new members join the team or if there are questions from Product Support. They are more detailed than the specs and clearly define expected behaviors.

Steps in Test Case Outlining

Research the Item to Be Tested

Start by really getting to know the item or area you are testing and its environment, customers, and dependencies.

- Read any specifications you may have, including those from prior releases.
- Talk to program managers and developers, if possible. Most of them are very willing to discuss their area and give you a tour of

it in the interests of furthering the test's efforts to create a comprehensive test case design.

■ Explore the item/product itself, including current releases and any mockups that are available.

■ If there are any standards your item is supposed to comply with, get a copy of those standards for reference.

■ Look at any bug histories for your item to give you additional ideas of test cases and failure scenarios.

Determine Starting TCO Format

Before you actually start drafting the initial outline, you should decide what format or tool that you are going to use to write your TCO in. Because a TCO is not tool dependent, you can use just about anything you are comfortable with and which will allow extensive revision and updation without requiring you to rewrite the TCO in its entirety.

As a personal preference, even if I will later translate the TCO into one of the test case management tools, I use Word's outline format. I find that this gives me the best ability to have multiple levels of depth, a good ability to cut and paste, and I have almost complete freedom for revision. It's also one of the easiest to produce readable and reviewable TCO documents from, which makes reviews much less painful.

Draft an Initial Outline

Now is where you start to break your product or area down to component parts. Sit down and make a list of major areas or components that you can organize testing around.

This is where the TCO process is driven by the needs of the product. Some examples are:

■ Functionality
■ Physical areas
■ Web pages
■ Server states
■ API methods

Here are a couple of very simple examples:

■ Toaster
  ■ Doneness dial
  ■ Start lever

- Toast slots
- Heat coils
- Power cord
- Outside casing
- Notepad
  - Menu
  - Document pane
  - Window appearance

At this point, you are simply trying to define the big buckets around which to organize the TCO itself.

Refine and Drill Down

Now you start taking each of your major areas and determining if there are discrete subareas that can be called out. Then, for each of those subareas, you continue this process until there are no other discernable subareas. It is helpful to look back at the specs and information you gathered during the research phase regularly while you carry out this step — both to avoid missing areas and to see if there are areas you see that are not in the specs and must be inquired about.

Remember that the goal at this point is to break the product down into smaller and smaller pieces until you get down to the actual testable behavior.

There is no perfect way to start a TCO. You will sometimes end up unhappy with the format you chase partway through and will rewrite it in a better format. Sometimes you will end up with a TCO that is so large that you will have to split it into separate documents to be able to review and maintain adequately.

Here are some of the refined versions of portions of the initial outlines from earlier examples.

- Toaster
  - Doneness dial
    - On
      - Set at 1
      - Set at 2
    - Off
  - Start lever
    - Up
    - Down
  - Toast slots
    - Left

- Right
- Both

- Notepad
  - Menu
    - File
      - New
      - Click
      - Shortcut (Ctrl + N)
      - Open
      - Save
    - Edit
    - Format
    - View
    - Help
      - Document pane
      - Window appearance

Here is a totally different TCO format for Notepad:

- Notepad
  - Files
    - Opening
      - Formats
      - Sizes
      - Storage media
      - Storage location
    - Saving
      - Save
      - Save as
  - Documents
    - Creating
    - Editing
    - Printing

Write Atomic/Predictive Statements of Behavior

"Atomic" or "predictive" statements of behavior are statements that say "When I do this, this happens" at the lowest possible level for your testing. This type of statement is a very binary statement, and if the actual behavior is identical to the statement, the case will be considered a pass, otherwise it fails. This is one of the fundamental reasons why TCOs have so many benefits.

Examples of these statements of behavior are:

■ When "xyz" is typed in field A and "Submit" is clicked, a new document file is created with the name "XYZ.doc" in the default directory.

■ When I insert a slice of wheat bread in the left slot of the toaster and set the doneness dial to maximum, then press down on the toast lever until it clicks, the bread is toasted for "x" s.

If you have a statement where you do not know the expected behavior, this should be clearly marked and followed up to obtain the expected behavior. If this was missing or unclear from the specification, the specification should be updated. If the developers need to provide the answer, follow up needs to be done with them. This clarification is another valuable benefit of writing TCOs.

Several important things to remember about these statements of behavior are:

■ You will often have several statements for a single action. The first of the two examples earlier may have several more statements that indicate any other actions that occur when Submit is clicked. These may verify things like the file date, the file icon, if a new document is opened at the same time the file is created, etc.

■ The predictive statements of behavior should be binary — there is only a yes or no answer — no gray area. The case either passes or fails. That's why each statement only tests one item, even if the behavior preceding the "x happens" really causes more than one event to occur. The granularity is built in, and the ambiguity level is far less.

■ If, however, you have multiple statements that are related, you can combine these into one scenario when the test pass is underway, as long as each statement is verified individually for a true/false or pass/fail result.

Use Equivalency Classes if Possible

This is the area where I really deviate from the original TCO theory as I was taught it. I now tend to use equivalency classes for my TCOs whenever possible. These are used if the input and expected results for individual test cases are equivalent.

Examples of common equivalency classes are:

- Data types
- Permission levels
- Document types
- Protocol types

For example, for text input fields I may decide that all alpha strings are equivalent and instead of calling out the exact string to input, I will use something like this:

- When Random Uppercase Alpha string (from Table 28.1) is typed in field A and "Submit" is clicked, a new document file is created in the default directory with name <Random Uppercase Alpha string>.doc.

Note that the input is different but equivalent, but the expected result is equivalent as well. In this case, I would have a separate statement of behavior that handled failure cases such as a 0 char string or a 256+ char string.

Exceptions in equivalency classes can be called out specifically or made separate equivalency classes of their own. So the above list may coexist in a TCO with a case that takes into account reserved words so certain letter combinations are disallowed. In this case, I would call out each specifically disallowed combination as a member of an equivalency class because the result should be the same. Then write statements of behavior around that equivalency class. Note that this is a greatly simplified example, as are all examples in this section.

This process does serve to compact a TCO without sacrificing much in the way of readability and usability. It has often been useful in pointing out more clearly to developers where there is a disparity between what the expected equivalencies are and what was actually coded.

This has also increased automateability of TCOs in the past for me because a single case can be easily shown to have variations of it with

Table 28.1   Random Uppercase Alpha

String Type	Length
Random Uppercase Alpha	1 char
Random Uppercase Alpha	255 chars
Random Uppercase Alpha	256 chars

the same expected outcome, and the job of whomever has to write the automation is simplified by having the variations all in one place.

Some other simple examples are:

- Toaster
    - Types of bread
    - Wall outlets
    - Doneness settings
    - Countertop surfaces
    - Toaster positions/orientation
    - Nonbread items
- Notepad
    - Types of files
    - General data sets
        - Alpha
        - Alphanumeric
        - Unicode
        - Extended characters
    - Fonts
    - Navigation methods

Look carefully at the pros and cons of using equivalency classes before you decide whether to use them or not.

Review, Review, Review

The rule of thumb I was taught originally and which I still advocate to this day is that you should spend no more than about 2 h working on your TCO without getting it peer-reviewed. Sometimes you will find yourself staring down a path that is unnecessarily complex or doesn't make sense and is not consistent; frequent reviews can help prevent a painful rewrite later.

I make it a practice to have my TCO reviewed in draft form by the development and program management as often as possible. The vastly different viewpoints and information that these two groups offer, in addition to reviews by test, have proved time and time again to be invaluable.

Reviewing a TCO should take about 30 min for the average-size TCO. If you find you have an exceptionally large TCO, try to break it into no more than 60-min segments to obtain the maximum benefit from the review time.

Some things to look for in a TCO review are:

- The organization and structure must be easy to understand.
- No missing equivalency classes or product areas.
- No missing product functionality.
- No unnecessary redundancy.
- No areas of fuzziness or unclear test cases.

TCO Formats

As I mentioned, TCOs can be written and stored in just about any format, but the real key is to let the TCO dictate the format instead of attempting to cram the TCO into a format unsuited for it.

It is important to keep only one copy of a TCO for a given area and release. If you have multiple copies of a TCO with different revisions, etc., it will be an endless source of confusion. I highly recommend keeping the TCO where it is viewable by anyone who wishes to review it, but limit the number of people who can modify it.

Some formats are:

> Word processor documents: Outline formats work particularly well. Spreadsheet documents: Large matrices often work well when entered into a spreadsheet program.
>
> Databases: This has the advantage of historical tracking but a good schema and interface are essential for it not to be really frustrating to write, maintain, and publish for reviews.
>
> Paper (hard copy): This option has a huge number of issues with upkeep but can sometimes be useful or required for reporting to management.
>
> Test case management tools: If you are using a commercial or in-house test case management tool, these need good organization. They share the issues of maintenance and publication for reviewing that databases have.
>
> CAD documents: This option works particularly well for server-state-based TCOs but requires a lot of fiddling to get it right, so be prepared.

TCO Maintenance

The more up-to-date a TCO is, the more accurate all the information derived from it will be — including the ability to hand it off to another tester or even to request temporary help with a section during "crunch mode."

TCOs should be kept updated constantly with information on:

- Test runs
- New cases
- Product changes

TCO to Scenario

To make running cases from a TCO easier, I mentioned that you can string together individual test cases in a logical order to create test scenarios. In this type of situation, each statement of behavior from the TCO becomes a validation point in the scenario.

An example of this would be the following set of predictive statements:

- Enter "xyz" in field A, and click "Submit." A new file named "xyz.doc" is created in the default directory.
- Enter "xyz" in field A, and click "Submit." A new file window is opened with the title of "xyz.doc."
- Enter "xyz" in Field A, and click "Submit." A new file window is opened with the default template font.

These could be combined into a scenario where the tester enters "xyz" in field A, clicks submit and then verifies the file is created. The file window is opened with the title of "xyz.doc" and the default template font.

The three cases remain three separate statements of behavior and are said to pass/fail individually, but the tester isn't running through the same steps three separate times. It is simply a matter of expedience.

Additional Sources of Information

Recommended Reading

Alberts, C. and Dorofee, A. *Managing Information Security Risks*. Addison-Wesley, Boston, MA, 2002.

Chase, S.G. and Thompson, H.H. *The Software Vulnerability Guide*. Charles River Media, Hingham, MA, 2005.

Erickson, J. *Hacking: The Art of Exploitation*. No Starch Press, San Francisco, CA, 2003.

Fadia, A. *The Unofficial Guide to Ethical Hacking*, 2nd ed. Thomson Course Technology, Boston, MA, 2006.

Gallagher, T., Jeffries, B., and Landauer, L. *Hunting Security Bugs*, Microsoft Press, Redmond, WA, 2006.

McGraw, G. *Software Security: Building Security In*. Pearson Education, Boston, MA, 2006.

Swiderski, F. and Snyder, W. *Threat Modeling*. Microsoft Press, Redmond, WA, 2004.

Recommended Web Sites and Mailing Lists

www.cert.org — CERT Coordination Center.

https://www.securecoding.cert.org/confluence/display/seccode/CERT+Secure+ Coding+Standards — CERT Secure Coding Standards Web page.

http://insecure.org/ — Insecure.org.

http://www.securityfocus.com/ — Security Focus Web site.

Index

\# character, in SQL injection, 228–229
500 Error Page, 228
302 Page Redirect, 228
419 scams, 48

A

Access control list (ACL), 8
Access control rules, inconsistent
    enforcement of, 135
Access path, control aspects, 101–102
Accidental discovery, 33–34
Active attacks, 45–46
Amplification attacks, 185
Anonymous proxy servers, 265
ANSI C functions, format string attack
    vulnerabilities in, 194
Antirepudiation validation, 144
APIs
    application process related
        considerations, 140
    input security considerations, 140
    language considerations, 141
    operational environment considerations,
        141
    security considerations, 140
    specialized considerations, 141
Application layer, in OSI Network Model,
    256
Application-level proxy firewalls, 252
Application modeling, 83–84

Application port numbers, in TCP, 269
Application processes
    API security considerations, 140
    considerations for stand alone
        applications, 138
    Web application security considerations,
        142
Application self-defense, 63
Arithmetic operations, integer
    overflows/underflows in, 206
ARP, 273–274
Asset-based threat profiles, 104
Asset list, 80
Assets
    defined, 75
    documenting in threat modeling, 79–80
Asymmetric encryption, 244–245
Atomic/predictive statements, in test case
    outlining (TCO), 280–281
Attack hypotheses, 84–85
Attack motivation, 112, 113
Attack naming, 7
Attack path, 75, 96
Attacker aspect matrix, 112
Attacker descriptions, for security personas,
    113
Attacker tools, 35–36
Attackers
    assumptions about, 35–37
    behavioral aspects, 100–101
    common targets of, 38–39
    defined, 8

identity of, 39
knowledge about, 35–38
motives, 39
technical aspects, 102–103
Attacks
defined, 8
sparse code needs for, 61
Authentication
encryption for, 242
inconsistent access control rule
    enforcement for, 135
security considerations, 134

B

Back Door, defined, 8
Back-end assumptions, 51
Backward compatibility, for stand-alone
    applications, 139
Basic script test, 180–181
Black-box testing
for buffer overruns, 161–162
for cookie tampering, 170–172
for cross-site scripting, 180–181
for format string vulnerabilities, 198
for integer overflows/underflows, 205
and sparse coding in attacks, 61
for SQL injection, 229
vs. white-box testing, 61–65
Blind spoofing, 222
Boot sector viruses, 42
BOOTP, 274
Boundary tests, 31
Brute force attacks, 213–214
exploit anatomy, 215
Brute force browsing
background description, 147–148
exploit anatomy, 149–150
non-URL type, 149
pseudonym, 147
real-world examples, 150
session replay attack, 148–149
test techniques, 150–151
URL guessing, 148
vulnerability case study, 147
Buffer overruns
attack modeling, 160–161
background description, 153–154
black-box testing for, 161–162
crash watches, 161

documenting entry points for, 160
exploit anatomy, 157–158
heap buffer overruns, 155–157
passing attack data to entry points, 161
pseudonyms for, 153
real-world examples, 158–160
sample buffer contents before and after,
    154
stack buffer overruns, 153, 154–155
test techniques, 160–162
vulnerability case study, 153
white-box testing for, 162
Bug fix bar, setting for fuzz testing, 235
Bug fixes
issues to consider, 68
prioritizing, 70
Bug reports, accuracy of, 69
Bugs, 17
reviewing existing, 120–122
Bugzilla DOM-based XSS, 177
By design test methods, 127

C

C datatype ranges, 202
Cache static content, and reverse proxies,
    263
Cached information, failure to safeguard,
    139
California State University-Northridge, xxiii
Case studies, fuzz testing, 238–239
Casts, integer overflows/underflows in, 206
Censoring proxies, 262
CERT Incident Report IN-99-02, 7
CGI proxies, 262
Char equivalents, in SQL injection, 229
Chat DoS attack, 189
Checksum value, and spoofing attacks, 222
Child nodes, 96
in threat trees, 94
Circular references, in DoS attacks, 190
Circumventor, 264
Client considerations, for Web and
    distributed applications,
    143–144
Client hijacking, 144
Code complexity, 32
Code coverage, 32–33
Code insertion, 173
Code maturity, 31–32

Commercial tools
  for test development, 127
  time to learn, 129
Communications
  presenting security issues effectively,
    67–72
  in SDC, 57
Company reputation, as data asset, 79
Compression, and reverse proxies, 264
Computer use, increase in U.S., 14
Computers, increased number of, 14
Condition, defined, 75
Confidentiality, encryption and, 242
Connection hijacking, 217
Consumers, *vs.* customers, 28–29
Conversions, integer overflows/underflows
    in, 206
Cookie inaccuracies, 167
Cookie misuse, 172
Cookie poisoning, 165, 167
  exploit anatomy, 169
Cookie tampering
  analyzing predictability of, 170
  background description, 165–166
  cookie inaccuracies, 167
  cookie poisoning, 167
  cookie risks, 166–168
  cookie theft, 166–167
  cross-site cooking, 167–168
  pseudonyms for, 165
  real-world examples, 169–170
  test techniques, 170–172
  vulnerability case study, 165
Cookie theft, 165, 166–167
  exploit anatomy, 168–169
  real-world examples, 169
Cookies, modifying, 171
Cracker, defined, 8
Cracking, defined, 8
Crash dump files/reports, access to, 137
Cross-site cooking, 165, 167–168
  exploit anatomy, 169
  real-world examples, 170
Cross-site scripting
  background description, 173–174
  Bugzilla DOM-based XSS, 177
  DOM-based or local, 175–176
  exploit anatomy, 176–177
  Microsoft Passport example, 178
  MySpace XSS worm example, 179
  nonpersistent/reflected, 174–175

PayPal XSS, 177–178
persistent/stored, 175
pseudonyms for, 173
real-world examples, 177–179
test techniques, 179–182
vulnerability case study, 173
Cryptography, 241
  asymmetric encryption, 244–245
  and cryptanalysis, 247
  encryption tools, 245–246
  future of, 248
  GPG, 246
  hash ciphers, 245
  key-based algorithms, 244–245
  key length issues, 246
  mechanisms of, 243–245
  obscurity issues, 247
  PGP, 245
  programmer error issues, 247
  purposes of encryption, 241–242
  S/KEY, 246
  security issues, 246–247
  single-key ciphers, 244
  SSH and SCP, 246
  SSL, 246
  universal security considerations, 136
  user error issues, 247
Custom packet formats, 142
Custom tools
  for test development, 127
  time to develop/learn, 129
Customer loyalty, loss of, 19
Customers, *vs.* consumers, 28–29
Cyber-terrorism, 39
Cyber-vandalism, 18

D

Daemon, defined, 8
Damage potential, 97
Data assets
  copies of data as, 88
  copies of production data outside
    production, 90
  database backups, 89
  employee or contractor access to, 1
  failover data, 90
  log files, 89
  physical disks or devices, 91–92
  temporary files, 89

Data consistency, 79
Data encoding, before action, 143
Data flow diagram, 83, 84
Data link layer, in OSI Network Model, 258
Data theft, 18, 39
Data transfer, security considerations for
        Web applications, 143
Database backups, as data assets, 89
Debug code, security considerations, 137
Dedicated software test teams, evolution of,
        12
Default accounts
    running API processes at, 140
    for Web and distributed applications,
        142
Default installations
    hard-coded install locations for, 134
    low permission levels to run, 134
    risky abilities enabled by default, 134
    security considerations, 133
    too many features enabled, 134
Default password cracking, 212
    exploit anatomy, 214
    real-world examples, 215
Defense in depth, 92
Denial of Service (DoS)
    amplification attacks, 185
    background description, 183–186
    Chat DoS attack, 189
    defined, 8
    distributed attacks, 186
    exploit anatomy, 186–187
    Gibson Research Corporation DDoS
        attack, 188–189
    ping flooding, 184
    ping of death, 184
    pseudonyms for, 183
    real-world examples, 187–189
    smurf attacks, 185
    spoofing attacks, 222–223
    in STRIDE model, 99
    SYN flooding attacks, 185–186
    teardrop attacks, 184
    test techniques, 189–190
    vulnerability case study, 183
    WorldPay DDoS attack, 187
Dependencies, segmenting as security area,
        118–119
Dependency changes, failure to track, 88
Design phase
    in SDC, 58–59

in SDLC, 53–54
Destination IP, and spoofing attacks, 222
Developer security focus, limitations of,
        50–51
Developers
    role in test prioritization, 126
    security testing needs, 65–66
DHCP, 274
Dictionary-based attacks, 213
    exploit anatomy, 214
Discoverability, 98
Disgruntled employees, 39
    data access by, 91
Distributed applications. *See also* Web
        applications
    security considerations, 142
Distributed Denial of Service (DDoS), 8,
        186. *See also* Denial of Service
        (DoS)
    vulnerability case study, 183
Documentation, comparing in black-box
        testing for cookie tampering,
        171
DOM-based cross-site scripting, 175–176
exploit anatomy, 177
Double dashes, in SQL injection, 228
Downstream dependents, interaction with,
        87
DREAD, 96–97
    affected users and, 97–98
    and damage potential, 97
    and discoverability, 98
    and exploitability, 97
    and reproducibility, 97
Dumb fuzz testing, 236

E

E-mail use, 15
Eavesdropping attacks, 207
Encoding, questioning for XSS testing, 180
Encoding test, 181
Encryption. *See also* Cryptography
    authentication and, 242
    and confidentiality, 242
    integrity and, 242
    key-based ciphers in, 243–244
    mechanisms of, 243–245
    methodology, 243
    and nonrepudiation, 242

purposes of, 241
and reverse proxies, 263
Encryption keys, storing in source code,
    145
Encryption tools, 245
    GPG, 246
    PGP, 245
    S/KEY, 246
    SSH and SCP, 246
    SSL, 246
Entry point list, 79
Entry points
    defined, 75–76
    documenting for buffer overruns, 160
    documenting in threat modeling, 78
    passing attack data to, 161
    in threat modeling, 74
Equivalency classes, in TCO, 281–283
Error pages, reviewing for SQL injections,
    227
Escalation of privilege, 8
Ethical hacker, defined, 8
Exit points
    defined, 76
    documenting in threat modeling, 78
Expiration data, and cookie tampering, 171
Exploitability, 97
Exploits
    brute force attacks, 215
    brute force browsing, 149–150
    buffer overruns, 157–158
    cookie poisoning, 169
    cookie theft, 168–169
    cost of, 68
    cross-site cooking, 169
    default password cracking, 214
    defined, 8
    dictionary-based password attacks, 214
    enormous costs of, 18–19
    format string attacks, 196
    insecure password storage, 214
    insecure password transmission, 214
    integer overflows/underflows, 203–204
    man-in-the-middle attacks, 209
    nonblind attacks, 223
    nonpersistent/reflected exploits, 176
    password cracking, 214
    password guessing, 214
    persistent/stored exploits, 176–177
    ping flooding, 187
    ping of death, 186

session hijacking, 219
smurf attacks, 187
spoofing attacks, 223
SQL injection, 227–229
SYN flooding, 187
teardrop attacks, 186
External dependency
    defined, 76
    documenting for initial threat model, 82
External security notes, 83
Extraneous code, security considerations,
    137–138
Extreme programming, and security testing,
    60–61

F

Faillover data, 90
Fallback mitigations, 92
File infector viruses, 43
Firewalls, 249
    application-level proxy type, 252
    defined, 8
    drawbacks to using, 253
    network address translation (NAT) type,
        252
    packet filtering type, 251
    packets and, 250
    and port scanners, 250
    ports and, 250
    stateful packet inspection type, 251–252
    and TCP/IP, 249–250
    types of, 251–252
Flawfinder, 199
Forceful browsing, 147. *See also* Brute force
        browsing
Format string attacks, 193
    sample, 195
Format string vulnerabilities
    ANSI C functions, 194
    background description, 193–196
    exploit anatomy, 196
    lprng (port 515/tcp), 197–198
    pseudonyms for, 193
    Ramen worm toolkit, 196–197
    real-world examples, 196–198
    rpc.statd (port 111/udp), 197
    software tools for, 199–200
    test techniques, 198–199
    vulnerability case study, 193

wu-ftpd (port 21/tcp), 197
Fragmentation variables, in IPv4, 272
Functional testing, 13
    differences from security testing, 3,
        27–33
    intent of, 29–30
    prioritization differences from security
        testing, 31–33
    test overlap and streamlining, 30–31
Fuzz testing, 233
    assumptions, 233–234
    building tools for, 236
    case studies, 238–239
    dumb, 236
    fixing vulnerabilities form, 237
    generation, 236
    iterative cycles of, 238
    mixed, 236
    mutation, 236
    prioritizing/choosing targets for,
        234–235
    process steps, 234–238
    results analysis, 237
    running tests, 237
    setting bug fix bar for, 235
    smart, 235
    tactics, 235–236
    UNIX case studies, 238
    Windows NT and Windows 2000 case
        studies, 238–239

G

Generation fuzz testing, 236
GET *vs.* POST, 182
Gibson Research Corporation DDoS attack,
    188–189
GPG encryption, 246
Graphic threat trees, 95
Group recognition, as motivation for
    exploits, 39
Guard-your-own-gates concept, 62
    Achilles' heel, 63–64
    application self-defense, 63
    and imperfect security, 65
    mitigation of damages, 64–65
    and reliance on outside protection, 63

H

Hacker, defined, 9
Hacker lack of interest, 50
Hard-coded install locations, 134
Harnesses, for fuzz testing, 236
Hash ciphers, 245
Heap buffer overruns, 153, 155–157
    real-world examples, 159–160
Heap buffers, 157
Heap smashing, 153
    real-world examples, 159–160
Hidden features, insecurity of, 50
Hidden fields, testing for cross-site
        scripting, 182
Hidden files, 137
Hidden form fields, validating, 143
Hijacking, defined, 9
Home-grown cryptography, 136
HTML contents, in shipped forms, 145
HTML tag equivalents, 179
Hub, defined, 9

I

ICMP, 273
Implementation phase
    in SDC, 59
    in SDLC, 54–55
In-house software, vulnerability of, 19
Incoming information, 117–118
Information disclosure
    defined, 9
    security considerations, 137
    in STRIDE model, 99
Information gathering, 119
    existing product bugs and known
        security issues, 120–122
    reviewing existing test automation, 123
    reviewing existing test plans and cases,
        122–123
    reviewing system specifications, 122
Infrastructure entry points, 76
Infrastructure vulnerabilities, 104–105
Initial threat model, 77
    application modeling for, 83–84
    asset documentation, 79–80
    entry and exit points documentation, 78
    external dependencies, 82
    external security notes for, 83

threat profile creation for, 84–86
trust levels, 81
use cases and use scenarios, 81–82
Input related security considerations
for APIs, 140
for authentication, 135
for Web applications, 142–143
Insecure password storage, 212–213
exploit anatomy, 214
real-world example, 215
test techniques for, 215
Insecure password transmission, 213
exploit anatomy, 214
real-world example, 215
test techniques for, 216
Insider attacks, 99
access path control aspects, 101–102
attacker behavioral aspects, 100–101
attacker technical aspects, 102–103
defense aspects, 103
Insider information, on vulnerabilities, 34
Insider threat study, 100
Integer manipulation bugs, 201
Integer overflows/underflows
background description, 201–203
C datatype ranges, 202
exploit anatomy, 203–204
pseudonyms for, 201
real-world examples, 204–205
test techniques, 205–206
two's complement translations, 203
unsigned short integer overflow, 203
vulnerability case study, 201
Integrity
and encryption, 242
encryption and, 242
Intended audience, 4
Intended purpose, 24
Intercepting proxies, 262–263
Internet shopping habits, 16
Internet use
increase in, 14–15
for specific tasks, 16
Interoperability, 119
Intrusion detection system (IDS), defined, 9
IP, 269–270
IPv4, 270–272
IPv6, 272–273
IP address spoofing, 221
ITS4 Security Scanner, 199

K

Key-based ciphers, 243–244
mechanism of, 244–245
Key length, in cryptography, 246
Known security issues, 120, 124
competitive systems, 121
in-house systems, 120–121
in interfacing systems, 121–122

L

Laptop theft, 91–92
Layered entry points, 76
Leaf conditions, 94, 96
Leetspeek, defined, 9
Load balancing, and reverse proxies, 263
Local cross-site scripting, 175–176
Log files, as data assets, 89
Logic bombs, 43–44
Logical addresses
in IPv4, 271
in IPv6, 272–273
lprng (port 515/tcp), 197–198

M

Macro viruses, 43
Mailing lists, recommended, 287
Malicious code, 173
Man-in-the-middle attacks
background description, 207–208
complete handshake, 208
exploit anatomy, 209
pseudonyms for, 207
real-world examples, 209–210
test techniques, 210
vulnerability case study, 207
Management decisions, handling for bug
fixes, 71
Master Boot Record (MBR) viruses, 42
Media Access Control (MAC) address, 9
MERIT, 99–100
insider threat study items of note, 100
Microsoft Corporation, xxiii, 4
Microsoft Passport, XSS example, 178
Microsoft Windows functionality, as
example case, 4

Misplaced trust, examples of, 24–25
Mitigation of damages, 64–65
    use of MERIT model for, 99
Mixed fuzz testing, 236
MTM attacks, 207
Multipartite viruses, 43
Mutation fuzz testing, 236
MySpace XSS worm, 179

N

Named pipes, 143
Negative testing, 30
Network address translation (NAT), 252
Network assets, 38–39
Network DoS attacks, test techniques,
    189–190
Network layer, in OSI Network Model,
    257–258
Networking protocols
    ARP, 273–274
    BOOTP, 274
    DHCP, 274
    ICMP, 273
    IP, 269–273
    RARP, 274
    TCP, 267–269
    UDP, 273
Nigerian scams, 48
Non-URL brute force browsing, 149
Nonblind spoofing, 222
    exploit anatomy, 223
Nonpersistent cross-site scripting, 174–175
    exploit anatomy, 176
Nonrepudiation, encryption and, 242

O

Obscurity, in cryptography, 247
OCTAVE/OCTAVE-S, 76, 103–104
    building asset-based profiles using, 104
    developing security strategy and plans
        for, 105
    infrastructure vulnerability identification
        for, 104–105
ODBC error pages, 227
Online activities, increase in, 15–17

Online communications, vulnerabilities of,
    17
Open proxies, 263
Operational environment
    API security considerations, 141
    hidden files and locations in, 137
    registry entries and, 136
    for stand-alone applications, 139–140
    system pathing considerations, 136
    universal security considerations, 136
Order value, and spoofing attacks, 222
OSI Network Model, 255
    application layer, 256
    data link layer, 258
    defined, 9
    network layer, 257–258
    physical layer, 258–259
    presentation layer, 256
    session layer, 256
    transport layer, 257
Outgoing information, 118
Output interceptability, 139
Output security considerations, for stand-
        alone applications, 138–139
Outside protection, reliance on, 63

P

Packet fields
    in IPv4, 270–271
    in IPv6, 272
Packet filtering, 251
Packets
    and firewalls, 250
    in IPv4/6, 270
Passive attacks, 46
Password cracking
    background description, 211–214
    brute force attacks, 213–214
    and default passwords, 212
    dictionary-based attacks, 213
    exploit anatomy, 214–215
    and insecure password storage, 212–213
    and insecure password transmission,
        213
    pseudonyms for, 211
    real-world examples, 215
    test techniques, 215–216, 216
    vulnerability case study, 211
    and weak passwords, 212

Password guessing, 211
 exploit anatomy, 214
Password length/complexity rules, 216
PayPal XSS, 177–178
Perimeter security, inadequacy of, 19–20
Permission levels, for installation *vs.*
 running, 134
Persistent cross-site scripting, 175
 exploit anatomy, 176–177
Personal experience data, for test
 prioritization, 126
Personal recognition, as motivation for
 exploits, 39
Personally Identifiable Information (PII), 9
Personas, 107
 creating, 107–109
 as customers *vs.* attackers, 111
 pitfalls, 111–112
 security personas, 111–112
 tunnel vision, 111
 using, 110
Phishing, 17, 46–47
 defined, 9
Physical access, pitfalls of forgetting, 93
Physical disks, as data assets, 91–92
Physical layer, in OSI Network Model,
 258–259
Ping flooding attacks, 184
 exploit anatomy, 187
Ping of death, 184
 exploit anatomy, 186
Port scanners, 250
Ports, and firewalls, 250
Positive testing, 30
Postmortems, 131
Potential downtime, 18
Presentation layer, in OSI Network Model,
 256
printf(), format parameters for, 194
Privilege
 API processes run at high, 140
 application processes run at high, 138
 elevation of, 99
 levels for Web and distributed
 applications, 142
Process tokens, 79
Production data, copies outside production,
 90
Program managers, security testing needs,
 66
Programmer error, in cryptography, 247

Programming language, security
 considerations, 141
Protection proxies, 262
Protocol stack, defined, 9
Protocol vulnerability, in network DoS
 attacks, 189
Proxies, *vs.* firewalls, 20
Proxy servers, 261
 anonymous, 265
 circumventor, 264
 intercepting proxies, 262–263
 open proxies, 263
 reverse proxies, 263–264
 split proxies, 264
 SSL proxies, 262
 types of, 261–264
 Web proxies, 261–262
Pscan, 199

R

Ramen worm toolkit, 196–197
RARP, 274
Recommended reading, 287
Reflected cross-site scripting, 174–175
Reformatting proxies, 262
Registry
 easy key accessibility, 140
 pitfalls of forgetting, 94
 security considerations for entries, 136
Release candidate, scheduling test time for,
 130
Release phase
 in SDC, 60
 in SDLC, 56
Remote administration, for Web and
 distributed applications, 144
Repair information, saving to hard-coded
 location, 139
Reproducibility, 97
Repudiation, in STRIDE model, 99
Requirements phase
 in SDC, 58
 in SDLC, 53
Resource availability, as data asset, 79
Restore information, saving to hard-coded
 location, 139
Returned code examination, 181
Reverse engineering, defined, 9
Reverse proxies, 263–264

Risk, defined, 76
Risk assessment, 73–74
Risk assessment charts, for test
       prioritization, 125–126
Risky activities, enabled by default, 134
Rogue servers, 144
Root threat, 94
Rootkit, defined, 9
Rough Auditing Tool for Security (RATS),
       199
Router, defined, 10
rpc.statd (port 111/udp), 197

S

S/KEY encryption, 246
Sample security considerations, 133
    for APIs, 140–141
    application process related, 138, 140,
       142
    authentication related, 134–135
    backward compatibility, 139
    client related, 143–144
    cryptographic considerations, 136
    data transfer related, 143
    for default installations, 133–134
    extraneous code, 137–138
    information disclosure, 137
    input-related, 135, 140, 142–143
    language related, 141
    operational environment related,
       139–140, 141
    for operational environments, 136–137
    output related, 138–139
    security validations, 135–136
    server related, 144
    for stand-alone applications, 138–140
    universal, 133–138
    for Web and distributed applications,
       142–145
SCP encryption, 246
Script injection, 225
Script kiddie, defined, 10
Secrecy, failure of security in, 36–37
Secure flag, and cookie tampering, 171
Security, increasing priority of, 13–17
Security areas, 117
    dependencies, 118–119
    incoming information, 117–118
    interactions/interoperability, 119

    outgoing information, 118
Security awareness, 17
    fostering, 71–72
Security bypass settings, 138
Security cases
    developing, 123
    known vulnerabilities for, 124
    unknown vulnerabilities, 124–125
Security cracks, 48–49
Security development cycle (SDC), 56–57
    communications in, 57
    design phase, 58–59
    extreme programming and security
       testing in, 60–61
    implementation phase, 59
    release phase, 60
    requirements phase, 58
    schematic diagram, 58
    secure by default, 57
    secure by design, 57
    secure in deployment, 57
    support and servicing phases, 60
    verification phase, 59–60
Security efforts, increasing visibility of,
       17–19
Security exploits, enormous costs of, 18–19
Security hindering phrases, 49
    back-end assumptions, 51
    developer security focus, 50–51
    hacker lack of interest, 50
    hidden features, 50
    testing errors, 52
    user interface reliance, 51
    user scenario, 49–50
Security interactions, 119
Security issues, presenting effectively,
       67–72
Security matrix, 40–41
Security notes, 83
Security personas, 112
    sample attacker aspect matrix, 112
    sample attacker descriptions, 113
Security terminology, 8–10
Security test plan
    approaches to creating, 3
    drafting, 116
    reviewing, 130
    reviewing existing, 122–123
    test passes, 131
Security test planning, 115
    developing security cases, 123–125

developing test plan of attack, 126–128
information gathering for, 119–123
postmorteming results, 131
process of, 4, 115–116
reviewing test plan and test cases, 130
running test passes, 131
schedule drafting, 128–130
system dissection, 117–119
test case documentation, 116–117
test case outline, 116–117
test documents, 116
test plan, 116
test prioritization, 125–126
Security testing, 1
in all testing efforts, 62
developers' needs, 65–66
extreme programming and, 60–61
intent of, 29–30
managers' needs, 66
positive *vs.* negative, 30
prioritization differences from functional
testing, 31–33
program managers' needs, 66
role of, 65–67
scarcity of resources for, 2
test overlap with functional testing,
30–31
vs. functional testing, 27–33
Security testing considerations, 27
assumptions about attackers, 35–37
black-box *vs.* white-box testing, 61–65
common security hindering phrases,
49–52
discovery of software vulnerabilities,
33–35
exploiting software vulnerabilities,
41–49
knowing your attackers, 35–38
presenting security issues effectively,
67–72
role of security testing, 65–67
security testing *vs.* functional testing,
27–33
software development life cycle *vs.*
security-testing life cycle, 52–61
Security testing life cycle, *vs.* software
development life cycle, 52
Security validations, 135
faulty, 136
processing in wrong order, 136
Security vocabulary, 7–10

Semicolons, in SQL injection, 228
Server related considerations, for Web and
distributed applications, 144
Servicing phase, in SDC, 60
Session cookies, weak or easily reused, 141
Session hijacking
background description, 217–218
exploit anatomy, 219
pseudonyms for, 217
real-world examples, 219
test techniques, 219–220
vulnerability case study, 217
Session-hijacking tools, 210
Session layer, in OSI Network Model, 256
Session persistence, 141
Session replay attack, 148–149, 149–150
test techniques, 151
Session theft, 217
Setup information, saving to hard-coded
location, 138
Single-key ciphers, 244
Single-layered security, pitfalls of, 92
Single quotes, in SQL injection, 228
Slow connection compensation, by reverse
proxies, 264
Smart fuzz testing, 235
Smatch, 199
Smurf attacks, 184
exploit anatomy, 187
Social engineering, 17, 44
and active attacks, 45–46
defined, 10
ease of, 37
and Nigerian scams, 48
and passive attacks, 46
and phishing, 46–47
and urban legends, 47
Software development life cycle
design phase, 53–54
implementation phase, 54–55
release phase, 56
requirements phase, 53
support phase, 56
verification phase, 55–56
vs. security testing life cycle, 52
waterfall method, 53
Software misuse, 24
Software testing
as discipline, 11–13
industrywide rethinking of, 12–13
lack of formal curriculum for, 11

Software tools
Flawfinder, 199
for format string vulnerabilities, 199
for fuzz testing, 236
ITS4 Security Scanner, 199
Pscan, 199
Rough Auditing Tool for Security
(RATS), 199
session-hijacking tools, 210
Smatch, 199
Splint, 200
Source code compromise, 35
Source IP, and spoofing attacks, 221
Splint, 200
Split proxies, 264
Spoofing attacks
background description, 221–223
blind spoofing, 222
defined, 10
denial of service attacks, 222–223
exploit anatomy, 223
nonblind spoofing, 222
pseudonyms for, 221
real-world examples, 223
testing techniques, 223
vulnerability case study, 221–223
Spoofing identity, 98
SQL injection
background description, 225–226
exploit anatomy, 227–229
pseudonyms for, 225
real-world examples, 229
test characters for, 230–231
test techniques, 229–231
vulnerability case study, 225
SQL Injection Testing, 3
SQL insertion, 225
SSH encryption, 246
SSL encryption, 246
SSL proxies, 262
Stack buffer overruns, 153, 154–155
real-world examples, 158–159
Stack frames, 156
Stack smashing, 153
real-world examples, 158–159
Stand-alone applications
application process considerations, 138
backward compatibility issues, 139
interceptability of output before final
destination, 139

operational environment considerations,
139–140
output security considerations, 138–139
processes running at high privilege, 138
saving repair-restore information to
hard-coded location, 139
saving setup information to hard-coded
location, 138
saving state information to hard-coded
location, 138
security considerations, 138
Starting TCO format, 278
State information, saving to hard-coded
location, 138
Stateful packet inspection, 251–252
Stored cross-site scripting, 175
Stored data, including in asset lists, 88
STRIDE, 98
denial of service, 99
elevation of privilege and, 99
information disclosure, 99
repudiation, 99
spoofing identity, 98
tampering with data, 98
threat classification with, 85
Support phase
in SDC, 60
in SDLC, 56
Switch, defined, 10
SYN flooding, 185–186
exploit anatomy, 187
System, defined, 76
System assets, 38
System dissection, 117
separation into security areas, 117–119
System pathing, security considerations,
136
System specifications, reviewing for
information gathering phase,
122

T

Tampering, with data, 98
Targets, 38–39
for fuzz testing, 234–235
TCO formats, 284
TCP, 267–268
common application port numbers, 269
flags, 268–269

packet fields in, 268
TCP/IP, firewalls and, 249–250
TCP packet, 268
Teardrop attacks, 184
   exploit anatomy, 186
Temporary files
   access to, 137
   as data assets, 89
Test automation
   evolution of, 13
   reviewing existing, 123
Test case outline/documentation, 116–117
Test case outlining (TCO), 275
   benefits of, 276–277
   defined, 276
   drafting initial outline, 278–279
   formats for, 284
   goals of, 275–276
   maintenance, 284–285
   refining, 279–280
   reviewing, 283–284
   starting TCO format, 278
   steps in, 277–284
   TCO to scenario, 285
   using equivalency classes in, 281–283
   writing atomic/predictive statements for, 280–281
Test cases, reviewing, 130
Test characters, for SQL injection, 230–231
Test harnesses, for fuzz testing, 236
Test hooks, security considerations, 137
Test passes, 131
Test plan of attack, 126
   commercial tools for developing, 127
   custom tools for, 127
   downsides of, 127–128
   normal or by design test methods, 127
   validation tools for, 127
Test prioritization, 125–126
   and developer communication, 126
   using personal experience data for, 126
Test techniques
   black-box testing, 161–162, 180–181
   buffer overruns, 160–162
   for cookie tampering, 170–172
   for cross-site scripting, 179–182
   denial of Service (DoS) attacks, 189–190
   format string vulnerabilities, 198–199
   for insecure password storage, 215
   for insecure password transmission, 216
   integer overflows/underflows, 205–206

for integer overflows/underflows, 205–206
   man-in-the-middle attacks, 210
   network DoS attacks, 189–190
   for password cracking, 216
   questioning filtering and encoding, 180
   session hijacking, 219–220
   session replay attacks, 151
   spoofing attacks, 223
   SQL injection, 229–231
   URL guessing, 150
   white-box testing, 162, 181–182
Testing errors, 52
Testing schedule, 128
   time to develop/learn tools, 129
   time to investigate issues, 129
   time to perform tests, 129
   time to rerun tests on release candidate, 130
Text threat trees, 95
Threat, defined, 10, 76
Threat analysis, to determine vulnerabilities, 85
Threat classification, 85
Threat model
   defined, 76
   updating, 86
Threat model tunnel vision, 87
Threat modeling, 73–74
   DREAD, 96–98
   initial modeling, 77–86
   MERIT, 99–103
   OCTAVE and OCTAVE-S, 103–105
   pitfalls of, 86–94
   STRIDE, 98–99
   terminology, 75–77
   and test prioritization, 125–126
   and threat trees, 94–96
   three required ingredients for, 74
   as time sink, 93
Threat modeling pitfalls, 86
   blindness to interaction with downstream dependents, 87
   failure to consider data copies as assets, 88–92
   failure to track dependency changes, 88
   forgetting physical access, 93
   forgetting registry, 94
   ignoring lower-priority vulnerabilities, 93
   modeling as time sink, 93

single-layered security, 92
threat model tunnel vision, 87
Threat modeling terms, 75
  assets, 75
  attack path, 75
  condition, 75
  entry points, 75
  exit points, 76
  external dependency, 76
  risk, 76
  system, 76
  threat, 76
  threat model, 76
  threat profile, 77
  trust levels, 77
  use scenario, 77
  vulnerability, 77
Threat profile, 77
  asset-based, 104
  creating for initial threat model, 84–86
Threat trees, 94–96
Total cost of ownership, 18
Traffic encryption, 143
Transaction limits, and DoS attacks, 190
Transitive assets, 80
Transport layer, in OSI Network Model, 257
Trickle-down effects, of bug exploits, 68
Trickle-up effects, of bug exploits, 68
Trojan Horse, 41–42
  alternate names for, 7
  defined, 10
Trust
  and external dependencies, 81
  misplacement of, 23–25, 28, 29
  secrecy *vs.* security, 36–37
  and security cracks, 48–49
  and social engineering, 44–48
Trust levels
  defined, 77
  documenting in initial threat model, 81
  in sample asset list, 80
Trust list, 80
Trustworthiness
  of data submission formats, 140
  of input contents, formats, sources, 135
Trustworthy Computing Security
      Development Lifecycle, 17–18
Two's complement translations, 203

U

UDP, 273
UML application modeling, 83
Universal security considerations, 133
  authentication related, 134–135
  cryptographic considerations, 136
  for default installations, 133–134
  extraneous code related, 137–138
  information disclosure, 137
  input related, 135
  operational environment related,
     136–137
  security validations, 135–136
Unshippable code, 128
Unsigned short integer overflow, 203
Untestable code, unshippability of, 128
Urban legends, 47
URL guessing, 148, 149
  test techniques, 150
Use cases
  documenting in initial threat model,
    81–82
  reviewing existing, 122–123
Use scenario
  defined, 77
  documenting in initial threat model,
    81–82
User assets, 38
User error issues, in cryptography, 247
User interface, limitations of reliance on, 51
User scenarios, 49–50

V

Valid information, 24
Validation
  antirepudiation, 144
  of data/request source, 140
Validation tools, 127
  time to develop/learn, 129
Verbose errors, display of, 137
Verification phase
  in SDC, 59–60
  in SDLC, 55–56
Virus naming, 7
Viruses, 42
  boot sector viruses, 42
  defined, 10
  file infector viruses, 43

macro viruses, 43
Master Boot Record (MBR) viruses, 42
multipartite, 43
Vulnerabilities, 4–5
   accidental discovery of, 33–34
   defined, 10, 77
   deliberate search efforts for, 34–35
   discovery of, 33–35
   ease of exploitation, 37
   exploiting in software, 41–49
   ignoring lower-priority, 93
   of in-house software, 19
   insider information on, 34
   known, 124
   mitigating, 86
   prioritizing, 86
   root problems behind, 3
   threat analysis to determine, 85
   Trojans, 41–42
   and trust, 16
   unknown, 124–125
   viruses, 42–43
   worms, 43–44
Vulnerability case study
   brute force browsing, 147–151
   buffer overruns, 153–162
   cookie tampering, 165–172
   cross-site scripting (XSS), 173–182
   denial of service/distributed denial of
      service, 183–190
   format string vulnerabilities, 193–200
   integer overflows and underflows,
      201–206
   man-in-the-middle attacks, 207–210
   password cracking, 211–216
   session hijacking, 217–220
   spoofing attacks, 221–223
   SQL injection, 225–232

W

Weak passwords, 212
Web applications
   application process related
      considerations, 142
   client related considerations, 143–144
   data transfer considerations, 143
   input related considerations, 142–143
   security considerations, 142
   server related considerations, 144
Web proxies, 261–262
Web sites, recommended, 287
What-why-who security matrix, 40–41
White-box testing, 1, 2
   for buffer overruns, 162
   for cookie tampering, 172
   for cross-site scripting, 181–182
   differences from black-box testing, 62
   for format string vulnerabilities, 198–199
      for integer overflows/underflows,
         206
   for SQL injection, 229, 231
   vs. black-box testing, 61–65
WorldPay DDoS attack, 187
Worms, 43
   logic bombs, 43–44
wu-ftpd (port21 tcp), 197

X

XSS, 173. *See also* Cross-site scripting

Z

Zero-day exploit, defined, 10